Swift for Beginners

DEVELOP AND DESIGN

Boisy G. Pitre

PEACHPIT PRESS
WWW.PEACHPIT.COM

Swift for Beginners: Develop and Design
Boisy G. Pitre

Peachpit Press
www.peachpit.com

To report errors, please send a note to errata@peachpit.com.

Peachpit Press is a division of Pearson Education.

Copyright 2015 by Boisy G. Pitre

Editor: Robyn G. Thomas
Copyeditor: Darren Meiss
Proofreader: Nancy Bell
Technical editor: Steve Phillips
Compositor: Danielle Foster
Indexer: Valerie Haynes Perry
Cover design: Aren Straiger

ISBN-13: 978-0-134-04470-5
ISBN-10: 0-134-04470-3

9 8 7 6 5 4 3 2 1

Printed and bound in the United States of America

To the girls: Toni, Hope, Heidi, Lillian, Sophie, and Belle

ACKNOWLEDGMENTS

When creating a book, it truly "takes a village," and I could not have had better support from the staff at Peachpit Press. Many thanks go to executive editor, Cliff Colby at Peachpit for providing me the opportunity; editor Robyn Thomas for her immensely helpful and invaluable editing skills and for keeping the project on track; technical editor Steve Phillips who meticulously commented on drafts of the book for technical correctness and whose contributions undoubtedly made this work better.

During my writing, I've drawn inspiration from the works of a number of friends who are authors in the iOS and Mac OS developer community: Chris Adamson, Bill Cheeseman, Bill Dudney, Daniel Steinberg, and Richard Warren.

I would be remiss if I didn't mention the MacTech Conference dynamic duo Ed Marczak and Neil Ticktin, as well as CocoaConf maestro Dave Klein, for the writing and speaking opportunities that they have provided me at those venues.

A tip of the hat to James Dempsey, whose band, the Breakpoints, and their excellent *Backtrace* album fueled several long writing and review sessions with their rollicking tunes. Java Square Café in downtown Opelousas, Louisiana provided a great place to write as well as tasty lattes. Also, thanks to *Dave et Ray's Camp Jam/Supper Club* and my friends there who served as inspiration for several of the coding examples I used.

Much appreciation goes to the minds at Apple for creating Swift, along with a host of great products over the years that have enhanced my own productivity and that of many, many others.

Finally, many thanks to my family, especially my wife, Toni, whose patience and encouragement while I worked on this book was abundant.

ABOUT THE AUTHOR

Boisy G. Pitre is Affectiva's Mobile Visionary and lead iOS developer, where his work has led to the creation of the first mobile SDK for delivering emotions to mobile devices for the leading emotion technology company and spin-off of the MIT Media Lab. Prior to that he was a member of the Mac Products Group at Nuance Communications where he worked with a team of developers on Dragon Dictate.

He also owns Tee-Boy, a software company focusing on Mac and iOS applications for the weather and data acquisition markets, and has authored the monthly *Developer to Developer* column in *MacTech Magazine*.

Along with Bill Loguidice, Boisy co-authored the book *CoCo: The Colorful History of Tandy's Underdog Computer* (2013), published by Taylor & Francis.

Boisy holds a Master of Science in Computer Science from the University of Louisiana at Lafayette, and resides in the quiet countryside of Prairie Ronde, Louisiana. Besides Mac and iOS development, his hobbies and interests include retro-computing, ham radio, vending machine and arcade game restoration, farming, and playing the French music of South Louisiana.

CONTENTS

INTRODUCTION

Welcome to *Swift for Beginners*! Swift is Apple's new language for developing apps for iOS and Mac OS, and it is destined to become the premier computer language in the mobile and desktop space. As a new computer language, Swift has the allure of a shiny new car—everybody wants to see it up close, kick the tires, and take it for a spin down the road. That's probably why you're reading this book—you've heard about Swift and decided to see what all the fuss is about.

The notion that Swift is an easy language to use and learn certainly has merit, especially when compared to the capable but harder-to-learn programming language it's replacing: Objective-C. Apple has long used Objective-C as its language of choice for developing software on its platforms, but that is changing with the introduction of Swift.

Not only is Swift easy to learn, it's extremely powerful. You'll get a taste of some of that power here in this book.

WHO IS THIS BOOK FOR?

This book was written for the beginner in mind. In a sense, we're all beginners with Swift because it's such a new language. However, many will want to learn Swift as a first or second computer language, many of whom haven't had any exposure to Objective-C or related languages, C and C++.

Ideally, the reader will have some understanding and experience with a computer language; even so, the book is styled to appeal to the neophyte who is sufficiently motivated to learn. More experienced developers will probably find the first few chapters to be review material and light reading because the concepts are ubiquitous among many computer languages but nonetheless important to introduce Swift to the beginner.

No matter your skill level or prior experience, *Swift for Beginners* will appeal to anyone who wants to learn about Swift.

HOW TO USE THIS BOOK

Like other books of its kind, *Swift for Beginners* is best read from start to finish. The material in subsequent chapters tends to build on the knowledge attained from previous ones. However, with few exceptions, code examples are confined to a single chapter.

The book is sized to provide a good amount of material, but not so much as to overwhelm the reader. Interspersed between the text are a copious number of screenshots to guide the beginner through the ins and outs of Swift as well as the Xcode tool chain.

HOW YOU WILL LEARN

The best way to learn Swift is to use it, and using Swift is emphasized throughout the book with plenty of code and examples.

Each chapter contains code that builds on the concepts presented. Swift has two interactive environments you will use to test out concepts and gain understanding of the language: the REPL and playgrounds. Later, you'll build two simple but complete apps: a loan calculator for Mac OS and a memory game for iOS.

Swift concepts will be introduced throughout the text—classes, functions, closures, and more, all the way to the very last chapter. You're encouraged to take your time and read each chapter at your leisure, even rereading if necessary, before moving on to the next one.

Source code for all the chapters is available at www.peachpit.com/swiftbeginners. You can download the code for each chapter, which cuts down considerably on typing; nonetheless, I am a firm believer in typing in the code. By doing so, you gain insight and comprehension you might otherwise miss if you just read along and rely on the downloaded code. Make the time to type in all of the code examples.

For clarity, code and other constructs such as class names are displayed in monospace font.

Highlighted code throughout the book identifies the portions of the code that are intended for you to type:

```
 1> let candyJar = ["Peppermints", "Gooey Bears", "Happy Ranchers"]
candyJar: [String] = 3 values {
  [0] = "Peppermints"
  [1] = "Gooey Bears"
  [2] = "Happy Ranchers"
}
 2>
```

You'll also find notes containing additional information about the topics.

> **NOTE:** To print or not to print? Remember, simply typing the name of the item without using print or println is acceptable when using the REPL. When doing so, the result of the expression is assigned to a temporary variable—in this case $R0.

WHAT YOU WILL LEARN

Ultimately, this book will show you how to use Swift to express your ideas in code. When you complete the final chapter, you should have a good head start, as well as a solid understanding of what the language offers. Additionally, you'll have the skills to begin writing an app. Both iOS and Mac OS apps are presented as examples in the later chapters.

What this book does not do is provide an all-inclusive, comprehensive compendium on the Swift programming language. Apple's documentation is the best resource for that. Here, the emphasis is primarily on learning the language itself; various Cocoa frameworks are touched on where necessary to facilitate the examples but are not heavily emphasized for their own sake.

WELCOME TO SWIFT

Swift is a fun, new, and easy-to-learn computer language from Apple. With the knowledge you'll gain from this book, you can begin writing apps for iOS and Mac OS. The main tool you'll need to start learning Swift is the Xcode integrated development environment (IDE). Xcode includes the Swift compiler, as well as the iOS and Mac OS software development kits (SDKs) that contain all the infrastructure required to support the apps you develop.

THE TECHNOLOGIES

The following technologies are all part of your journey into the Swift language.

SWIFT

Swift is the language you'll learn in this book. Swift is a modern language designed from the ground up to be easy to learn as well as powerful. It is language that Apple has chosen to fuel the continued growth of apps, which make up their iOS and Mac OS ecosystem.

XCODE

Xcode is Apple's premier environment for writing apps. It includes an editor, debugger, project manager, and the compiler tool chain needed to take Swift code and turn it into runnable code for iOS or Mac OS. You can download Xcode from Apple's Mac App Store.

LLVM

Although it works behind the scenes within Xcode, LLVM is the compiler technology that empowers the elegance of the Swift language and turns it into the digestible bits and bytes needed by the processors that power Apple devices.

THE REPL

The Read-Eval-Print-Loop (REPL) is a command-line tool you can use to try out Swift code quickly. You run it from the Terminal application on Mac OS.

PLAYGROUNDS

The interactivity and immediate results from Xcode's playgrounds are a great way to try out Swift code as you learn the language.

SECTION I

The Basics

Learning something new always starts with "the basics." The Swift language is no exception. This section covers everything you need to know about this cool new language to start making your next great app!

CHAPTER 1

Introducing Swift

Welcome to the brave new world of Swift! If you've been paying attention to the buzz, you may have heard that Swift is an entirely new programming language created by Apple to empower developers to write iOS and Mac apps more easily and efficiently. Swift is so easy to learn that you'll be writing simple apps before you know it.

Swift gives you powerful new ways to write code. Its readability is refreshingly simple compared to its worthy and powerful predecessor, Objective-C. With Swift, you'll find new and interesting ways to express yourself as a developer, and learn the language and its capabilities.

You'll find that expressing your ideas is easy in this innovative language. It also delivers power and flexibility in both its capabilities and its syntax.

Since Swift is so new, it is subject to changes and additions by Apple. Never before has a computer language with such exposure and potential usage been subject to near-immediate modifications and revisions. It's all part of the excitement and innovation that Swift represents.

EVOLUTIONARY, YET REVOLUTIONARY

Language is the vehicle in which we share, exchange, and co-opt information. As humans, we express intent through language to our friends, family members, and co-workers. It's no different when we communicate with a computer system—the basic tenet remains the same.

Just like human languages, computer languages aren't new—in fact, they have been with us in some form or another for many, many years. Their *raison d'etre* has always been to allow us to communicate with and instruct a computer to perform a specific operations.

What has changed and evolved are the computer languages themselves. Early computer pioneers understood that telling a computer what to do in terms of 0's and 1's was tedious and error prone. Compromises between the richness of a language's syntax and the computing power needed to process and interpret that language were made along the way, and languages such as C and C++ became the entrenched *lingua franca* of modern computer applications.

And while C and C++ were widely adopted and used on major computing platforms, Apple brought something different to the party with Objective-C. Built upon the foundation of C, this rich language welded the power of the long-used language with object-oriented design methodologies to the programmer's toolbox. For many years Objective-C has been the underpinning of applications written for Apple's ecosystem of Macintosh computers and iOS devices.

Yet, despite its power and elegance, Objective-C carried the baggage of its namesake, C. For many of us who know C quite well, this isn't an impediment; however, the crop of new developers who have come to the Mac and iOS platforms in recent years pined for something easier to comprehend and develop with.

Apple answered the call and at the same time lowered the barrier to entry. Now, writing apps has just become much easier, and our ability to express what we want our apps to do is one step closer to "easy."

PREPARING FOR SUCCESS

You may be wondering what you need to learn Swift successfully. Actually, you've taken your first step by starting to read this book. Learning a new computer language can be daunting, and that's why this book was written for the Swift beginner. If you are new to Swift, this book is for you. If you have never used C, C++, or Objective-C, this book is also for you. Yet even if you are a seasoned developer with knowledge of the aforementioned languages, you'll still find this book helpful in getting up to speed with Swift.

While not an absolute necessity, possessing a basic understanding of, and familiarity with, an existing programming language is valuable while reading this book. This book isn't written to teach you how to program, or provide you the underlying fundamentals of developing software. It assumes a certain familiarity with the basic concepts of computer languages; therefore, you should have *some* exposure to a computer language already.

Despite this requirement, the book is written to help you along as much as possible. Terminology is explained thoroughly when it is introduced, and concepts are described as clearly as possible.

TOOLS OF THE TRADE

So you're ready to learn Swift. Great! First, you need to get your "supplies" in order. Thinking back to when you were in grade school, just prior to the start of the term, your parents were given a list of supplies you needed: notebooks, scissors, construction paper, glue, no. 2 pencils, and the like. Well, you won't need those for this book, but you must nevertheless prepare for learning Swift by obtaining the proper tools of the trade.

First, we highly recommend that you interactively run the code presented here, and to do that, you will need a Macintosh computer running OS X 10.9 Mavericks or 10.10 Yosemite. You'll also need Xcode 6, which has the Swift compiler and accompanying environment. Most importantly, you will want to become a member of the Apple Developer Proram in order to get the most out of Yosemite and Xcode 6. If you're not already a memory of the Apple Developer Program, you can read all about joining by visiting https://developer.apple.com/programs.

Once you've downloaded and installed Xcode 6 on your Mac, you're ready to learn Swift.

INTERACTING WITH SWIFT

To start out, we'll be exploring the Swift language through a fun and interactive environment known as the REPL. REPL stands for Read-Eval-Print-Loop and indicates the nature of the tool: It reads instructions, evaluates them, prints the results, and loops back around to do it all over again.

In fact, this interactivity is one of Swift's nifty features that evades many compiled languages such as C and Objective-C. This isn't something new if you're coming from scripting languages like Ruby or Python, which offer their own REPL environments, but for a compiled language, it is a novel idea. Ask C, C++, or Objective-C developers how many times they've wished for a way to "try out" code without the overhead of creating a source file with debug statements, compiling it, running it, and then observing the results. The beauty of the Swift REPL is that it makes that kind of long-winded, repetitious workflow a thing of the past.

Another huge benefit of this interactivity is that it helps to make the inherently strenuous task of learning a new language much, much easier. You can put off learning the complexity of compiler tool chains and the nuances of integrated development environments, and instead focus on the language. In fact, very early on in this book, you'll be exploring, testing, and prodding the nooks and crannies of Swift. You'll quickly find that doing this interactively will help you formulate an understanding of the language much quicker.

Having the ability to run your code in real time, without the context of an encompassing run-time environment, may feel odd at first, but you'll soon fall in love with the instant gratification it provides. In fact, the REPL reminds some of us "old-timers" of the interactive nature of early interpretive languages like BASIC, which was around in the early days of the home computer revolution. Talk about coming full circle!

READY, SET...

FIGURE 1.2 The Go menu in the Finder menu bar

FIGURE 1.1 Using Spotlight to find the Terminal application

FIGURE 1.3 Locating Terminal from the Finder

FIGURE 1.4 The Terminal window

OK, have you downloaded Xcode 6? Very good. Now, forget about Xcode for the time being. Actually, I encourage you to explore Xcode 6 and its new features, but we're going to focus our attention completely on the REPL in the Terminal for the first few chapters.

If you haven't run the Terminal app before, don't worry. It's accessible from the Utilities folder, which is located in your Mac's Applications folder. The easiest way to get to it is to click the Spotlight icon and type **Terminal** (**Figure 1.1**).

Alternatively, you can click the Finder icon in the Dock and then choose Go > Utilities (**Figure 1.2**).

A new Finder window shows the contents of this folder; you may have to scroll down in the window to find the Terminal app (**Figure 1.3**). Double-click the icon to launch the app.

When you launch Terminal, you'll see a window similar to **Figure 1.4**. The text and background color of your Terminal may vary from what you see here.

You're almost ready to start your first foray into Swift. But before you start your adventure, you'll need to type a few commands in this newly created Terminal window.

Start by typing this line and pressing Return:

```
sudo xcode-select -s /Applications/Xcode.app/Contents/Developer/
```

You'll be prompted for your administrator password; type it. This command is necessary because it ensures that Xcode 6 is the default version of Xcode running on your Mac. It is required just in case you've already installed a previous version of Xcode. The good news is that you'll have to type this command only once. The setting stays in place, and you need not worry about typing it again, unless you want to switch to another version of Xcode.

Typing this next command and pressing Return takes you into the Swift REPL:

```
xcrun swift
```

Depending on your previous use of Xcode, you may be presented with a dialog asking for your password, similar to **Figure 1.5**. If so, type the password as instructed.

In short order, you're greeted with this message:

```
Welcome to Swift!  Type :help for assistance.
  1>
```

Congratulations for making this far! Now the adventure begins.

DIVING INTO SWIFT

So here you are running the Swift REPL as it sits in the Terminal window and patiently awaits your command. Swift is in control and gently reminds you that you can type something by showing you a prompt. Every time you start the REPL, the prompt is shown with the number 1 followed by the greater-than sign. Let's do a sanity check by pressing Return:

```
Welcome to Swift!  Type :help for assistance.
  1>
  2>
```

As you type a line, the prompt increments to the next ordinal position—easy enough. The constantly increasing number acts as a reference point as you type commands.

HELP AND QUIT

Swift has built-in help for REPL commands. Typing `:help` at the prompt will show a list of these commands, which are always prepended with a colon character. This is how Swift distinguishes a REPL command from a Swift statement. Go ahead and type `:help` (which is itself a command) to see the list of commands. There are quite a few of them in the list, and you'll notice a number of commands are related to debugging. We won't worry about most of these commands.

If you want to quit Swift at any time and return back to the Terminal's default shell, you can type the `:quit` command. If you do quit the REPL, you can simply retype the `xcrun swift` command at the shell prompt to get right back into Swift.

HELLO WORLD!

All right, this is the moment you've been waiting for. Every programmer's introduction to a new language involves the initial ritual of writing the necessary code to tell the world "Hello!" In Swift, it's surprisingly easy, as you'll soon see.

Whet your appetite a bit by typing a one-liner, which is emblematic of your first encounter with this new language. Let's tell the world hello... in French. Type the following text and press Return at the 2> prompt:

```
print("Bonjour, monde")
```

And you see the following:

```
Welcome to Swift!  Type :help for assistance.
  1>
  2> print("Bonjour, monde")
  3>
```

Congratulations on writing your first line of code in Swift. Granted, it's a bit minimal, but hey, it's a start. And it shows just how quickly you can get something working.

It's a rather innocuous line. `print` is a Swift method that directs the computer to display whatever is enclosed in quotation marks (the *string*) and bounded by parentheses. A *method* is a term used to describe a collection of instructions that can be executed by invoking a given name. The `print` method is just one of many common Swift methods you'll be using throughout the book. You'll use it often.

At this point, you may be asking yourself, "Wait, didn't I just tell it to print something?" Indeed, you did. And Swift obediently followed your direction. Computers are never wrong, right? Swift followed your command, just as you gave it. So what gives? Have you encountered your first bug already?

It turns out that the `print` method doesn't "flush" its contents to the screen straight away. Instead, it buffers the data, awaiting the point where another method comes into play. The related method that adds a new line character, which forces everything to appear, is `println`.

Let's use that method to print a character:

```
3> println("!")
Bonjour, monde!
4>
```

Now the full text appears on a line by itself. Note that the initial text we expected to appear, did not. However, it wasn't gone forever. It was just waiting for a new line to "flush it out."

All right, you've mastered the very basics… you can tell Swift to print a string of text. This is a small, but important start to your understanding of the language. Let's take things a little further by looking at some basic but important Swift constructs.

THE POWER OF DECLARATION

If you harken back to your high school algebra class, you'll remember that a variable is a placeholder that represents some quantity. When you say "x equals 12" or "y equals 42" you are in essence making a *declaration*. You declare that some variable is equal to some number.

Swift would make your algebra teacher proud, because it too can declare variables, albeit with a slightly different syntax. Type the following:

```
4> var x = 12
x: Int = 12
5>
```

We've just declared our first variable using Swift's var keyword. Line 4 instructed Swift to declare the variable x to be equal to 12, and Swift dutifully followed that instruction by declaring that indeed, x is now equal to 12. Not only that, but it went further: Swift declares that "x is an Int whose value is equal to 12."

What is Int? It's short for "integer," which is simply a whole number with no fractional component. By typing the number 12 as we did, Swift inferred something about the variable it was being assigned to: x is a number whose value is 12, and furthermore, x is an integer. In Swift's response, it uses the notation of x: Int as a way of advertising the variable's type. We'll see this notation again in a short while.

OK, so we've declared a variable named x with seemingly little effort. Let's up the ante a bit by declaring a second variable, with a twist:

```
5> var y = 42.0
y: Double = 42
6>
```

Here, you've added a decimal point followed by a zero. That nomenclature is enough of a hint to Swift that y is a Double, which simply means a number with a fractional component; it's not a whole number but a representation of a real number, also known as a *floating point number*.

Here's a quick review. What Swift has done in both of these cases is assign a type to the variable. The two variables x and y exist as an integer and as a double, respectively, and will hold that distinction for as long as this REPL session runs.

Variables can be assigned different values once they have been declared. For example, you assigned x the number 12 earlier. Giving a different value to the variable is as simple as using the equals sign:

```
6> x = 28
7>
```

Notice that Swift is silent on the assignment of x to the number 28. Now verify the new value has been assigned:

```
7> println(x)
28
```

And as we expected, x is shown to hold the value of its last assignment, 28.

Variables can also be assigned the contents of other variables. Test this idea by assigning the variable y to the variable x. What do you think will happen?

```
8> x = y
<REPL>:8:5: error: 'Double' is not convertible to 'Int'
x = y
    ^

8>
```

Swift's errors are very detailed, providing both the line number and the column location separated by a colon (in this case, line 8 and column 5) where the error occurred. The content of the line is even reprinted after the error, with a caret reinforcing the error position. Finally, due to the error, the succeeding prompt did not increase to number 9. Instead you received a prompt with the number 8 once more (it's Swift's way of saying "hey, relax... try again!").

So what went wrong here? Very simply, you attempted to assign the variable y, whose type is Double, to the variable x, whose type is Int. Such assignments are a violation of Swift's type rules. We'll get into types in more detail in a little while, but for now, let's see if this "rule" can be bent.

Assume that you stubbornly want to assign the value of y to x, even though they are of different types. You can do it after all, but it takes a little persuasion. Recall that x is an Int and y is a Double. With this in mind, type the following statements:

```
 8> x = Int(y)
 9> println(x)
42
10>
```

With some coaxing, the assignment worked. So what's going on here?

On line 8, we are "casting" the Double value of y into an Int, which is the type of x. Swift allows such assignments if they are explicitly written. We'll talk more about casting shortly.

For good measure, we used the println command to show the value of x. And as we would expect, x is now equal to the integer value of 42.

CONSTANTS ARE CONSISTENT

Variables are useful in so many ways because their values can change over time. They come in handy for iterating loops, holding temporary numbers, strings, and other objects that we'll discuss later.

Another construct in Swift can hold values... the *constant*. Constants are just what their name implies: They hold a value constantly and unwaveringly. Unlike a variable, the value of a constant doesn't change once it's assigned. It's literally locked into place. Yet like a variable, a constant has a type, and types, once assigned, never change.

Let's see constants in action by declaring a new variable and assigning a new constant z to the value of the variable x:

```
10> let z = x
z: Int = 42
11>
```

On line 10, we're using the let command, which is Swift's keyword for creating a constant. The constant z has taken on both the type and the value of the variable x: It's an integer with a value of 42.

Now, if a constant is truly constant, we should not be able to assign another number or variable to it. Let's test that theory:

```
11> z = 4
<REPL>:11:3: error: cannot assign to 'let' value 'z'
z = 4
~ ^


11>
```

The attempt to reassign the constant z to a value raised an error. Again, Swift's concise error reporting leads the way, advertising the line number (11) and the column number (3) where the offense took place.

So why does Swift have constants *and* variables? Isn't a variable more flexible, since it can change, and constants cannot? These are good questions, and the answers lie in the underlying compiler technology. The Swift compiler can make better decisions and code optimizations when it knows that a location in memory holding a value will not change. Always use constants in your code when this is the case. Only use variables when you truly anticipate that the value will change at some point. In short, constants don't require as much overhead as variables, precisely because they don't change.

As you learn to develop with Swift, you'll find yourself using constants in more and more situations where you recognize that a value doesn't change. Indeed, Apple encourages their use in your code for that very reason.

THIS THING CALLED A TYPE

Earlier, did you notice that Swift inferred the type of our declared variables automatically? Recall that you didn't have to do any extra typing to tell Swift that a variable was an integer or a double. Swift infers the type of a variable or a constant by simply looking at what is on the right side of the equals sign.

A type is a construct that computer languages use to classify values and the containers that hold them. Types bring clarity of intent to code and eliminate ambiguity by clearly defining the characteristics of a value, variable, or constant. They tightly couple a variable or constant to its value, like an ironclad contract. Swift is very much a type-aware language, and you've seen this already in some of the previous examples.

Table 1.1 illustrates Swift's basic types. There are others, and as you'll see later, you can create our own types, but for now, you'll work with these:

TABLE 1.1 Variable Types

TYPE	CHARACTERISTICS	EXAMPLES
Bool	A binary type that is either true or false	true, false
Int, Int32, Int64	A 32- or 64-bit positive or negative whole number value used to represent larger numbers; no fractional component	3, 117, −502001, 10045
Int8, Int16	An 8- or 16-bit positive or negative whole number value used to represent smaller numbers; no fractional component	−11, 83, 122
UInt, UInt32, UInt64	A 32- or 64-bit positive whole number value used to represent larger numbers; no fractional component	3, 117, 50, 10045
UInt8, UInt16	An 8- or 16-bit positive whole number value used to represent smaller numbers; no fractional component	44, 86, 255
Float, Double	A positive or negative floating point number; may have a fractional component	324.147, −2098.8388, 16.0
Character	A single letter, number, or other symbol bounded by double quotes	"A", "!", "*", "5"
String	A sequence of characters bounded by double quotes	"Jambalaya", "Crawfish Pie", "Filet Gumbo"

You have already learned about Int, but Int8, Int32, and Int64 may be new to you, as well as UInt, UInt8, UInt32, and UInt64. Integers that can be positive and negative are known as *signed integers* and come in 8, 16, 32, and 64 bits of representation; integers that are positive only are known as *unsigned integers*. They also come in 8-, 16-, 32-, and 64-bit flavors. If you don't specify 32- or 64-bit types, the 64-bit values are assumed in Int and UInt. In fact, in development you rarely need to concern yourself with the size of a type. For now, don't worry about this detail.

TESTING THE LIMITS

Each of the numeric types in Table 1.1 has an upper and lower limit. That is, each type can store a number that can be no smaller than its minimum and no larger than its maximum. That's because numeric types have a finite amount of bits that can be used to represent them. Swift conveniently allows you to interrogate each type for its minimum and maximum stored value:

```
 11> println(Int.min)
-9223372036854775808
 12> println(Int.max)
9223372036854775807
 13> println(UInt.min)
0
 14> println(UInt.max)
18446744073709551615
 15>
```

By adding .min or .max to the end of the type name, you can determine its minimum and maximum value capacity. Lines 11 through 14 show the ranges for the Int and UInt type. Feel free to explore the ranges of the other types listed in the table.

CAN A LEOPARD CHANGE ITS STRIPES?

Since types are an inherent characteristic of a value, constant, or variable, you may be curious as to what the rules are when different types interact with each other. Remember in the earlier example where you tried assigning a variable of one type to the variable of another? The initial assignment attempt caused an error, and some nudging was required to convince Swift to assign the Double variable to an Int one. Let's look at that example again (don't retype it; just scroll up in the Terminal to see what you typed earlier):

```
  4> var x = 12
x: Int = 12
  5> var y = 42.0
y: Double = 42
```

We assigned x and y values of Int and Double, respectively, and then shortly thereafter attempted to assign the value of y to x:

```
  8> x = y
<REPL>:8:5: error: 'Double' is not convertible to 'Int'
x = y
    ^

  8> x = Int(y)
  9> println(x)
42
```

The assignment of the newly declared variable x to the number 12 on line 4 established it as an Int, followed by declaring y as a Double. Then an assignment of y to x failed with the error, which forced us to cast y into an Int on line 8. We refer to this process as *casting*, whereby a value of one type is coerced into being a value of another type. In computer language–speak, this feature is known as *type conversion*. Every language has rules for handling type conversions, and Swift is certainly no exception.

One typical rule is that type conversions can only take place between "like" types. In popular computer languages such as C, you can convert an integer to a double, or vice versa, because both are numeric types. However, coercing an integer to become a string is not a valid type conversion because the types are inherently different. Swift is a bit more flexible in this regard, however. Try the following:

```
 15> var t = 123
t: Int = 123
 16> var s = String(t)
s: String = "123"
 17>
```

Here, the variable t is being declared and assigned what is clearly an Int number. That is followed by another declaration of the variable s to the String type casted version of the Int variable t.

Can we cast a string into an Int, or even a Double?

```
 17> var u = Int(s)
<REPL>:17:9: error: cannot invoke 'init' with an argument of type
 →  '@lvalue String'
var u = Int(s)
        ^~~~~~
```

```
 17> var v = Double(s)
<REPL>:17:9: error: cannot invoke 'init' with an argument of type
 →  '@lvalue String'
var v = Double(s)
        ^~~~~~~~~
```

Here is where Swift draws its line in the sand. Although casting a numeric type to a String type is possible, it doesn't work the other way around. But don't fret; you can convert a String's contents to an Int or Double, without type casting:

```
 17> var myConvertedInt = s.toInt()
myConvertedInt: Int? = 123
 18>
```

The String type has a special method for converting its contents to an integer: toInt(). This method evaluates the string's contents and if it consists of characters composed of a valid integer, it provides the integer representation. On line 17, myConvertedInt is declared and assigned an Int value on the same line.

You are probably puzzled by the Int? shown in Swift's response for line 17, and rightly wondering "What is that question mark doing there?" It's an indicator that myConvertedInt is a special type of Int: an optional Int. We'll talk a lot more about optionals later, but for now, just know that they allow a variable to take on a special value known as nil.

BEING EXPLICIT

Having Swift infer the type of your variables or constants is pretty handy. You don't have to tell Swift what an integer is, or what a number with a fractional component is—it just knows. However, sometimes you may want to explicitly declare a variable or constant to be a certain type. Swift allows you to advertise the type as part of the declaration:

```
 18> var myNewNumber : Double = 3
myNewNumber: Double = 3
 19>
```

Declaring a variable or constant with a specific type is as easy as adding a colon, followed by the type name, after the variable or constant name. Here, you've declared myNewNumber as a Double and assigned the number 3 to it, and Swift dutifully reports the declaration.

What would have happened if you left off the : Double on line 18? Swift would have evaluated the assignment, determined that the value was an Int, and made myNewNumber that type. In this particular case, we overrode Swift's inherent assumption, and forced it to type the variable according to our wishes.

Let's consider what happens if we leave off the assignment of the variable or constant to a value:

```
 19> var m : Int
:19:5 error: variables currently must have an initial value when entered at the
→  top level of the REPL
 20> let rr : Int
<REPL>:20:5: error: 'let' declarations require an initializer expression
let rr : Int
      ^
```

On line 19, a variable named m was declared to be an Int, but did not assign a value at declaration time. Swift returned an error indicating that an initial value must be assigned in the context of the REPL.

On the next line, the let command declares rr as an Int, but does not assign a value. Notice that Swift returns an error indicating that an initializer expression is required. Since constants are just that—constant—the value must be assigned when the constant is declared.

STRINGS AND THINGS

So far, you've delved a bit into the numeric types, but another type in Swift is used quite a bit: the String type. As you saw earlier, a string in Swift is one or more characters bounded by double quotes ("").

Here is a perfectly valid declaration of a string:

```
20> let myState = "Louisiana"
myState: String = "Louisiana"
21>
```

So is this:

```
21> let myParish : String = "St. Landry"
myParish: String = "St. Landry"
22>
```

Again, these examples underscore type inference versus type explicitness. In the first case, Swift looks at the value to determine the type; in the second case, you specified the type explicitly. Both are correct.

STRINGING THINGS TOGETHER

Strings can be connected, or *concatenated* together to form larger strings using the plus sign (+) operator. Here are a number of constant declarations that are used to form a larger constant string:

```
22> let noun = "Wayne"
noun: String = "Wayne"
23> let verb = "drives"
verb: String = "drives"
24> let preposition = "to Cal's gym"
preposition: String = "to the gym"
25> let sentence = noun + " " + verb + " " + preposition + "."
sentence: String = "Wayne drives to Cal's gym."
26>
```

On line 25, we concatenated six individual pieces of text together and assigned that result to the sentence constant.

CHARACTERS HAVE CHARACTER

So far, you've seen three types in action: Int (for whole numbers), Double (for numbers with a fractional component), and String (for a series of characters). Another type you will use in Swift is the Character type, which is actually a special case of a String. A variable or constant of type Character contains a single character bound in double quote marks.

It's worth a try:

```
26> let myFavoriteLetter = "A"
myFavoriteLetter: String = "A"
 27>
```

You may be scratching your head wondering why the variable myFavoriteLetter is identified by Swift as a String. Without explicitly specifying the type Character, Swift assumes a string type when even just one letter is enclosed in double quotes. The Character type is one type that isn't inferred by Swift. Let's rectify this:

```
27> let myFavoriteLetter : Character = "A"
myFavoriteLetter: Character = "A"
 28>
```

Now we get the result we expect!

If a String is a composition of one or more Character types, you should be able to build a String from a Character. And indeed you can, using the same plus sign (+) operator we used earlier for strings, but with a caveat: The character must be cast to a String type.

```
28> let myFavoriteLetters = String(myFavoriteLetter) +
    → String(myFavoriteLetter)
myFavoriteLetters: String = "AA"
 29>
```

If you are coming from languages like C or Objective-C where string concatenation is much more obtuse, this should feel extremely simple. After all, bringing characters and strings together with a simple plus sign operator is a lot less typing that using C's strcat() function or Objective-C's Foundation class NSString method stringWithFormat: to perform string concatenation. You're witnessing the conciseness and beauty of the Swift language in action here. String concatenation is as naturally expressive as adding two numbers. Speaking of adding numbers, let's get back to them, and take a look at doing some simple math in Swift.

MATH AND MORE

Swift can do math very, very well. We just saw how the String type uses the plus sign for concatenating strings. However, the plus sign is used for more than just bringing together strings. It's also the universal expression for addition, and now is as good a time as any to explore Swift's math capabilities. Let's look at a few simple arithmetic examples of mathematical expressions:

```
29> let addition = 2 + 2
addition: Int = 4
30> let subtraction = 4 - 3
subtraction: Int = 1
31> let multiplication = 10 * 5
multiplication: Int = 50
32> let division = 24 / 6
division: Int = 4
33>
```

The basic four operations are here: addition (+), subtraction (-), multiplication (*), and division (/). Swift gave us the answers we anticipated and also typed the constants as we would expect: Int. Again, this decision to type the constants as integers is based on the value on the right side of the equals sign.

We can also perform the modulo math operation (using the % operator), which returns the remainder value of a division operation:

```
33> let modulo = 23 % 4
modulo: Int = 3
34>
```

In Swift, the modulo operator even works with Double values:

```
34> let modulo = 23.5 % 4.3
modulo: Double = 2.0000000000000009
35>
```

In addition, the plus and minus signs are honored as unary operators. Prepending a + to the value infers a positive number, while a - implies a negative number:

```
35> var positiveNumber : Int = +33
positiveNumber: Int = 33
36> var negativeNumber : Int = -33
negativeNumber: Int = -33
37>
```

EXPRESSIONS

Mathematical expressions are fully supported, including the standard operator order of precedence (multiplication and division evaluated first from left to right, and then addition and subtraction):

```
 37> let r = 3 + 5 * 9
r: Int = 48
 38> let g = (3 + 5) * 9
g: Int = 72
 39>
```

Line 37 yields the result of multiplying 5 times 9 first and then adding 3, while line 38 yields the same expression with parentheses around the first two values to enforce the addition first, and then the multiplication of the result by 9. Swift honors the canonical order of precedence of mathematical operations just like other modern languages.

MIXING NUMERIC TYPES

What happens if we get clever and mix a number with a fractional component with an integer?

```
 39> let anotherDivision = 48 / 5.0
anotherDivision: Double = 9.5999999999999996
 40>
```

Here we are dividing an integer 48 by a number 5 with a decimal point and a 0 behind it. The decimal point is just enough of a hint to Swift that its type is Double. Even the type of the resulting constant anotherDivision is assigned a type of Double. What you are witnessing here is Swift's notion of *type promotion*. The Int 48 has been promoted to a Double simply by the presence of another Double in the equation. Likewise, the type of the constant being assigned also takes on the same type. It's a good idea to be aware of this rule.

When numeric values of different types are used in a common expression, type promotion always goes from the type with the least possible representation to the type with the most possible representation. Since a Double can represent Int value, but not the other way around, Int values are promoted to Double values.

NUMERIC REPRESENTATIONS

Numeric values can be represented different ways in Swift. Up to now, we've been focused on the most common and natural way of thinking of numbers: decimal, or base 10. Let's explore other ways to express a numeric value.

BINARY, OCTAL, AND HEXADECIMAL NOTATION

If you have done any amount of programming, you've encountered base 2, base 16, and possibly even base 8 numbers. Known as binary, hexadecimal, and octal, respectively, these number systems come up often enough in software development that having a shorthand notation to refer to them in their natural state is helpful:

```
40> let binaryNumber = 0b110011
binaryNumber: Int = 51
 41> let octalNumber = 0o12
octalNumber: Int = 10
 42> let hexadecimalNumber = 0x32
hexadecimalNumber: Int = 50
 43>
```

The prefix for binary numbers is 0b, for octal numbers it's 0o, and for hexadecimal numbers it's 0x. Of course, no prefix implies a decimal number.

SCIENTIFIC NOTATION

An alternate way of representing a number is to provide it in scientific notation. Such notation is useful to express numbers with a large number of decimal places in a compact form:

```
43> let scientificNotation = 4.434e-10
scientificNotation: Double = 0.00000000044339999999999999
 44>
```

The e represents the exponent of a base 10 number, in this case 4.434×10^{-10}.

LARGE NUMBER NOTATION

If you've ever sat in front of your Mac counting the number of zeros behind a number to determine its magnitude, you'll love this next feature. Swift allows you to demark large numbers in such a way that their size is immediately clear:

```
44> let fiveMillion = 5_000_000
fiveMillion: Int = 5000000
 45>
```

The underscores are ignored but help immensely with the readability of the number.

TRUE OR FALSE

Another type that Swift supports is Bool, or the Boolean type; it holds a single value: true or false and is often used in comparative expressions to answer questions like "is 12 greater than 3?" or "does 55 equal 12?" These logical comparisons are used heavily in software development, from terminating the iteration of a list of objects to determining the execution path of a set of conditional statements:

```
 45> 100 > 50
$R0: Bool = true
 46> 1.1 >= 0.3
$R1: Bool = true
 47> 66.22 < 7
$R2: Bool = false
 48> 44 <= 1
$R3: Bool = false
 49> 5.4 == 9.3
$R4: Bool = false
 50> 6 != 7
$R5: Bool = true
 51>
```

The comparisons above are: greater than, greater than or equal, less than, less than or equal, equal to, and not equal to. Based on the "trueness" of the comparison, a Bool of either true or false is returned. We're also comparing both Int and Double literals to illustrate that both numeric types are comparable, even amongst each other.

THE RESULT

Notice that we have not used the let or var keyword to assign the result of the Boolean expression to a variable or constant. Also, the results of the conditional expression evaluations are different, as in the result of line 48:

```
$R3: Bool = false
```

What is $R3? This is known in the Swift REPL as a temporary variable, and it holds the value of the result, in this case, false. You can reference a temporary variable as though it were a variable:

```
51> println($R3)
```
false
```
52>
```

You can assign values to these temporary variables as though they were declared variables as well.

WHAT ABOUT STRINGS?

Wouldn't it be great if you could use the same comparator operators to test the equality of strings? If you've come from C or Objective-C, you know how tedious testing for equality of two strings is.

In C, it's like this:

```
int result = strcmp("this string", "that string")
```

In Objective-C, it's like this:

```
NSComparisonResult result = [@"this string" compare:@ "that string"];
```

Swift makes this operation super easy to read and type:

```
52> "this string" == "that string"
$R6: Bool = false
53> "b" > "a"
$R7: Bool = true
54> "this string" == "this string"
$R8: Bool = true
55> "that string" <= "a string"
$R9: Bool = false
56>
```

The results speak for themselves: Swift's string comparison feature is much more natural and expressive.

PRINTING MADE EASY

So far we have used the `print` and `println` methods to print strings in the REPL. Let's revisit these methods, and examine how we can use them to construct more complex strings.

One of the conveniences of the `print` and `println` methods is their ability to effortlessly print the contents of variables in-line with other text. If you happen to know C or Objective-C, you'll recall that the amount of typing required to express formatted text is rather large, with `printf` in C and `NSLog()` in Objective-C being prime examples. Consider this Objective-C code excerpt:

```
NSString *myFavoriteCity = "New Orleans";
NSString *myFavoriteFood = "Seafood Gumbo";
NSString *myFavoriteRestaurant = "Mulates";
NSInteger yearsSinceVisit = 3;
NSLog(@"When I visited %@ %d years ago, I went to %@ and ordered %@.",
 → myFavoriteCity, yearsSinceVisit, myFavoriteRestaurant, myFavoriteFood);
```

If this looks familiar to you, you know that it's problematic for several reasons. First, the variables are not in the exact position they would be when the string is printed, which requires us to "line up" variables in the correct order or else we will get unexpected results. Second, we are dealing with two different types of variables with different formatting codes: `NSString`, which uses `%@`, and `NSInteger`, which uses `%d`. (If you aren't familiar with the concept of formatting codes, don't worry, you won't use them in Swift.)

With Swift you avoid the cumbersome dance of using a format string and worrying about ordering and formatting codes. Instead, you can simply place your variables right inside the string, exactly where they would naturally go, and they will be printed right alongside the other text. Here's the Swift version of the Objective-C code:

```
 56> let myFavoriteCity = "New Orleans"
myFavoriteCity: String = "New Orleans"
 57> let myFavoriteFood = "Seafood Gumbo"
myFavoriteFood: String = "Seafood Gumbo"
 58> let myFavoriteRestaurant = "Mulates"
myFavoriteRestaurant: String = "Mulates"
 59> let yearsSinceVisit = 3
yearsSinceVisit: Int = 3
 60> println("When I visited \(myFavoriteCity) \(yearsSinceVisit) years ago,
     → I went to \(myFavoriteRestaurant) and ordered \(myFavoriteFood).")
When I visited New Orleans 3 years ago, I went to Mulates and ordered
 → Seafood Gumbo.
 61>
```

The markup to do this on line 60 is amazingly simple. There, the embedded notation \() is used to reference all four constants you declared earlier on lines 56 through 59. This notation is very handy, especially when compared to how the aforementioned languages handle this feature.

Of course, assigning the result of the string to a variable or constant is just as easy as printing it:

```
61> let sentence = "When I visited \(myFavoriteCity) \(yearsSinceVisit) years
  → ago, I went to \(myFavoriteRestaurant) and ordered \(myFavoriteFood)."
sentence: String = "When I visited New Orleans 3 years ago, I went to Mulates
→ and ordered Seafood Gumbo."
62>
```

USING ALIASES

We talked about types earlier and how they are central to Swift's idea of identifying and classifying variables and constants. As an *immutable* (non-changing) property, the type is an integral component of every number and string in your program. Sometimes, however, you may want to enhance the readability of your source code by using a type alias.

A *type alias* is simply a way of telling Swift to give an alternate name to a type:

```
62> typealias EightBits = UInt8
63> var reg : EightBits = 0
reg: EightBits = 0
64>
```

Here, the native Swift type UInt8 has been aliased to EightBits, which can then be used in subsequent declarations. You can even get clever and assign a type alias to another type alias:

```
64> typealias NewBits = EightBits
65> var reg2 : NewBits = 0
reg2: NewBits = 0
66>
```

Of course, NewBits and EightBits are really a UInt8 under the hood. Nothing really new has been created in terms of a type, but the readability of your code changes. Although type aliases are great ways to enhance your code, they should be used with care and their use documented, especially if you are sharing your work with other developers. Nothing can be more confusing than encountering a new type and not knowing exactly what it is or represents.

GROUPING DATA WITH TUPLES

Sometimes bringing different data elements together to form a larger type is useful. Up to now, you've worked with single pieces of data: integers, strings, and so on. These elemental types are the foundation of Swift's data storage and manipulation capabilities, but they can also be combined in interesting ways as you'll see throughout the book.

One such combination that we will explore here is the *tuple*. A tuple is a grouping of one or more variables, constants, or literal values into a single entity. A tuple is defined by a comma-separated list bounded with parentheses:

```
66> let myDreamCar = (2014, "Mercedes-Benz", "M-Class")
myDreamCar: (Int, String, String) = {
  0 = 2014
  1 = "Mercedes-Benz"
  2 = "M-Class"
}
67>
```

The constant myDreamCar is defined as a tuple with three elements: an Int and two String literals. Note that Swift inferred the type of each member of the tuple, as you did not provide an explicit type. Also, the members of the tuple retain the order in which they are defined.

So now that you've defined a tuple, what can you do with it? You can inspect it, of course. Using dot notation, you can explore the tuple's contents, starting with the 0 index element as follows:

```
67> println(myDreamCar.0)
2006
68> println(myDreamCar.1)
Ford
69> println(myDreamCar.2)
Mustang
70> println(myDreamCar)
(2006, Ford, Mustang)
71>
```

If you attempt to reference a non-existing member of the tuple, Swift will remind you with an error:

```
71> println(myDreamCar.3)
<REPL>:71:9: error: '(Int, String, String)' does not have a member named '3'
println(myDreamCar.3)
        ^           ~

71>
```

You will encounter the use of tuples later in this book; as you'll see, they will come in handy for quite a few things.

OPTIONALS

You may recall earlier that we used the toInt() method on a String variable s to convert its contents to an Int so that it could be assigned to a new variable of the same type:

```
17> var myConvertedInt = s.toInt()
myConvertedInt: Int? = 123
18>
```

We glossed over the question mark following the type designator returned by Swift. That question mark signifies that myConvertedInt is more than just an Int. It's an *optional* Int.

So what exactly is an optional? It's actually a qualifier on a type that alerts Swift that the variable or constant could be nothing, or *nil*. The value nil has long standing in programming languages. In Objective-C, it's also known as nil and in C/C++, it's NULL. The meaning is essentially the same: empty.

Let's consider the code above in a different context: where s is not "123" but "abc":

```
71> let s = "abc"
s: String = "abc"
72> var myConvertedInt = s.toInt()
myConvertedInt: Int? = nil
73>
```

Notice that myConvertedInt is still of type Int? (an optional Int), but its value is not 123. It's nil. And that is precisely because there is no numeric representation for the letters "abc" to convert to an Int. Returning nil is Swift's way of admitting defeat. The optional gives a variable an alternate path to success. In this case, the String class's toInt() method is returning nil as a way of saying "I cannot convert this into a number."

Declaring a variable as an optional is as simple as adding a question mark at the end of the type at declaration time:

```
73> var v : Int?
v: Int? = nil
74>
```

Swift responds with the indication that v is indeed an optional Int. Since you didn't provide an assignment to a value at declaration time, the default assigned value is not 0, but nil.

Try setting the variable to an actual value:

```
74> v = 3
75>
```

Finally, let's show the value. Instead of using the println method, we'll just type the name of the variable; Swift will assign it to a temporary.

```
75> v
$R10: Int? = 3
76>
```

And as you can see, Swift reports that the value is indeed 3.

Optionals work on more than just Int types. In fact, any type can be declared as an optional. Here's an example of two variables, one String and one Character, as declared optionals:

```
76> var s : String? = "Valid text"
s: String? = "Valid text"
77> var u : Character? = "a"
u: Character? = "a"
78> u = nil
79>
```

On line 78, u is set to the nil value, underscoring that any variable declared as an optional can be set to nil.

We'll explore optionals much more in a subsequent chapter. For now, knowing that they exist and recognizing the notation surrounding them is enough.

SUMMARY

Congratulations, Swift beginner... you've made it through the first chapter. And what a whirlwind it has been. You have been thrown quite a lot of information to digest, so don't hesitate to go back and review the chapter if you need to.

Here are the topics that were introduced in this chapter:

- Variables
- Constants
- The `print` method
- Types (`Int`, `Double`, `Character`, and `String`, just to name a few)
- Mathematical operators
- Numeric notations (binary, hexadecimal, scientific, and so on)
- String concatenation
- Type inference and explicit declarations
- Type aliases
- Tuples
- Optionals

Remember: These are the basic concepts you need to master in order to become a Swift artisan. Know and understand them well because in subsequent chapters we'll build on what you learned here and discuss even more features of the language.

CHAPTER 2

Working with Collections

The last chapter covered a lot of the basics of Swift, with plenty of examples (including intentional mistakes) in order to reinforce the concepts of variables, constants, and types. As you'll see going forward, the Chapter 1 information will come in handy in this and subsequent chapters.

For this chapter, get ready to turn your attention to the notion of collections.

When you think of a collection, what comes to mind? Here are several examples of collections you might have had at one time or another:

- Assortment of toy action figures and accessories
- Postage stamps or coins from different countries
- Shopping list of items to buy at the grocery store

Collections can also be more general categorizations:

- Make and model of vehicles in a parking lot
- Names of people on a wedding invitation list

All these examples evoke the notion of a grouping or organization of individual elements or items (toys, stamps, vehicles, and so on). Collections of related (or even unrelated) items is an important part of the Swift language. And as you'll see shortly, collections come in different flavors.

For the bulk of this chapter, you'll focus on collections, which are essentially structures that allow you to group information and data in various ways. You'll use collections quite a bit later in this book and in your general Swift development, so take the time to understand them.

THE CANDY JAR

Let's explore the idea of collections in Swift by imagining an empty candy jar sitting on a store counter. Now, think of all the various candies you could put into that jar. Let's call the jar a *container*, which holds one or more candies, or *values*. Representing that candy jar and its contents in Swift can be modeled in a number of ways, starting with an *array*.

An array is nothing more than an ordered list of values of some length. Arrays are common constructs in computer languages, and declaring one in Swift is easy.

Here is an array of three candy values that would go into the virtual candy jar:

```
1> let candyJar = ["Peppermints", "Gooey Bears", "Happy Ranchers"]
candyJar: [String] = 3 values {
  [0] = "Peppermints"
  [1] = "Gooey Bears"
  [2] = "Happy Ranchers"
}
  2>
```

Recognize the let keyword? That's the constant declaration keyword. In this case you're declaring a constant named candyJar and using a special notation: the opening and closing brackets [and]. The items in the array are bounded by these two characters, and this is how Swift recognizes that an array is being declared.

This array has three String constants:

- "Peppermints"
- "Gooey Bears"
- "Happy Ranchers"

The comma between each value in the array denotes where one value ends and the other begins. Also, notice that once again, Swift inferred the types of each of these items by simply looking at how they are represented—as strings. That's because each value is surrounded by double quotes.

We'll continue to use the REPL to explore concepts. The line numbers shown in the code snippets in this chapter start with line number 1, which presumes we have restarted the REPL. Remember: To quit the REPL, type:

```
:quit
```

and to restart the REPL from the Terminal, type:

```
xcrun swift
```

Notice how Swift reported the declaration to us after you typed it. It explicitly points to candyJar being an array of String values:

```
candyJar: [String] = 3 values {
  [0] = "Peppermints"
  [1] = "Gooey Bears"
  [2] = "Happy Ranchers"
}
```

Here, Swift is confirming that the array holds three values, and that they are ordered, starting with the number 0. In fact, all arrays in Swift begin with the "0th value" and continue in ordinal fashion. This number is known as the *array index* and maps directly to the value it represents.

So far, so good? Great. Now, let's learn how to interrogate an array for a particular value. Let's say you wanted to see the second element in the array. Remember, since arrays are ordered starting at 0, the second element will have an index of 1.

```
2> candyJar[1]
$R0: String = "Gooey Bears"
3>
```

> **NOTE:** To print or not to print? Remember, simply typing the name of the item without using print or println is acceptable when using the REPL. When doing so, the result of the expression is assigned to a temporary variable—in this case $R0.

Swift politely responds with the value "Gooey Bears" as the second element in the array and also reminds us of the type: String.

As expected, replacing the [1] with another array index will reference the value at that location:

```
3> candyJar [2]
$R1: String = "Happy Ranchers"
4>
```

That notation is quite handy. You can access individual elements in the array simply by using the index number bounded by brackets.

Now, what happens if you reference a nonexistent location? Use an index that is clearly out of the range of the currently available index values:

```
4> candyJar[5]
fatal error: Array index out of range
Execution interrupted. Enter Swift code to recover and continue.
Enter LLDB commands to investigate (type :help for assistance.)
  5>
```

Not surprisingly, you have hit a nerve with Swift because you requested a nonexistent element. The array doesn't have a sixth element (the array has only three elements, with subscripts 0, 1, and 2). Being the ever so careful language that it is, Swift reminds us of the infraction with a fatal error.

And here's where Swift is ahead of the pack compared to some other computer languages: It emphasizes *safety*. Swift creates a safe environment where exceptional and anomalous behavior, like referencing nonexisting array subscripts, is not tolerated. If you have any experience with arrays in C, you might already know accessing nonexistent parts of an array is possible. In fact, very similar methods have been used in the past by writers of Trojan horse software to compromise computer systems.

This error presents an opportunity to bring up a very good question: "What if I wanted to add more values to an array? How would I do that?" Swift has a special method that works on arrays: append(). To add a value to an array, simply append it. Let's add my favorite candy to the jar:

```
5> candyJar.append("Candy Canes")
/var/folders/2c/pbfh6lvx6gl73t448cwt47v00000gn/T//lldb/3609/expr.mdR66C.
→ swift:2:1: error: immutable value of type '[String]' only has mutating
→ members named 'append'
candyJar.append("Candy Canes")
^               ~~~~~~

  5>
```

Another error! It seems you just can't catch a break. We all learn by making mistakes, though, and this is certainly part of learning the ins and outs of Swift.

Can you spot why this error occurred? Look carefully at the text of the error message:

error: immutable value of type '[String]' only has mutating members named 'append'

Swift is telling you that the array of String values is immutable (nonchangeable), and you are trying to change the contents of a constant array. Remember, you declared the array as a constant array with let. You cannot modify the value of a constant, and that includes arrays declared as constants.

You'll need to create a second array, a mutable (changeable) one. You can do that easily, and at the same time, start with the contents of the immutable array:

```
5> var refillableCandyJar = candyJar
refillableCandyJar: [String] = 3 values {
  [0] = "Peppermints"
  [1] = "Gooey Bears"
  [2] = "Happy Ranchers"
}
  6>
```

That was easy! You just declared a variable refillableCandyJar and initialized it with the contents of the candyJar constant array. All the same values that exist in the constant array are now part of this variable array.

BIRDS OF A FEATHER...

Can an array contain values of different types? Try the following:

```
6> var arrayTest = ["x", 3]
/var/folders/2c/pbfh6lvx6gl73t448cwt47v00000gn/T//lldb/3866/expr.xiaPT9.
→ swift:2:17: error: 'String' is not convertible to 'Int'
var arrayTest = ["x", 3]
                ^


  6>
```

Clearly, Swift prevents this from happening, underscoring that indeed, values in an array must be of the same type.

Speaking of types, what if you want to be specific about the value type in the array declaration itself?

```
6> var h2o : [String] = ["Hydrogen", "Hydrogen", "Oxygen"]
h2o: [String] = 3 values {
  [0] = "Hydrogen"
  [1] = "Hydrogen"
  [2] = "Oxygen"
}
  7>
```

Declaring an array to hold specific type values involves adding the colon, followed by the name of the type bounded by brackets [ ].

EXTENDING THE ARRAY

Let's bring our focus back to the `refillableCandyJar` array, which is a mutable array, thanks to the previous assignment on line 5. Now, can you actually append to this new array? Let's find out:

```
 7> refillableCandyJar.append("Candy Canes")
 8>
```

Other than the prompt, there's no indication whether or not this was successful. But hey, at least you didn't get an error. Let's see the contents of the variable array and verify that Candy Canes was added:

```
 8> refillableCandyJar
$R2: [String] = 4 values {
  [0] = "Peppermints"
  [1] = "Gooey Bears"
  [2] = "Happy Ranchers"
  [3] = "Candy Canes"
}
 9>
```

And indeed, it occupies the fourth location (array subscript 3) in the array, just as we hoped it would.

Let's add a few more candies to the jar. This time, use a different syntax:

```
 9> refillableCandyJar += ["Peanut Clusters"]
10> refillableCandyJar += ["Banana Taffy", "Bubble Gum"]
11> refillableCandyJar
$R3: [String] = 7 values {
  [0] = "Peppermints"
  [1] = "Gooey Bears"
  [2] = "Happy Ranchers"
  [3] = "Candy Canes"
  [4] = "Peanut Clusters"
  [5] = "Banana Taffy"
  [6] = "Bubble Gum"
}
12>
```

Instead of adding a single `String` value, lines 9 and 10 instead append another array, which demonstrates the flexibility that Swift brings here. You can simply add the contents of one array to another with the += operator. Finally, on line 11, you requested the contents of the variable `refillableCandyJar`, which shows the entire contents of the virtual candy jar—all seven delicious varieties.

So far, you have created a constant array and a variable array. You've also assigned the constant array to the variable array, creating a mutable array that can be changed. And you've successfully modified the array contents using both the append() method and the += operator. Let's do some further exploration into arrays.

REPLACING AND REMOVING VALUES

Replacing an array value is as simple as specifying the array subscript and assigning it a new value. Let's replace Happy Ranchers with another type of candy:

```
12> refillableCandyJar[2] = "Lollipops"
13> refillableCandyJar
$R4: [String] = 7 values {
  [0] = "Peppermints"
  [1] = "Gooey Bears"
  [2] = "Lollipops"
  [3] = "Candy Canes"
  [4] = "Peanut Clusters"
  [5] = "Banana Taffy"
  [6] = "Bubble Gum"
}
 14>
```

Replacements work great. But what if you want to remove a value? Perhaps you don't like Gooey Bears. Can it be removed from the virtual candy jar? Of course. You've grown a variable array by appending to it, now you'll remove some items completely:

```
14> refillableCandyJar.removeAtIndex(1)
$R5: String = "Gooey Bears"
15> refillableCandyJar
$R6: [String] = 6 values {
  [0] = "Peppermints"
  [1] = "Lollipops"
  [2] = "Candy Canes"
  [3] = "Peanut Clusters"
  [4] = "Banana Taffy"
  [5] = "Bubble Gum"
}
 16>
```

On line 14, you employed the array method removeAtIndex(), which takes a single parameter: the index of the value you wish to remove. The method's result is the value removed, and the value is assigned to $R5.

A quick review of the variable refillableCandyJar on line 15 shows that indeed, the Gooey Bears are gone, and the contents of the entire array have "shifted" up. Instead of seven items in the candy jar, you have six now.

Remember, any time an item is removed from an array, the other values "fill in the gap" and move up to accommodate the empty space.

Here's another handy way to remove the last value of the array:

```
16> refillableCandyJar.removeLast()
$R7: String = "Bubble Gum"
17>
```

Again, the removed value is returned, and the array is shortened from six to five values:

```
17> refillableCandyJar
$R8: [String] = 6 values {
  [0] = "Peppermints"
  [1] = "Lollipops"
  [2] = "Candy Canes"
  [3] = "Peanut Clusters"
  [4] = "Banana Taffy"
}
18>
```

INSERTING VALUES AT A SPECIFIC LOCATION

So far, you have added values (via the append() method) to the end of an array, and you have directed Swift to remove a value at a specific position from the array. Now, let's see how easy inserting a value is.

Let's add "Twirlers" at the position where "Candy Canes" is currently. That's position 2, or the third position in the array:

```
18> refillableCandyJar.insert("Twirlers", atIndex: 2)
19>
```

Now let's review the contents of the array to see if it worked:

```
19> refillableCandyJar
$R9: [String] = 6 values {
  [0] = "Peppermints"
  [1] = "Lollipops "
  [2] = "Twirlers"
  [3] = "Candy Canes"
  [4] = "Peanut Clusters"
  [5] = "Banana Taffy"
20>
```

And indeed it did. "`Twirlers`" now occupies location 2. The values have also been shifted down one place to accommodate the new value thanks to the `insert()` method.

Notice that the `insert()` method took two parameters: the value to insert into the array, as well as the index (or position) where the insertion takes place. What's interesting to note about this method is the second parameter. These named parameters increase the readability of Swift's code by providing context for the parameter being passed. You'll learn more about the composition of method names in Swift a little later.

COMBINING ARRAYS

Swift's syntax for combining arrays together is natural for concatenating strings. To illustrate, create another candy jar array with a different set of confectionaries:

```
20> var anotherRefillableCandyJar = [ "Sour Tarts", "Cocoa Bar",
    → "Coconut Rounds" ]
anotherRefillableCandyJar: [String] = 3 values {
  [0] = "Sour Tarts"
  [1] = "Cocoa Bar"
  [2] = "Coconut Rounds"
}
21>
```

Now create a third array with the array combination syntax using the earlier array, `refillableCandyJar` with six values, and the new `anotherRefillableCandyJar` with three values:

```
21> var combinedRefillableCandyJar = refillableCandyJar +
    → anotherRefillableCandyJar
combinedRefillableCandyJar: [String] = 9 values {
  [0] = "Peppermints"
  [1] = "Lollipops"
  [2] = "Twirlers"
  [3] = "Candy Canes"
  [4] = "Peanut Clusters"
  [5] = "Banana Taffy"
  [6] = "Sour Tarts"
  [7] = "Cocoa Bar"
  [8] = "Coconut Rounds"
}
22>
```

The new array has nine values (six from the first array, and three from the second). Also, the values are ordered in the same way they were in the original arrays.

We've covered a lot about arrays. They are excellent for storing lists of values, whether they are related or not. They can be immutable (by declaring them constant with the let command), or they can be mutable arrays that can change (values can be added, removed, or replaced). And finally, all values within an array must be of the same type.

The next section takes a look at another type of collection: the dictionary.

THE DICTIONARY

When you think of a dictionary, Daniel Webster probably comes to mind. The dictionary on a shelf in the library is composed of pages of definitions for words. You look up a word in alphabetical order to determine its definition. In Swift, dictionaries work in a similar fashion.

Like an array, a dictionary in Swift is composed of one or more entities. Unlike an array, the entity in a dictionary contains two distinct components: a *key* and a *value*. Although the key and the value themselves can be different types, all keys must be of the same type; likewise, all values must also share the same type.

To start out learning about dictionaries, I'll use one of my favorite food additives: peppers. Some peppers are hotter than others, and this "heat" can be quantified using a measurement known as Scoville units. You'll use a dictionary to define a subset of the Scoville scale. The key for each entry will be the name of the pepper, and the value will be the Scoville unit for that pepper:

```
22> var scovilleScale = ["Poblano" : 1_000, "Serrano" : 700, "Red Amazon" :
    → 75_000, "Red Savina Habanero" : 500_000]
scovilleScale: [String : Int] = {
  [0] = {
    key = "Poblano"
    value = 1000
  }
  [1] = {
    key = "Red Savina Habanero"
    value = 500000
  }
  [2] = {
    key = "Red Amazon"
    value = 75000
  }
  [3] = {
    key = "Serrano"
    value = 700
```

```
    }
}
  23>
```

You've just created a dictionary with four entries: Poblano with a score of 1,000, Serrano with a score of 700, Red Amazon with a score of 75,000, and Red Savina Habanero with a score of 500,000! (That's a really hot pepper!)

> **NOTE:** How Swift orders the dictionary depends on the version of Xcode used. However, Swift will always use the order that is the most efficient for retrieval and access.

When you declared the dictionary, Swift once again inferred the type of both the key and the value. The key is clearly a `String` type; the value is an `Int` type. This is confirmed by the REPL report showing the result of the declaration. Also, the underscore was used to visually mark the thousands place in the number. Remember, this is purely syntactic sugar. It has no bearing on the value of the `Int`; the numbers show up without underscores in the result.

Do you notice something unusual? Look closely at the REPL output. The order in which you declared the dictionary and the order in which the dictionary is reported is not the same. Swift ordered the dictionary differently than you declared it. This difference illustrates an important tenet of dictionaries: Swift orders keys to determine the best method for quick retrieval and access. You cannot rely on the order in which you declared a dictionary to be the order in which it will be stored.

LOOKING UP AN ENTRY

Accessing an entry in a dictionary looks very similar to accessing a value in an array... except for the value bounded in the brackets. Recall that in an array, the ordinal position of the value is used (0, 1, 2, 3, and so on). In a dictionary, you use the actual key to look up the value of that entry:

```
  23> scovilleScale["Serrano"]
$R10: Int? = 700
  24>
```

Notice the question mark again following the `Int` declaration. Remember that the question mark signifies an optional value—one that can be `nil`. The return value of a dictionary value is always an optional, but that doesn't mean we can use `nil` as a value, as shown in this example:

```
  24> var myNilArray = ["someKey" : nil]
/var/folders/2c/pbfh6lvx6gl73t448cwt47v00000gn/T//lldb/8622/expr.6ydWX5.
 ⇢ swift:2:18: error: type 'StaticString' does not conform to protocol
 ⇢ 'Hashable'
var myNilArray = ["someKey" : nil]
                 ^
  24>
```

The somewhat mystical error is telling us that `nil` is not a valid value. Nor would it be for the key:

```
24> var myNilArray = [nil : "x"]
/var/folders/2c/pbfh6lvx6gl73t448cwt47v00000gn/T//lldb/8622/expr.vsuqMC.
→ swift:2:18: error: cannot convert the expression's type 'Dictionary' to
→ type 'NilLiteralConvertible'
var myNilArray = [nil : "x"]
                  ^~~~~~~~~~~~~~~~

24>
```

So why would Swift bother to return a value as an optional type when you ask for a value in a dictionary? Let's consider the dictionary of Scoville units again:

```
24> scovilleScale
$R11: [String : Int] = {
  [0] = {
    key = "Poblano"
    value = 1000
  }
  [1] = {
    key = "Red Savina Habanero"
    value = 500000
  }
  [2] = {
    key = "Red Amazon"
    value = 75000
  }
  [3] = {
    key = "Serrano"
    value = 700
  }
}
25>
```

You still have the same four entries in the dictionary. What if you asked for a value with a key that didn't exit? Let's find out if there is a Scoville unit for the Tabasco pepper:

```
25> scovilleScale["Tabasco"]
$R12: Int? = nil
26>
```

Lo and behold, the value returned is `nil`. This is precisely why Swift dictionary values return an optional type: the possibility that the dictionary will be queried with a nonexistent key.

ADDING AN ENTRY

Now that you've established what happens when you ask our Scoville unit dictionary for a nonexistent pepper, let's add that same pepper to our dictionary. Remember, because the dictionary was created as a mutable dictionary with var, extending it with the following syntax is possible:

```
26> scovilleScale["Tabasco"] = 50_000
27>
```

And for verification:

```
27> scovilleScale
$R13: [String : Int] = {
  [0] = {
    key = "Poblano"
    value = 1000
  }
  [1] = {
    key = "Red Savina Habanero"
    value = 500000
  }
  [2] = {
    key = "Tabasco"
    value = 50000
  }
  [3] = {
    key = "Red Amazon"
    value = 75000
  }
  [4] = {
    key = "Serrano"
    value = 700
  }
}
28>
```

Notice that the newly added pepper finds its way in the dictionary in an unpredictable order.

UPDATING AN ENTRY

If you really know your peppers, you may have realized that the Serrano's Scoville unit is actually wrong. The value is off by an order of magnitude: Its Scoville rating is 7,000, not 700. Let's fix that:

```
28> scovilleScale["Serrano"] = 7_000
29>
```

The syntax for updating a dictionary entry is the same as assigning a new value to a new key. Swift simply replaces the old value, 700, with the new value, 7,000:

```
29> scovilleScale
$R14: [String : Int] = {
  [0] = {
    key = "Poblano"
    value = 1000
  }
  [1] = {
    key = "Red Savina Habanero"
    value = 500000
  }
  [2] = {
    key = "Tabasco"
    value = 50000
  }
  [3] = {
    key = "Red Amazon"
    value = 75000
  }
  [4] = {
    key = "Serrano"
    value = 7000
  }
}
30>
```

REMOVING AN ENTRY

Removing a dictionary entry looks a lot like the previous two examples:

```
30> scovilleScale["Tabasco"] = nil
31>
```

Setting the key value to `nil` effectively removes that dictionary entry:

```
31> scovilleScale
$R15: [String : Int] = {
  [0] = {
    key = "Poblano"
    value = 1000
  }
  [1] = {
    key = "Red Savina Habanero"
    value = 500000
  }
  [2] = {
    key = "Red Amazon"
    value = 75000
  }
  [3] = {
    key = "Serrano"
    value = 7000
  }
}
32>
```

Another way to remove a dictionary item is to use the `removeValueForKey()` method:

```
32> scovilleScale.removeValueForKey("Poblano")
$R16: Int? = 1000
33>
```

In this case, the entry's value is returned (1000). Sometimes this is the preferred method of removing an entry, as you'll see in later chapters.

ARRAYS OF ARRAYS?

The parts of this chapter on arrays and dictionaries used a very specific set of data: strings and integers. But what if you wanted to declare an array of dictionaries? Or a dictionary of arrays? In Swift, arrays and dictionaries are types, just like strings and integers, so they can contain references to each other.

Let's take the candy jar analogy a bit further. Mr. Arceneaux has a candy route with three stores: Fontenot's Grocery, Dupre's Quick Mart, and Smith's Pick-n-Sack. Each store has its own candy jar, and every week, Mr. Arceneaux's route takes him to each store to fill the candy jars.

Mr. Fontenot's customers like Choppers and Jaw Bombs, while Mr. Dupre's customers are inclined to purchase chocolate candies like Butterbar, Mrs. Goodbuys, and Giggles. Mr. Smith's customers prefer Jelly Munchers and Gooey Bears.

How could you model this assortment of candies and stores using either arrays or dictionaries? To make things easy, start from the bottom up: with the candy jars.

```
33> var fontenotsCandyJar = [ "Choppers", "Jaw Bombs" ]
fontenotsCandyJar: [String] = 2 values {
  [0] = "Choppers"
  [1] = "Jaw Bombs"
}
34> var dupresCandyJar = [ "Butterbar" , "Mrs. Goodbuys", "Giggles" ]
dupresCandyJar: [String] = 3 values {
  [0] = "Butterbar"
  [1] = "Mrs. Goodbuys"
  [2] = "Giggles"
}
35> var smithsCandyJar = [ "Jelly Munchers", "Gooey Bears" ]
smithsCandyJar: [String] = 2 values {
  [0] = "Jelly Munchers"
  [1] = "Gooey Bears"
}
36>
```

Three arrays represent three candy jars. The variable names indicate the jars' owners.

Now it's simply a matter of creating an array:

```
36> let arceneauxsCandyRoute = [ fontenotsCandyJar, dupresCandyJar,
    ↪ smithsCandyJar ]
arceneauxsCandyRoute: [[String]] = 3 values {
  [0] = 2 values {
    [0] = "Choppers"
    [1] = "Jaw Bombs"
```

```
  }
  [1] = 3 values {
    [0] = "Butterbar"
    [1] = "Mrs. Goodbuys"
    [2] = "Giggles"
  }
  [2] = 2 values {
    [0] = "Jelly Munchers"
    [1] = "Gooey Bears"
  }
}
 37>
```

Swift denotes the type of arceneauxCandyRoute as "an array of an array of strings" with the [[String]] nomenclature.

Interrogating the array for the first element yields the first value in the array, which itself is an array:

```
 37> arceneauxsCandyRoute[0]
$R17: [String] = 2 values {
  [0] = "Choppers"
  [1] = "Jaw Bombs"
}
 38>
```

Notice that while the candy jars are now part of the route array, there isn't really an indication of which store goes with the array. That's because the variable name is not encapsulated within the array itself, just the values.

Let's bring some clarity to this example. Instead of using an array to hold the candy jar arrays, let's use a dictionary:

```
 38> let arceneauxsOtherCandyRoute = ["Fontenot's Grocery" :
     → fontenotsCandyJar, "Dupre's Quick Mart" : dupresCandyJar,
     → "Smith's Pick-n-Sack" : smithsCandyJar]
arceneauxsOtherCandyRoute: [String : [String]] = {
  [0] = {
    key = "Dupre's Quick Mart"
    value = 3 values {
      [0] = "Butterbar"
      [1] = "Mrs. Goodbuys"
      [2] = "Giggles"
    }
  }
```

```
    [1] = {
      key = "Smith's Pick-n-Sack"
      value = 2 values {
        [0] = "Jelly Munchers"
        [1] = "Gooey Bears"
      }
    }
    [2] = {
      key = "Fontenot's Grocery"
      value = 2 values {
        [0] = "Choppers"
        [1] = "Jaw Bombs"
      }
    }
  }
 39>
```

Swift denotes the type of arceneauxsOtherCandyRoute with [String : [String]]. In English, this is "a dictionary whose key is a string and whose value is an array of strings."

The difference between this dictionary of arrays and the array of arrays earlier is that the key (of type String) is the descriptive term that defines the value, the candy jar. Instead of using a somewhat anonymous index value to obtain the value you want, you can now specify the value by its key:

```
 39> arceneauxsOtherCandyRoute["Smith's Pick-n-Sack"]
$R18: [String]? = 2 values {
  [0] = "Jelly Munchers"
  [1] = "Gooey Bears"
}
```

Depending on what you are trying to model, you may find that a mixture of arrays, dictionaries, or both may be appropriate. Practice certainly makes perfect.

STARTING FROM SCRATCH

Up to now, the arrays and dictionaries you have created have been initialized at declaration time. At times in Swift development, however, creating an array or dictionary without initializing it will be necessary. Perhaps the values are not known at that time in the application, or an empty array or dictionary will need to be populated by a method in a library or framework.

THE EMPTY ARRAY

Two nomenclatures are used to declare an empty array:

```
40> var myEmptyArray : Array<Int> = []
myEmptyArray: [Int] = 0 values
41>
```

This is the "longhand" form of declaring an array, and involves the keyword `Array` along with the type of the array bounded by angle brackets `< >`. Swift gives us a second "short form" style we can also employ:

```
41> var myEmptyArray = [Int]()
myEmptyArray: [(Int)] = 0 values
42>
```

In these examples, you have declared an empty mutable array that will hold `Int` values. Because it's a mutable array, you can change it or populate it as you normally would any other array. Let's add three integers to the array:

```
42> myEmptyArray += [33, 44, 55]
43> myEmptyArray
$R19: [(Int)] = 3 values {
  [0] = 33
  [1] = 44
  [2] = 55
}
44>
```

You can also remove all elements of an array by assigning the variable to the "empty array":

```
44> myEmptyArray = []
45> myEmptyArray
$R20: [(Int)] = 0 values
46>
```

The array is now void of its original values, and you can reuse it for storing other data.

THE EMPTY DICTIONARY

Creating a new, empty dictionary is similar to creating an empty array. The syntax involves the actual word `Dictionary` along with a set of angle bracket characters:

```
46> var myEmptyDictionary = Dictionary<String, Double>()
myEmptyDictionary: [String : Double] = {}
47>
```

In this example, you specified the specific key type and the value that will be allowed in the dictionary: The key type is String, and the value type is Double. These types are bounded by the angle bracket characters < > and separated by a comma. You can then add entries into the dictionary as follows:

```
 47> myEmptyDictionary = ["MyKey" : 1.125]
 48> myEmptyDictionary
$R21: [String : Double] = {
  [0] = {
    key = "MyKey"
    value = 1.125
  }
}
 49>
```

ITERATING COLLECTIONS

Now that you've covered the basic collection types (arrays and dictionaries), it's time to explore *iterating* them. Iterating a collection is the act of examining each value in an array or dictionary and potentially performing some work on it.

Iterating is something that we all do in our daily work. When you're following a written list of steps to complete a task, you are iterating over that list. Working with data is no different. Iteration is a very common coding task, and as you'll see shortly, Swift provides several constructs to make iterating over collections a breeze.

ARRAY ITERATION

If you're coming from another programming language like C, you are intimately familiar with the notion of the for loop. Swift has several flavors of this same construct that are more naturally expressive than C's version. Even if you have little prior programming experience, you'll pick up the concept right away.

The for-in loop is constructed in the following manner:

```
for itemName in list {
    ... do something with itemName
}
```

The itemName is any name you wish to use. It becomes a variable assigned to each value in the list as the iteration occurs. The list is the object being iterated, and everything that appears between the curly braces is code that is executed.

Let's revisit the combinedRefillableCandyJar array from earlier in the chapter:

```
 49> combinedRefillableCandyJar
$R22: [String] = 9 values {
  [0] = "Peppermints"
  [1] = "Lollipops"
  [2] = "Twirlers"
  [3] = "Candy Canes"
  [4] = "Peanut Clusters"
  [5] = "Banana Taffy"
  [6] = "Sour Tarts"
  [7] = "Cocoa Bar"
  [8] = "Coconut Rounds"
}
 50>
```

The following is a segment of code that uses Swift's for-in construct to print individual array values. This is a multiline code segment; as you type it in the REPL, the prompt changes from a number followed by a greater-than sign to a number followed by a period. This is triggered by the addition of the opening curly brace {, which tells the REPL that a new code block is beginning.

Because of this behavior, the results don't appear until the last line, which contains the closing curly brace }, is entered:

```
 50> for candy in combinedRefillableCandyJar {
 51.     println("I enjoy eating \(candy)!")
 52. }
I enjoy eating Peppermints!
I enjoy eating Lollipops!
I enjoy eating Twirlers!
I enjoy eating Candy Canes!
I enjoy eating Peanut Clusters!
I enjoy eating Banana Taffy!
I enjoy eating Sour Tarts!
```

```
I enjoy eating Cocoa Bar!
I enjoy eating Coconut Rounds!
 53>
```

Here's the breakdown of this code block: Each item in the combinedRefillableCandyJar array is assigned to the candy variable. Since there are nine values in the array, the for-in loop iterates nine times; each time, the code bounded in the curly braces is executed. In this case, the value is combined with a formatted String value and printed to the screen.

Another variation of the for-in loop provides both the value and the index of that value in the array:

```
53> for (index, candy) in enumerate(combinedRefillableCandyJar) {
54.     println("Candy \(candy) is in position \(index) of the array")
55. }
Candy Peppermints is in position 0 of the array
Candy Lollipops is in position 1 of the array
Candy Twirlers is in position 2 of the array
Candy Candy Canes is in position 3 of the array
Candy Peanut Clusters is in position 4 of the array
Candy Banana Taffy is in position 5 of the array
Candy Sour Tarts is in position 6 of the array
Candy Cocoa Bar is in position 7 of the array
Candy Coconut Rounds is in position 8 of the array
 56>
```

Here, Swift's enumerate() method wraps the previously defined array named combinedRefillableCandyJar. This method conveniently returns a tuple containing both the index of the value and the value itself in the array. The variables index and candy are then referenced to create a combined string. (You will recall that tuples were introduced in Chapter 1.)

DICTIONARY ITERATION

Iterating through a dictionary using the for-in construct is identical to that of the array example we just covered. To illustrate, let's reuse the dictionary you created earlier for Mr. Arceneaux's other candy route.

```
56> for (key, value) in arceneauxsOtherCandyRoute {
57.     println("\(key) has a candy jar with the following contents:
            → \(value)")
58. }
Dupre's Quick Mart has a candy jar with the following contents:
→ [Butterbar, Mrs. Goodbuys, Giggles]
```

```
Smith's Pick-n-Sack has a candy jar with the following contents:
→ [Jelly Munchers, Gooey Bears]
Fontenot's Grocery has a candy jar with the following contents:
→ [Choppers, Jaw Bombs]
 59>
```

Since dictionaries are composed of keys and values, they automatically return a tuple. That tuple is captured, and its contents are assigned to the variables key and value. Notice that value is itself an array, and the println method displays that array quite handily.

To further illustrate iterations, let's go for the gold and expand the first for-in loop to contain another for-in loop as follows:

```
59> for (key, value) in arceneauxsOtherCandyRoute {
60.     for (index, candy) in enumerate(value) {
61.         println("\(key)'s candy jar contains \(candy) at position
            → \(index)")
62.     }
63. }
Dupre's Quick Mart's candy jar contains Butterbar at position 0
Dupre's Quick Mart's candy jar contains Mrs. Goodbuys at position 1
Dupre's Quick Mart's candy jar contains Giggles at position 2
Smith's Pick-n-Sack's candy jar contains Jelly Munchers at position 0
Smith's Pick-n-Sack's candy jar contains Gooey Bears at position 1
Fontenot's Grocery's candy jar contains Choppers at position 0
Fontenot's Grocery's candy jar contains Jaw Bombs at position 1
 64> :quit
```

This is an example of a *nested* for-in loop. For each iteration through arceneauxsOtherCandyRoute (a dictionary), Swift is capturing the value in the variable value (an array) and using the enumerate() method on that variable to perform further iteration.

SUMMARY

The whirlwind tour of collections has come to an end. As you have seen, arrays and dictionaries are great structures for organizing and grouping different types of data, from text to numbers. These collection types can even contain other collections, allowing you to concoct very elaborate data referencing schemes. Finally, you've witnessed Swift's flexible syntax for declaring new arrays and dictionaries. You can literally take your pick on how you want your code to read when creating new collections.

In the next chapter, you will begin flexing your programming muscles with control structures, which is where things will begin to get interesting.

CHAPTER 3

Taking Control

In the last chapter, you spent some time getting to know Swift's collections: arrays and dictionaries. Then you started looking at ways to iterate through those collections. In this chapter, you'll continue looking at iterating, and then move on to Swift's ability to take directions on what to do at specific intervals.

If you haven't already done so, start up the REPL in the Terminal application (remember, you can type xcrun `swift` to get it going). The line numbers in the figures in this chapter assume that you are starting with a fresh REPL session.

FOR WHAT IT'S WORTH

As you saw in the previous chapter, Swift's ability to iterate through a collection, be it an array or a dictionary, uses the for-in loop. Other variations of the for-in loop are also useful for iterating, and not just through collections.

COUNTING ON IT

One common use for the for-in loop is as an enumeration mechanism. Using a special syntax Swift provides, you can construct a for-in loop that counts a specific range of numbers. The construction of this for-in loop is as follows:

```
for loopVariable in startNumber...endNumber
```

Just as in the previous chapter, the for-in loop requires a loop variable, which will hold the value for each iteration. What follows the in keyword for this variation of the loop is a start number, followed by three periods (...), followed by the end number.

The three periods is your way of telling Swift that the start and end number are part of a range. The for loop will then start by assigning the start number to the loop variable, execute the loop, add 1 to the loop variable, and compare it to the end number. As long as the loop variable is less than or equal to the end number, the loop will continue to execute.

Try the following code snippet:

```
  1> var loopCounter : Int = 0
loopCounter: Int = 0
  2> for loopCounter in 1...10 {
  3.      println("\(loopCounter) times \(loopCounter) equals \(loopCounter *
         → loopCounter)")
  4. }
1 times 1 equals 1
2 times 2 equals 4
3 times 3 equals 9
4 times 4 equals 16
5 times 5 equals 25
6 times 6 equals 36
7 times 7 equals 49
8 times 8 equals 64
9 times 9 equals 81
10 times 10 equals 100
  5>
```

On line 1, you declared an Int variable loopCounter that will be used as the loop variable. Line 2 has the for-in loop with the ... variation, setting 1 as the start number and 10 as the end number.

On line 3 is a print command that will show the result of the multiplication of the loopCounter variable times itself. Finally, on line 4 the closing bracket cues the REPL that the for-in loop should be executed. Swift then emits 10 lines showing the squaring of numbers from 1 to 10.

INCLUSIVE OR EXCLUSIVE?

Another variation on the ... syntax for specifying a range is the ..< syntax, which tells Swift to iterate the loop *one value less* than the end number. Using the previous example again, replace ... with ..< and notice the difference:

```
5> for loopCounter in 1..<10 {
6.      println("\(loopCounter) times \(loopCounter) equals \(loopCounter *
   → loopCounter)")
7. }
1 times 1 equals 1
2 times 2 equals 4
3 times 3 equals 9
4 times 4 equals 16
5 times 5 equals 25
6 times 6 equals 36
7 times 7 equals 49
8 times 8 equals 64
9 times 9 equals 81
   8>
```

The loop ended with the number 9, one less than the ending number specified, 10.

You may be wondering why this is useful. After all, couldn't you just replace the 10 with 9, use the ... range specifier, and obtain the same effect?

Actually, the syntax is useful when iterating through a collection like the array, which has an index that always starts at 0. Enter the following lines of code:

```
8> let numbersArray = [ 11, 22, 33, 44, 55, 66, 77, 88, 99 ]
 → numbersArray: [Int] = 9 values {
  [0] = 11
  [1] = 22
  [2] = 33
  [3] = 44
  [4] = 55
  [5] = 66
  [6] = 77
  [7] = 88
  [8] = 99
}
  9> for loopCounter in 0..<9 {
 10.    println("value at index \(loopCounter) is \
          → (numbersArray[loopCounter])")
 11. }
value at index 0 is 11
value at index 1 is 22
value at index 2 is 33
value at index 3 is 44
value at index 4 is 55
value at index 5 is 66
value at index 6 is 77
value at index 7 is 88
value at index 8 is 99
 12>
```

Using the array size as the loop limit value might look more natural. No matter your preference, remember that arrays always start their index at 0, which means the last element's index is one less than the total number of elements in the array. Don't' forget to compensate for that fact when iterating through an array.

FOR OLD TIME'S SAKE

Swift has yet another variation of the `for` loop, one that you might recognize if you're familiar with the C language. It doesn't use the `in` keyword, but instead has three distinct parts:

for *initialization*; *evaluation*; *modification*

- *initialization*: Here, the loop variable is initialized.
- *evaluation*: A test is made at this location; as long as the result is true, the loop executes.
- *modification*: This is typically where the loop variable is modified.

One advantage to this form of `for` loop is that it allows the modification step to be more than just a simple increment of 1. It can also be an increment of another number, or even a decrement.

```
12> for loopCounter = 0; loopCounter < 9; loopCounter = loopCounter + 2 {
13.     println("value at index \(loopCounter) is \(numbersArray
        ↦ [loopCounter])")
14. }
value at index 0 is 11
value at index 2 is 33
value at index 4 is 55
value at index 6 is 77
value at index 8 is 99
15>
```

The choice of 2 as an increment value in the `for` loop modification component causes the iteration to skip every other element in the array. You can even construct the loop to go backward, paying close attention not to go below 0, the index of the first element of the array:

```
15> for loopCounter = 8; loopCounter >= 0; loopCounter = loopCounter - 2 {
16.     println("value at index \(loopCounter) is \(numbersArray
        ↦ [loopCounter])")
17. }
value at index 8 is 99
value at index 6 is 77
value at index 4 is 55
value at index 2 is 33
value at index 0 is 11
18>
```

The flexibility of this `for` loop's form makes it ideal for traversing collections in non-ordinal fashion, or for any number of computational variations.

WRITING SHORTHAND

In the previous two examples, the modification step of the for loop looks like this:

```
loopCounter = loopCounter + 2
loopCounter = loopCounter - 2
```

The first line adds 2 to loopCounter; the second line subtracts 2.

It's a little long, isn't it? Don't worry. Swift has a more succinct syntax for adding or subtracting a number from a variable:

```
 18> var anotherLoopCounter = 3
anotherLoopCounter: Int = 3
 19> anotherLoopCounter += 2
 20> anotherLoopCounter
$R0: Int = 5
 21>
```

Line 18 assigns 3 to the anotherLoopCounter variable. On line 19, the += syntax takes the place of typing the variable again. It's a shorthand method of saying "add the value on the right to the variable on the left." On line 20, typing the variable name by itself causes the REPL to show the value and assign it to a temporary variable.

The same logic works for subtraction, too:

```
 21> anotherLoopCounter -= 3
 22> anotherLoopCounter
$R1: Int = 2
 23>
```

It gets better! If you simply want to increment the number by 1, you can use an even shorter syntax, ++:

```
 23> anotherLoopCounter++
$R2: Int = 2
 24>
```

Did you catch that? anotherLoopCounter was 2 before the increment. Why did it return 2 after the increment? Shouldn't it be 3 if you are incrementing by 1?

What you are seeing here is a side effect of the increment operation. The position of the ++ after the variable name causes the value *prior* to the increment to be returned. So the value, 2, is assigned to the temporary variable $R2. If you request the REPL to show the variable again, it will contain the incremented value:

```
 24> anotherLoopCounter
$R3: Int = 3
 25>
```

This is called a *post increment*. The increment is happening *after* the evaluation of the variable. This also works for subtraction as a *post decrement*:

```
 25> anotherLoopCounter--
$R4: Int = 3
 26> anotherLoopCounter
$R5: Int = 2
 27>
```

Just as there is a post increment, there's also a *pre increment*:

```
 27> ++anotherLoopCounter
$R6: Int = 3
 28>
```

Notice that anotherLoopCounter, which was 2 on line 26, is now 3. Showing another-LoopCounter again should reveal the same number:

```
 28> anotherLoopCounter
$R7: Int = 3
 29>
```

And so it is.

Finally, here's the *pre decrement*:

```
 29> --anotherLoopCounter
$R8: Int = 2
 30> anotherLoopCounter
$R9: Int = 2
 31>
```

You'll see more of these shorthand increment/decrement operators later. Just remember, they save you some typing so be sure to recognize them in code and use them to add or subtract a number from a variable.

IT'S TIME TO PLAY

Up to this point in your journey, you've used the Swift REPL to type code and see results. The REPL works well for short, quick lines of code that provide immediate feedback. However, as we move forward, you'll be writing more and more code. Being able to save and load that code and easily edit it requires interacting with Xcode 6, Apple's development environment for writing Swift apps for iOS and OS X.

FIGURE 3.1 Finder showing Xcode 6

FIGURE 3.2 The Xcode startup window

FIGURE 3.3 Saving the playground

FIGURE 3.4 The newly created playground window

One of the new and fun features of Xcode 6 is *playgrounds*. A playground is an interactive slate where you can type Swift instructions and see instant results—much like the REPL but way easier to edit and change your source code.

Since you downloaded Xcode 6 in Chapter 1 in order to work with the REPL, you have everything you need to get started. To begin, use the Finder (**Figure 3.1**) to launch Xcode 6 from your Applications folder.

When starting Xcode 6, you'll be greeted with the dialog in **Figure 3.2**.

The first option is "Get started with a playground." Click it, and a new window appears, asking you to give a name to your playground and select the target platform (either iOS or OS X) (**Figure 3.3**).

For now, keep the suggested name **MyPlayground**, and leave the Platform set to OS X. Click Next. Select a location on your system, and click Create.

After the playground is saved, a new window appears (**Figure 3.4**). This is your new playground! It's like a fresh canvas with no paint—ready for you to type Swift code to your heart's content.

```
1   // Playground - noun: a place where people can play
2
3   import Cocoa
4
5   var str = "Hello, playground"
6   |
```

FIGURE 3.5 The default code in the initial playground window

"Hello, playground"

FIGURE 3.6 The Results sidebar

The playground window is composed of two panes. The left pane shows the Swift code that you type, one line at a time, along with the line number. This pane is very similar to the REPL sessions you've used up to now, but more interactive.

The right pane shows the results of the code, corresponding to the line. This is the real power and convenience of playgrounds—seeing your code run live, along with the results. As you'll see, playgrounds are excellent for learning Swift because you can try new concepts without the overhead of waiting for the compiler to do its work.

Let's go over the five lines of code that already appear in the window (**Figure 3.5**).

Line 1 is a comment; Xcode shows comment text in green. A comment in Swift begins with two forward slashes. The Swift compiler ignores whatever follows the two forward slashes, up to the end of the current line. Developers use comments to add source code commentary, usually for the benefit of other developers who might read the code someday. Adding code comments is akin to being a good citizen; comments help others understand your app's intent. Comments also help document your own work so that months (or years) later you can quickly remember what you did.

Line 3 is an import statement. This statement tells Swift that your program needs resources (code and data) from Cocoa, which is Apple's framework for writing iOS and OS X apps.

Line 5 should look familiar; it's a variable declaration, implicitly declaring a string type and assigning "Hello, playground" to the variable.

Turn your attention to the Results sidebar on the right (**Figure 3.6**). The text "Hello, playground" appears there. This is the result of Swift executing the code in the left pane.

Playgrounds make writing, editing, and understanding code so much easier. Throughout our use of playgrounds in this book, you'll appreciate that your work is preserved, and you can scroll back and modify or alter previously written code.

PLAYGROUND RULES

Wherever you use playgrounds throughout the remainder of this book, you'll see a listing of the code to type, accompanied by the code appearing in the playground along with the results. This is intended to guide you line by line through the code and show you exactly how your results will look onscreen.

MAKING DECISIONS

Can computers "think?" It's an oft-debated topic. Part of thinking is making decisions, and in that regard, computers certainly do well. An integral part of any app is decision making, and knowing what to do and where to go is critical in the flow of a program.

Program flow is simply one long series of decisions: "if this is true then go here, else go there." Or, "while this is not true, continue doing this operation until it is." Our lives are filled with such decision-making instances—we don't even give it a second thought. Tasks like deciding which pair of shoes to wear, what time to leave for work, or when it's appropriate to cross the street are all part of the decision matrix we encounter each day.

It's no different for your Mac, iPhone, or iPad. When you're writing your app in Swift, it gives you a rich set of ways to specify what your program should do, and when. We'll spend a good part of the rest of this chapter looking at Swift's control flow constructs.

THE DECISIVENESS OF "IF"

"If" is everywhere around us. It's in our speech and is a constant presence in our mind as we go through our day making decisions. It usually indicates the start of a sentence that contains the word "then," as in:

If the light is red, **then** *apply the brake.*
If the coffee is hot, **then** *drink it.*

Swift's version isn't as wordy as the English variants, but is nonetheless easy to read. Here's the general form of the Swift if statement:

```
if predicate {
    // do something
}
```

The *predicate* is evaluated by Swift, and if found to be true will cause statements in the first set of curly braces to execute; otherwise the evaluation is false, and the code in the curly braces is ignored.

It can also include the word "else." Carrying the previous sentence further:

If the light is red, **then** *apply the brake,* **else** *stomp on the accelerator!*
If the coffee is hot, **then** *drink it,* **else** *throw it away.*

These sentences carry a predicate and two possible outcomes, depending on the "truthfulness" of the predicate in question. Is the light red? Is the coffee hot? If so, do something; otherwise do something else. In programing, we call this construct the if/then/else clause.

FIGURE 3.7 Using `if` in the playground

```
●○○                    MyPlayground.playground — Edited
      MyPlayground.playground                                    +
⊞  ◄  ►  ⓘ MyPlayground.playground ⟩ No Selection
 1   // Playground - noun: a place where people can play
 2
 3   import Cocoa
 4
 5   var str = "Hello, playground"                              "Hello, playground"
 6
 7   var trafficLight = "Red"                                   "Red"
 8
 9   if trafficLight == "Red" {
10       print("Stop!")                                         "Stop!"
11   } else {
12       print("Go!")
13   }
14
```

Here's the general form of the `if`/`then`/`else` as expressed in Swift:

```
if predicate {
    // do something
}
else {
{
    // do something else
}
```

When Swift encounters an `if` clause, it evaluates the predicate. If the predicate's result is true, the code in the first set of curly braces executes. The `else` clause provides a fallback; if the predicate evaluates to false, the code in the second set of curly braces executes.

As an illustration, let's set up the traffic light analogy in Swift's parlance. Start by typing the following code as lines 7 through 13 in the MyPlayground window (**Figure 3.7**).

```
var trafficLight = "Red"

if trafficLight == "Red" {
    print("Stop!")
} else {
    print("Go!")
}
```

On line 7, you are declaring a variable named trafficLight and assigning it the string "Red".

Line 9 contains the `if` statement. Our predicate here is the comparison of the variable trafficLight to the string "Red", which is true because trafficLight was assigned the value "Red" on line 7.

In the Results sidebar, you can see that "Stop!" is shown because the comparison of trafficLight to the string "Red" is true.

How would you get the Results sidebar to show "Go!" instead of "Stop!"?

FIGURE 3.8 Executing
the else clause

FIGURE 3.9 An alter-
nate execution of the
else clause

You could set the trafficLight variable to something other than "Red" on line 7
(**Figure 3.8**).

Now the Results sidebar shows "Go!" as you would expect, since the comparison of
trafficLight to "Red" on line 9 is false.

Another approach would be to leave the variable on line 7 set to the string "Red" and
modify the comparison operator on line 9 (**Figure 3.9**).

The comparison operator != means does not equal, which is the opposite of ==. The logic
of the sentence on line 9 is inverted, and literally reads: "if the trafficLight variable does
not equal Red, print Stop! Otherwise print Go!"

TESTING FOR EQUALITY IN SWIFT

Up to this point, you've seen a single equals sign when assigning a value to a variable
or constant. When doing a comparison between two values, variables, or constants, the
double equal (==) is used. Line 9 in Figure 3.7 uses this comparison operator, and we'll go
over additional comparison operators shortly.

FIGURE 3.10
Comparing numbers in
an if statement

So far, you've been comparing strings. Let's try comparing numbers and look at a few new comparison operators. Just for grins, keep the existing code on lines 7 through 13, and just add the following new code beginning on line 15 (**Figure 3.10**):

```
var number1 : Int = 33
var number2 : Int = 101

if number1 >= number2 {
    print("33 is greater than 101")
} else {
    print("33 is less than 101")
}
```

Line 18 shows the greater-than (>) symbol as a comparison operator. In the example, number1 (value of 33) is less than number2 (value of 101) so the expression is false, and the code in the second clause executes. If you replace the greater-than symbol on line 18 with the less-than (<) symbol, the condition becomes true, and the code in the first clause executes. Go ahead and try it... that's what playgrounds are for!

There are more operators you can use. Swift supports the equality tests in **Table 3.1**.

TABLE 3.1 Swift's Equality Operations

OPERATOR	TEST
==	Equal
!=	Not equal
>	Greater than
<	Less than
>=	Greater than or equal
<=	Less than or equal

FIGURE 3.11 String comparisons

These operators also work on more than just numbers. You can use them to compare strings, too. Strings can be compared to each other based on alphabetical order. Consider lines 24 through 29 in **Figure 3.11**.

```
let tree1 = "Oak"
let tree2 = "Pecan"
let tree3 = "Maple"

let treeCompare1 = tree1 > tree2
let treeCompare2 = tree2 > tree3
```

On lines 24 through 26, three constant strings are declared: Oak, Pecan, and Maple. Line 28 shows the comparison of tree1 (Oak) to tree2 (Pecan) and the resulting value (false). It's obvious that tree1 is not greater than tree2, because alphabetically, Oak comes before Pecan. Line 29 indicates a result of true, because tree2 (Pecan) indeed is greater than (or comes after) tree3 (Maple).

WHEN ONE CHOICE IS NOT ENOUGH

Sometimes a comparison yields more than just an either/or scenario. Take for example, the three tree constants you just created. Each type of tree is associated with a type of product. What if you wanted to return a product for each tree type? Type the following code on lines 31 through 43 (**Figure 3.12**) and let's talk about the results.

FIGURE 3.12 Multiple
if statements wrapped
in a for loop

```
8
9    if trafficLight == "Red" {
10       print("Stop!")                                    "Stop!"
11   } else {
12       print("Go!")
13   }
14
15   var number1 : Int = 33                                33
16   var number2 : Int = 101                               101
17
18   if number1 >= number2 {
19       print("33 is greater than 101")
20   } else {
21       print("33 is less than 101")                      "33 is less than 101"
22   }
23
24   let tree1 = "Oak"                                      "Oak"
25   let tree2 = "Pecan"                                    "Pecan"
26   let tree3 = "Maple"                                    "Maple"
27
28   let treeCompare1 = tree1 > tree2                       false
29   let treeCompare2 = tree2 > tree3                       true
30
31   var treeArray = [tree1, tree2, tree3]                 ["Oak", "Pecan", "Maple"]
32
33   for tree in treeArray {
34       if tree == "Oak" {
35           println("Furniture")                          "Furniture"
36       }
37       else if tree == "Pecan" {
38           println("Pie")                                "Pie"
39       }
40       else if tree == "Maple" {
41           println("Syrup")                              "Syrup"
42       }
43   }
44
```

```
var treeArray = [tree1, tree2, tree3]

for tree in treeArray {
    if tree == "Oak" {
        println("Furniture");
    }
    else if tree == "Pecan" {
        println("Pie");
    }
    else if tree == "Maple" {
        println("Syrup")
    }
}
```

This code snippet combines several concepts. On line 31, you declare an array composed of the three tree constants declared earlier.

On line 33, the for statement is used to iterate through the newly created array, with the variable tree holding each array element throughout the iteration process. Lines 34, 37, and 40 all do a comparison of the variable tree to the known strings that were assigned earlier, and if a match is made, the product for that tree is printed.

FIGURE 3.13
The switch-case state-
ment wrapped in a for
loop

```
24   let tree1 = "Oak"                              "Oak"
25   let tree2 = "Pecan"                            "Pecan"
26   let tree3 = "Maple"                            "Maple"
27
28   let treeCompare1 = tree1 > tree2               false
29   let treeCompare2 = tree2 > tree3               true
30
31   var treeArray = [tree1, tree2, tree3]          ["Oak", "Pecan", "Maple"]
32
33   for tree in treeArray {
34       if tree == "Oak" {
35           println("Furniture")                   "Furniture"
36       }
37       else if tree == "Pecan" {
38           println("Pie")                         "Pie"
39       }
40       else if tree == "Maple" {
41           println("Syrup")                       "Syrup"
42       }
43   }
44
45   treeArray += ["Cherry"]                         ["Oak", "Pecan", "Ma... ⊚
46
47   for tree in treeArray {
48       switch tree {
49           case "Oak":
50               println("Furniture")               "Furniture"
51           case "Pecan":
52               println("Pie")                     "Pie"
53           case "Maple":
54               println("Syrup")                   "Syrup"
55           default:
56               println("Wood")                    "Wood"
57       }
58   }
59
```

SWITCHING THINGS AROUND

In the previous example, the three if statements handled the available cases, but what happens if there are more possibilities to compare? Long lists of repeating if statements can be tedious to type and difficult to read. Swift gives you an alternative when handling more than just a handful of predicates: the switch statement.

You'll find that this new construct comes in handy in a number of coding scenarios. Type in the following code, and study the results in **Figure 3.13** to see exactly what is happening.

```
treeArray += ["Cherry"]

for tree in treeArray {
    switch tree {
        case "Oak":
            println("Furniture")
        case "Pecan":
            println("Pie")
        case "Maple":
            println("Syrup")
        default:
            println("Wood")
    }
}
```

FIGURE 3.14 The effect on the `switch-case` statement when adding to the array

Line 48 shows the `switch` keyword, followed by the `tree` variable, which is assigned each member in the `treeArray` throughout the `for` loop iteration on line 47. A closing curly brace contains the various `case` statements that fall below it. Swift stops at each `case` statement and evaluates the `tree` variable for a match. When one is found, the code bounded between the triggered `case` statement and the next `case` statement is executed.

You may be wondering what the `default` keyword does. It is a "catch-all" case whose code is executed when all other cases fail. Here, it is never executed because all three tree types are covered in `case` statements, but what if you were to add a fourth tree in the array? Line 55 in **Figure 3.14** does just that:

Now the `default` case is activated because the new value in the array does not have a matching `case` statement, and `"Wood"` is printed when `"Cherry"` is encountered in the `for` loop.

WHERE'S THE BREAK?

If you're familiar with Objective-C, you may have used `switch-case` statements in that language, and are wondering where the `break` statement is in each case. Simply put, Swift does not require it. It's implicitly understood that execution will "fall through" the remaining `case` statements on a match, and the intervening code won't be executed.

FIGURE 3.15 Multiple constants on a single case

```
45   treeArray += ["Cherry"]                                              ["Oak", "Pecan", "Ma... ⊙
46
47   for tree in treeArray {
48       switch tree {
49           case "Oak":
50               println("Furniture")                                      "Furniture"
51           case "Pecan", "Cherry":
52               println("Pie")                                            (2 times)
53           case "Maple":
54               println("Syrup")                                          "Syrup"
55           default:
56               println("Wood")
57       }
58   }
59
```

Cherry wood certainly seems less appealing than cherry pie. How could you alter the statement to accommodate printing the word "Pie" for both Pecan and Cherry? Obviously, you could add another case statement to catch the case of the variable tree being equal to "Cherry" and that would certainly work, but there is a much more neat and tidy alternative. Swift allows you to combine two or more values in a single case for evaluation. Modify line 51 to case "Pecan", "Cherry": as in **Figure 3.15**, and notice the output in the Results sidebar.

Swift duly notes that in the case of "Pecan" and "Cherry", the code to print "Pie" was executed two times. You don't have to stop there. As an exercise, you can add other names like "Lemon" and "Apple" to line 51. This flexibility makes switch-case a powerful alternative to other normally used conditional constructs.

Up to this point, you've been using switch-case to evaluate strings. That is more than can be done in languages like Objective-C and C, which can evaluate only numbers. Numbers in Swift, including ranges, are easy to compare. The following code snippet illustrates this by using a switch-case statement to append the appropriate ordinal abbreviation to a number between 1 and 9 (**Figure 3.16**).

```
var position = 8

switch position {
    case 1:
        println("\(position)st")

    case 2:
        println("\(position)nd")

    case 3:
        println("\(position)rd")

    case 4...9:
        println("\(position)th")

    default:
        println("Not covered")
}
```

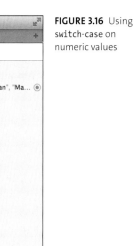

FIGURE 3.16 Using switch-case on numeric values

```
42          }
43      }
44
45      treeArray += ["Cherry"]                              ["Oak", "Pecan", "Ma... ⊙
46
47      for tree in treeArray {
48          switch tree {
49              case "Oak":
50                  println("Furniture")                     "Furniture"
51              case "Pecan", "Cherry":
52                  println("Pie")                           (2 times)
53              case "Maple":
54                  println("Syrup")                         "Syrup"
55              default:
56                  println("Wood")
57          }
58      }
59
60      var position = 8                                     8
61
62      switch position {
63          case 1:
64              println("\(position)st")
65
66          case 2:
67              println("\(position)nd")
68
69          case 3:
70              println("\(position)rd")
71
72          case 4...9:
73              println("\(position)th")                     "8th"
74
75          default:
76              println("Not covered")
77      }
78
```

On line 60, `position` is declared as a variable with the number 8 and execution falls through to the `switch-case` where the variable is evaluated against the possible cases. Since numbers 4 through 9 always end in "th", line 72 takes advantage of Swift's range (`...`) operator to specify every whole number between 4 and 9, with the remaining cases being covered on the previous lines.

Feel free to experiment with this code by changing the value of `position` on line 60. The Results sidebar will update to indicate the code being executed when you make your change.

WHILE YOU WERE AWAY…

Up to this point, you've seen some of Swift's powerful control and iterative capabilities with `if`, `for`, and `switch-case`, but additional constructs can provide other natural ways of expressing intent.

Sometimes in the course of developing software you want to express the logic of a loop in terms of an unknown iteration count. For example, you want to iterate on something *until* a specific set of criteria is met. For example, let's say you want to compute a table of values, but don't want to stop until the computed value is greater than some number.

The `while` loop is a Swift loop construct that allows you to continue executing the same code, over and over, until a condition of your choosing is met. Its basic form is:

```
while someCondition {
    // execute code
}
```

FIGURE 3.17 Iterating a value in a while loop

The condition someCondition is a Boolean expression that can be either true or false. If true, the code in the curly braces is executed, and control goes back to the while loop. If the condition result is false, execution moves past the encapsulated code.

To see the while loop in action, type the following code on lines 79 through 85 (**Figure 3.17**), and watch the results in the Results sidebar.

```
var base = 2
var target = 1000
var value = 0

while value > target {
    value += base
}
```

A variation of the while loop is the do-while. This type of loop executes the code *and then* evaluates the expression before deciding whether to continue the execution or move on. Here's the form of this style of loop:

```
do {
    // execute code
} while someCondition
```

FIGURE 3.18
A do-while loop

```
 ●○○                    MyPlayground.playground — Edited
        MyPlayground.playground                                            +
 ⊞  ◄  ►    MyPlayground.playground > No Selection
55            default:
56                println("Wood")
57        }
58  }
59
60  var position = 8                                              8
61
62  switch position {
63      case 1:
64          println("\(position)st")
65
66      case 2:
67          println("\(position)nd")
68
69      case 3:
70          println("\(position)rd")
71
72      case 4...9:
73          println("\(position)th")                             "8th"
74
75      default:
76          println("Not covered")
77  }
78
79  var base = 2                                                  2
80  var target = 1000                                             1,000
81  var value = 0                                                 0
82
83  while value < target {
84      value += base                                            (500 times)
85  }
86
87  do
88  {
89      value += base                                            1,002
90  } while value < target
91  |
```

The condition someCondition is the same Boolean expression expected in the while loop, but is evaluated after the code in the curly braces is executed initially. In **Figure 3.18**, lines 87 through 90 show a do-while loop executing the same code as the earlier while loop in lines 83 through 85. Notice the difference in the value for the do-while loop: It is 1002 instead of the while loop's value of 1000. Why?

```
do
{
    value += base
} while value < target
```

When you entered the do-while loop, in lines 87 through 90, value was already 1000, due to being previously set by the while loop in lines 83 through 85. The do-while loop enforced the execution of the code, which added base (2) to value (1000), and *then* evaluated the expression. At that point, value (1002) was *not* less than target (1000); the condition was false, and the do-while loop exited.

FIGURE 3.19 The speed limit code snippet

```
92    // Speed Limit Simulation
93    var speedLimit = 75                                                          75
94    var carSpeed = 0                                                             0
95
96    while (carSpeed < 100) {
97        carSpeed++                                                               (76 times)
98        switch carSpeed {
99        case 0..<20:
100           println("\(carSpeed): You're going really slow")                     (19 times)
101
102       case 20..<30:
103           println("\(carSpeed): Pick up the pace")                             (10 times)
104
105       case 30..<40:
106           println("\(carSpeed): Tap the accelerator")                          (10 times)
107
108       case 40..<50:
109           println("\(carSpeed): Hitting your stride")                          (10 times)
110
111       case 50..<60:
112           println("\(carSpeed): Moving at a good clip")                        (10 times)
113
114       case 60..<70:
115           println("\(carSpeed): Now you're cruising!")                         (10 times)
116
117       case 70...speedLimit:
118           println("\(carSpeed): Warning... approaching the speed limit")       (6 times)
119
120       default:
121           println("\(carSpeed): You're going too fast!")                       "76: You're going too f...
122
123       }
124
125       if carSpeed > speedLimit {
126           break
127       }
128   }
129
```

INSPECTING YOUR CODE

One feature of playgrounds we've glossed over so far is the ability to inspect and see the output of the code. In the Results sidebar, Swift is constantly analyzing the code you type, even reporting how many times a code segment runs. This is helpful for analyzing how many times a loop runs, and can even be used in certain scenarios to optimize and make your code run faster and better.

The playgrounds environment actually offers more ways to inspect your code in the Results sidebar. Type the following code snippet, and study the results of the code on lines 92 through 128 in **Figure 3.19**. This code uses a combination of while and switch-case to monitor the increasing speed of a car.

```
// Speed Limit Simulation
var speedLimit = 75
var carSpeed = 0

while (carSpeed < 100) {
    carSpeed++
    switch carSpeed {
```

```
        case 0..<20:
            println("\(carSpeed): You're going really slow")

        case 20..<30:
            println("\(carSpeed): Pick up the pace")

        case 30..<40:
            println("\(carSpeed): Tap the accelerator")

        case 40..<50:
            println("\(carSpeed): Hitting your stride")

        case 50..<60:
            println("\(carSpeed): Moving at a good clip")

        case 60..<70:
            println("\(carSpeed): Now you're cruising!")

        case 70...speedLimit:
            println("\(carSpeed): Warning... approaching the speed limit")

        default:
            println("\(carSpeed): You're going too fast!")

    }

    if carSpeed > speedLimit {
        break
    }
}
```

This example monitors the ever-increasing speed of a car. On line 93, the speed limit is set to 75 (miles per hour), and on the following line, the car's speed variable is set to 0. The while loop on line 96 contains the condition that the speed is less than 100. As the loop progresses, the car's speed is incremented by 1 on line 97, then evaluated in a `switch-case` statement.

Each case handles a range of speeds, providing feedback on each value. After you type in the code, notice that the number of times each case is executed appears in the Results sidebar. If you hover your mouse over any of those lines in the Results sidebar, you'll see an "eye" icon and a circle.

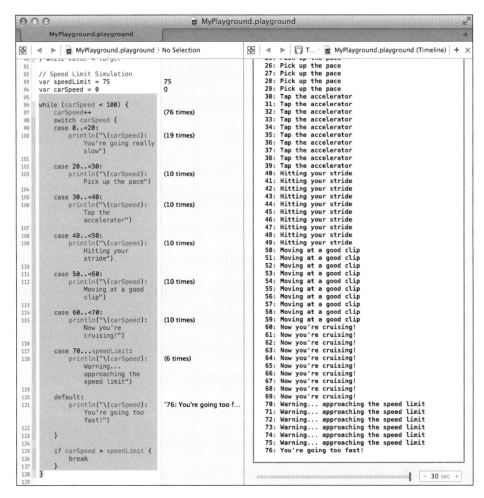

Clicking the circle (shown in **Figure 3.20**) to the right of the results line brings up the Timeline pane, which shows details about the values in the playground. It gives you a blow-by-blow account of what your code is doing. As you scroll through this new pane, you'll notice some interesting panels of data that appear. We'll ignore most of these for now. Scroll all the way down and view the output of the `println` method showing the speed and the message "You're going too fast!"

With the Timeline pane (**Figure 3.21**), you can review the exact behavior of your code, even down to the messages that were output, how many times they were output, and their order. This is a very insightful part of playgrounds, scroll around and get a taste of what else is in this pane. When you're finished exploring, click the X in the upper-right corner to close it, making room for your code and the Results sidebar.

FIGURE 3.22 Using break to exit the while loop early

```
96   while (carSpeed < 100) {
97       carSpeed++                                              (76 times)
98       switch carSpeed {
99       case 0..<20:
100          println("\(carSpeed): You're going really slow")    (19 times)
101
102      case 20..<30:
103          println("\(carSpeed): Pick up the pace")            (10 times)
104
105      case 30..<40:
106          println("\(carSpeed): Tap the accelerator")         (10 times)
107
108      case 40..<50:
109          println("\(carSpeed): Hitting your stride")         (10 times)
110
111      case 50..<60:
112          println("\(carSpeed): Moving at a good clip")       (10 times)
113
114      case 60..<70:
115          println("\(carSpeed): Now you're cruising!")        (10 times)
116
117      case 70...speedLimit:
118          println("\(carSpeed): Warning... approaching the    (6 times)
                 speed limit")
119
120      default:
121          println("\(carSpeed): You're going too fast!")      "76: You're going too fast!"
122
123      }
124
125      if carSpeed > speedLimit {
126          break
127      }
128  }
129
```

GIVE ME A BREAK!

Sometimes in the process of using a loop you may find yourself wanting to exit early. The previous code snippet provides such an opportunity. Once the car is speeding past the speed limit, the message "You're going too fast!" continues to print all the way to the car going to 100 miles per hour. What if you wanted to stop the while loop once the car exceeded the speed limit? This is achievable using the break keyword. Using break allows you to exit early from a loop or switch-case statement, allowing control to go immediately to the nearest encompassing block of code. Lines 125 through 127 of **Figure 3.22** show how this is done.

The if statement on line 125 checks to see if the car's speed has exceeded the speed limit, and if so, issues a break. Note that this breaks the encompassing while loop, effectively ending the iteration.

SUMMARY

In this chapter, you've seen Swift's control constructs in action, and have tamed the wild west of while and do-while loops. You've also been exposed to one of Swift and Xcode 6's neatest features: playgrounds. These interactive documents let you play with your code like putty in your hands, allowing you to see changes in near real time, as well as analyze the results. They're a great way to experiment and learn the Swift language.

Give your mind a rest and get ready for the next chapter, where there's more Swift goodness coming!

Writing Functions and Closures

We've covered a lot up to this point in the book: variables, constants, dictionaries, arrays, looping constructs, control structures, and the like. You've used both the REPL command-line interface and now Xcode 6's playgrounds feature to type in code samples and explore the language.

Up to this point, however, you have been limited to mostly experimentation: typing a line or three here and there and observing the results. Now it's time to get more organized with your code. In this chapter, you'll learn how to tidy up your Swift code into nice clean reusable components called functions.

Let's start this chapter with a fresh, new playground file. If you haven't already done so, launch Xcode 6 and create a new playground by choosing File > New > Playground, and name it **Chapter 4**. We'll explore this chapter's concepts with contrived examples in similar fashion to earlier chapters.

THE FUNCTION

Think back to your school years again. This time, remember high school algebra. You were paying attention, weren't you? In that class your teacher introduced the concept of the *function*. In essence, a function in arithmetic parlance is a mathematical formula that takes an input, performs a calculation, and provides a result, or output.

Mathematical functions have a specific notation. For example, to convert a Fahrenheit temperature value to the equivalent Celsius value, you would express that function in this way:

$$f(x) = \frac{(x - 32) * 5}{9}$$

The important parts of the function are:

- Name: In this case the function's name is f.
- Input, or independent variable: Contains the value that will be used in the function. Here it's x.
- Expression: Everything on the right of the equals sign.
- Result: Considered to be the value of $f(x)$ on the left side of the equals sign.

Functions are written in mathematical notation but can be described in natural language. In English, the sample function could be described as:

A function whose independent variable is x and whose result is the difference of the independent variable and 32, with the result being multiplied by 5, with the result being divided by 9.

The expression is succinct and tidy. The beauty of this function, and functions in general, is that they can be used over and over again to perform work, and all they need to do is be called with a parameter. So how does this relate to Swift? Obviously I wouldn't be talking about functions if they didn't exist in the Swift language. And as you'll see, they can perform not just mathematical calculations, but a whole lot more.

CODING THE FUNCTION IN SWIFT

Swift's notation for establishing the existence of a function is a little different than the mathematical one you just saw. In general, the syntax for declaring a Swift function is:

```
func funcName(paramName : type, ...) -> returnType
```

Take a look at an example to help clarify the syntax. **Figure 4.1** shows the code in the Chapter 4.playground file, along with the function defined on lines 7 through 13. This is the function discussed earlier, but now in a notation the Swift compiler can understand.

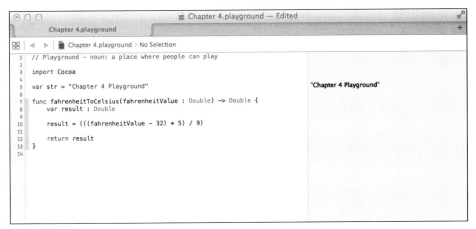

FIGURE 4.1 Tempera-
ture conversion as a
Swift function

Start by typing in the following code.

```swift
func fahrenheitToCelsius(fahrenheitValue : Double) -> Double {
    var result : Double

    result = (((fahrenheitValue - 32) * 5) / 9)

    return result
}
```

As you can see on line 7, there is some new syntax to learn. The `func` keyword is Swift's way to declare a function. That is followed by the function name (`fahrenheitToCelsius`), and the independent variable's name, or parameter name in parentheses. Notice that the parameter's type is explicitly declared as `Double`.

Following the parameter are the two characters `->`, which denote that this function is returning a value of a type (in this case, a `Double` type), followed by the open curly brace, which indicates the start of the function.

On line 8, you declare a variable of type `Double` named `result`. This will hold the value that will be given back to anyone who calls the function. Notice it is the same type as the function's return type declared after the `->` on line 7.

The actual mathematical function appears on line 10, with the result of the expression assigned to `result`, the local variable declared in line 8. Finally on line 12, the result is returned to the caller using the `return` keyword. Any time you wish to exit a function and return to the calling party, you use `return` along with the value being returned.

The Results sidebar doesn't show anything in the area where the function was typed. That's because a function by itself doesn't *do* anything. It has the potential to perform some useful work, but it must be called by a caller. That's what you'll do next.

FIGURE 4.2 The result of calling the newly created function

```
                        Chapter 4.playground — Edited
        Chapter 4.playground

    ◄  ►   Chapter 4.playground ⟩ No Selection
1   // Playground — noun: a place where people can play
2
3   import Cocoa
4
5   var str = "Chapter 4 Playground"                    "Chapter 4 Playground"
6
7   func fahrenheitToCelsius(fahrenheitValue : Double) -> Double {
8       var result : Double
9
10      result = (((fahrenheitValue - 32) * 5) / 9)     31.2222222222222
11
12      return result                                   31.2222222222222
13  }
14
15  var outdoorTemperatureInFahrenheit = 88.2           88.2
16  var outdoorTemperatureInCelsius = fahrenheitToCelsius  31.2222222222222
        (outdoorTemperatureInFahrenheit)
17
18  |
```

EXERCISING THE FUNCTION

Now it's time to call on the function you just created. Type in the following two lines of code, and pay attention to the Results sidebar in **Figure 4.2**.

```
var outdoorTemperatureInFahrenheit = 88.2
var outdoorTemperatureInCelsius = fahrenheitToCelsius(outdoorTemperature
→ InFahrenheit)
```

On line 15, you've declared a new variable, outdoorTemperatureInFahrenheit, and set its value to 88.2 (remember, Swift infers the type in this case as a Double). That value is then passed to the function on line 16, where a new variable, outdoorTemperatureInCelsius, is declared, and its value is captured as the result of the function.

The Results sidebar shows that 31.222222 (repeating decimal) is the result of the function, and indeed, 31.2 degrees Celsius is equivalent to 88.2 degrees Fahrenheit. Neat, isn't it? You now have a temperature conversion tool right at your fingertips.

Now, here's a little exercise for you to do on your own: Write the inverse method, celsiusToFahrenheit using the following formula for that conversion:

$$f(x) = \frac{x * 9}{5} + 32$$

Go ahead and code it up yourself, but resist the urge to peek ahead. Don't look until you've written the function, and then check your work against the following code and in **Figure 4.3**.

FIGURE 4.3 Declaring the inverse function, celsiusToFahrenheit

```
func celsiusToFahrenheit(celsiusValue : Double) -> Double {
    var result : Double

    result = (((celsiusValue * 9) / 5) + 32)

    return result
}
```

```
outdoorTemperatureInFahrenheit = celsiusToFahrenheit(outdoorTemperature
→ InCelsius)
```

The inverse function on lines 18 through 24 simply implements the Celsius to Fahrenheit formula and returns the result. Passing in the Celsius value of 31.22222 on line 26, you can see that the result is the original Fahrenheit value, 88.2.

You've just created two functions that do something useful: temperature conversions. Feel free to experiment with other values to see how they change between the two related functions.

FIGURE 4.4 A multi-parameter function

MORE THAN JUST NUMBERS

The notion of a function in Swift is more than just the mathematical concept we have discussed. In a broad sense, Swift functions are more flexible and robust in that they can accept more than just one parameter, and even accept types other than numeric ones.

Consider creating a function that takes more than one parameter and returns something other than a Double (**Figure 4.4**).

```swift
func buildASentence(subject : String, verb : String, noun : String) -> String {
    return subject + " " + verb + " " + noun + "!"
}
```

```swift
buildASentence("Swift", "is", "cool")
buildASentence("I", "love", "languages")
```

After typing in lines 28 through 33, examine your work. On line 28, you declared a new function, buildASentence, with not one but three parameters: subject, verb, and noun, all of which are String types. The function also returns a String type as well. On line 29, the concatenation of those three parameters, interspersed with spaces to make the sentence readable, is what is returned.

For clarity, the function is called twice on lines 32 and 33, resulting in the sentences in the Results sidebar. Feel free to replace the parameters with values of your own liking and view the results interactively.

FIGURE 4.5 Variable parameter passing in a function

PARAMETERS AD NAUSEAM

Imagine you're writing the next big banking app for the Mac, and you want to create a way to add some arbitrary number of account balances. Something so mundane can be done a number of ways, but you want to write a Swift function to do the addition. The problem is you don't know how many accounts will need to be summed at any given time.

Enter Swift's variable parameter passing notation. It provides you with a way to tell Swift, "I don't know how many parameters I'll need to pass to this function, so accept as many as I will give." Type in the following code, which is shown in action on lines 35 through 48 in **Figure 4.5**.

```
// Parameters Ad Nauseam
func addMyAccountBalances(balances : Double...) -> Double {
    var result : Double = 0

    for balance in balances {
        result += balance
    }
```

FIGURE 4.6 Adding
additional variable
parameters results in
an error.

```
 8        var result : Double
 9
10        result = (((fahrenheitValue - 32) * 5) / 9)        31.2222222222222
11
12        return result                                       31.2222222222222
13  }
14
15  var outdoorTemperatureInFahrenheit = 88.2                 88.2
16  var outdoorTemperatureInCelsius = fahrenheitToCelsius     31.2222222222222
        (outdoorTemperatureInFahrenheit)
17
18  func celsiusToFahrenheit(celsiusValue : Double) -> Double {
19        var result : Double
20
21        result = (((celsiusValue * 9) / 5) + 32)            88.2
22
23        return result                                       88.2
24  }
25
26  outdoorTemperatureInFahrenheit = celsiusToFahrenheit      88.2
        (outdoorTemperatureInCelsius)
27
28  func buildASentence(subject : String, verb : String, noun : String) -
        > String {
29        return subject + " " + verb + " " + noun + "!"       (2 times)
30  }
31
32  buildASentence("Swift", "is", "cool")                     "Swift is cool!"
33  buildASentence("I", "love", "languages")                 "I love languages!"
34
35  // Parameters Ad Nauseam
36  func addMyAccountBalances(balances : Double..., names : String) ->
        Double {
37        var result : Double = 0        '...' must be on the last parameter  (3 times)
38
39        for balance in balances {
40            result += balance                                (9 times)
41        }
42
43        return result                                        (3 times)
44  }
45  |
```

```
    return result

}
```

```
addMyAccountBalances(77.87)
addMyAccountBalances(10.52, 11.30, 100.60)
addMyAccountBalances(345.12, 1000.80, 233.10, 104.80, 99.90)
```

This function's parameter, known as a *variadic parameter*, can represent an unknown number of parameters.

On line 36, our balances parameter is declared as a Double followed by the ellipsis (...) and returns a Double. The presence of the ellipsis is the clue: It tells Swift to expect *one or more* parameters of type Double when this function is called.

The function is called three times on lines 46 through 48, each with a different number of bank balances. The totals for each appear in the Results sidebar.

You might be tempted to add additional variadic parameters in a function. **Figure 4.6** shows an attempt to extend addMyAccountBalances with a second variadic parameter, but it results in a Swift error.

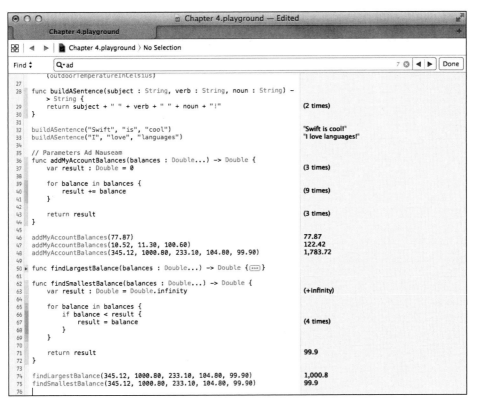

FIGURE 4.7 Functions to find the largest and smallest balance

This is a no-no, and Swift will quickly shut you down with an error. Only the *last* parameter of a function may contain the ellipsis to indicate a variadic parameter. All other parameters must refer to a single quantity.

Since we're on the theme of bank accounts, add two more functions: one that will find the largest balance in a given list of balances, and another that will find the smallest balance. Type the following code, which is shown on lines 50 through 75 in **Figure 4.7.**

```
func findLargestBalance(balances : Double...) -> Double {
  var result : Double = -Double.infinity

  for balance in balances {
    if balance > result {
      result = balance
    }
  }

  return result
}
```

```
func findSmallestBalance(balances : Double...) -> Double {
   var result : Double = Double.infinity

   for balance in balances {
      if balance < result {
         result = balance
      }
   }

   return result
}
```

```
findLargestBalance(345.12, 1000.80, 233.10, 104.80, 99.90)
findSmallestBalance(345.12, 1000.80, 233.10, 104.80, 99.90)
```

Both functions iterate through the parameter list to find the largest and smallest balance. Unless you have an account with plus or minus infinity of your favorite currency, these functions will work well. On lines 74 and 75, both functions are tested with the same balances used earlier, and the Results sidebar confirms their correctness.

FUNCTIONS FLY FIRST CLASS

One of the powerful features of Swift functions is that they are *first-class objects*. Sounds pretty fancy, doesn't it? What that really means is that you can handle a function just like any other value. You can assign a function to a constant, pass a function as a parameter to another function, and even return a function from a function!

To illustrate this idea, consider the act of depositing a check into your bank account, as well as withdrawing an amount. Every Monday, an amount is deposited, and every Friday, another amount is withdrawn. Instead of tying the day directly to the function name of the deposit or withdrawal, use a constant to point to the function for the appropriate day. The code on lines 77 through 94 in **Figure 4.8** provides an example.

```
var account1 = ( "State Bank Personal", 1011.10 )
var account2 = ( "State Bank Business", 24309.63 )

func deposit(amount : Double, account : (name : String, balance : Double)) ->
→ (String, Double) {
   var newBalance : Double = account.balance + amount
   return (account.name, newBalance)
}
```

FIGURE 4.8
Demonstrating
functions as first-class
types

```
func withdraw(amount : Double, account : (name : String, balance : Double)) ->
→ (String, Double) {
  var newBalance : Double = account.balance - amount
  return (account.name, newBalance)
}


let mondayTransaction = deposit
let fridayTransaction = withdraw


let mondayBalance = mondayTransaction(300.0, account1)
let fridayBalance = fridayTransaction(1200, account2)
```

For starters, you create two accounts on lines 77 and 78. Each account is a tuple consisting of an account name and balance.

On line 80, a function is declared named deposit that takes two parameters: the amount (a Double) and a tuple named account. The tuple has two members: name, which is of type String, and balance, which is a Double that represents the funds in that account. The same tuple type is also declared as the return type.

At line 81, a variable named newBalance is declared, and its value is assigned the sum of the balance member of the account tuple and the amount variable that is passed. The tuple result is constructed on line 82 and returned.

The function on line 85 is named differently (withdraw) but is effectively the same, save for the subtraction that takes place on line 86.

On lines 90 and 91, two new constants are declared and assigned to the functions respectively by name: deposit and withdraw. Since deposits happen on a Monday, the mondayTransaction is assigned the deposit function. Likewise, withdrawals are on Friday, and the fridayTransaction constant is assigned the withdraw function.

Lines 93 and 94 show the results of passing the account1 and account2 tuples to the mondayTransaction and fridayTransaction constants, which are in essence the functions deposit and withdraw. The Results sidebar bears out the result, and you've just called the two functions by referring to the constants.

THROW ME A FUNCTION, MISTER

Just as a function can return an Int, Double, or String, a function can also return another function. Your head starts hurting just thinking about the possibilities, doesn't it? Actually, it's not as hard as it sounds. Check out lines 96 through 102 in **Figure 4.9**.

```
func chooseTransaction(transaction: String) -> (Double, (String, Double)) ->
→ (String, Double) {
    if transaction == "Deposit" {
       return deposit
    }


    return withdraw
}
```

On line 96, the function chooseTransaction takes a String as a parameter, which it uses to deduce the type of banking transaction. That same function returns a function, which itself takes a Double, and a tuple of String and Double, and returns a tuple of String and Double. Phew!

That's a mouthful. Let's take a moment to look at that line closer and break it down a bit. The line begins with the definition of the function and its sole parameter: transaction, followed by the -> characters indicating the return type:

```
func chooseTransaction(transaction: String) ->
```

After that is the return type, which is a function that takes two parameters: the Double, and a tuple of Double and String, as well as the function return characters ->:

```
(Double, (String, Double)) ->
```

And finally, the return type of the returned function, a tuple of String and Double.

FIGURE 4.9
Returning a function from a function

```
65        for balance in balances {
66            if balance < result {
67                result = balance                     (4 times)
68            }
69        }
70
71        return result                                 99.9
72    }
73
74    findLargestBalance(345.12, 1000.80, 233.10, 104.80, 99.90)     1,000.8
75    findSmallestBalance(345.12, 1000.80, 233.10, 104.80, 99.90)    99.9
76
77    var account1 = ( "State Bank Personal", 1011.10 )    (.0 "State Bank Personal", .1 1,011.1)
78    var account2 = ( "State Bank Business", 24309.63 )   (.0 "State Bank Business", .1 24,309.63)
79
80    func deposit(amount : Double, account : (name : String, balance : Double)) ->
          (String, Double) {
81        var newBalance : Double = account.balance + amount    1,311.1
82        return (account.name, newBalance)                     (.0 "State Bank Personal", .1 1,311.1)
83    }
84
85    func withdraw(amount : Double, account : (name : String, balance : Double)) -
        > (String, Double) {
86        var newBalance : Double = account.balance - amount    23,109.63
87        return (account.name, newBalance)                     (.0 "State Bank Business", .1 23,109.63)
88    }
89
90    let mondayTransaction = deposit                    (Function)
91    let fridayTransaction = withdraw                   (Function)
92
93    let mondayBalance = mondayTransaction(300.0, account1)   (.0 "State Bank Personal", .1 1,311.1)
94    let fridayBalance = fridayTransaction(1200, account2)    (.0 "State Bank Business", .1 23,109.63)
95
96    func chooseTransaction(transaction: String) -> (Double, (String, Double)) ->
          (String, Double) {
97        if transaction == "Deposit" {
98            return deposit
99        }
100
101       return withdraw
102   }
103
```

What functions did you write that meet this criteria? The deposit and withdraw functions, of course! Look at lines 80 and 85. Those two functions are bank transactions that were used earlier. Since they are defined as functions that take two parameters (a Double and a tuple of String and Double) and return a tuple of Double and String, they are appropriate candidates for return values in the chooseTransaction function on line 96.

Back to the chooseTransaction function: On line 97, the transaction parameter, which is a String, is compared against the constant string "Deposit" and if a match is made, the deposit function is returned on line 98; otherwise, the withdraw function is returned on line 101.

Ok, so you have a function which itself returns one of two possible functions. How do you use it? Do you capture the function in another variable and call it?

Actually, there are two ways this can be done (**Figure 4.10**).

```
// option 1: capture the function in a constant and call it
let myTransaction = chooseTransaction("Deposit")
myTransaction(225.33, account2)


// option 2: call the function result directly
chooseTransaction("Withdraw")(63.17, account1)
```

FIGURE 4.10 Calling the returned function in two different ways

```
72   }
73
74   findLargestBalance(345.12, 1000.80, 233.10, 104.80, 99.90)          1,000.8
75   findSmallestBalance(345.12, 1000.80, 233.10, 104.80, 99.90)         99.9
76
77   var account1 = ( "State Bank Personal", 1011.10 )                   (.0 "State Bank Personal", .1 1,011.1)
78   var account2 = ( "State Bank Business", 24309.63 )                  (.0 "State Bank Business", .1 24,309.63)
79
80   func deposit(amount : Double, account : (name : String, balance : Double)) ->
         (String, Double) {
81       var newBalance : Double = account.balance + amount             (2 times)
82       return (account.name, newBalance)                              (2 times)
83   }
84
85   func withdraw(amount : Double, account : (name : String, balance : Double)) -
       > (String, Double) {
86       var newBalance : Double = account.balance - amount             (2 times)
87       return (account.name, newBalance)                              (2 times)
88   }
89
90   let mondayTransaction = deposit                                    (Function)
91   let fridayTransaction = withdraw                                   (Function)
92
93   let mondayBalance = mondayTransaction(300.0, account1)             (.0 "State Bank Personal", .1 1,311.1)
94   let fridayBalance = fridayTransaction(1200, account2)             (.0 "State Bank Business", .1 23,109.63)
95
96   func chooseTransaction(transaction: String) -> (Double, (String, Double)) ->
         (String, Double) {
97       if transaction == "Deposit" {
98           return deposit                                            (Function)
99       }
100
101      return withdraw                                               (Function)
102  }
103
104  // option 1: capture the function in a constant and call it
105  let myTransaction = chooseTransaction("Deposit")                   (Function)
106  myTransaction(225.33, account2)                                    (.0 "State Bank Business", .1 24,534.96)
107
108  // option 2: call the function result directly
109  chooseTransaction("Withdraw")(63.17, account1)                     (.0 "State Bank Personal", .1 947.93)
110
```

On line 105 you can see that the returned function for making deposits is captured in the constant myTransaction, which is then called on line 106 with account2 increasing its amount by $225.33.

The alternate style is on line 109. There, the chooseTransaction function is being called to gain access to the withdraw function. Instead of assigning the result to a constant, however, the returned function is immediately pressed into service with the parameters 63.17 and the first account, account1. The results are the same in the Results sidebar: The withdraw function is called and the balance is adjusted.

A FUNCTION IN A FUNCTION IN A…

If functions returned by functions and assigned to constants isn't enough of an enigma for you, how about declaring a function inside of another function? Yes, such a thing exists. They're called *nested functions*.

Nested functions are useful when you want to isolate, or hide, specific functionality that doesn't need to be exposed to outer layers. Take, for instance, the code in **Figure 4.11**.

```
// nested function example
func bankVault(passcode : String) -> String {
  func openBankVault(Void) -> String {
    return "Vault opened"
  }
```

FIGURE 4.11 Nested functions in action

```
func closeBankVault(Void) -> String {
    return "Vault closed"
}
if passcode == "secret" {
    return openBankVault()
}
else {
    return closeBankVault()
}
}

println(bankVault("wrongsecret"))
println(bankVault("secret"))
```

On line 112, a new function, bankVault, is defined. It takes a single parameter, passcode, which is a String, and returns a String.

Lines 113 and 116 define two functions inside of the bankVault function: openBankVault and closeBankVault. Both of these functions take no parameter and return a String.

On line 119, the passcode parameter is compared with the string "secret" and if a match is made, the bank vault is opened by calling the openBankVault function. Otherwise, the bank vault remains closed.

```
91     let fridayTransaction = withdraw                                    (Function)
92
93     let mondayBalance = mondayTransaction(300.0, account1)              (.0 "State Bank Personal", .1 1,311.1)
94     let fridayBalance = fridayTransaction(1200, account2)              (.0 "State Bank Business", .1 23,109.63)
95
96     func chooseTransaction(transaction: String) -> (Double, (String, Double)) ->
           (String, Double) {
97         if transaction == "Deposit" {
98             return deposit                                             (Function)
99         }
100
101        return withdraw                                                (Function)
102    }
103
104    // option 1: capture the function in a constant and call it
105    let myTransaction = chooseTransaction("Deposit")                   (Function)
106    myTransaction(225.33, account2)                                    (.0 "State Bank Business", .1 24,534.96)
107
108    // option 2: call the function result directly
109    chooseTransaction("Withdraw")(63.17, account1)                     (.0 "State Bank Personal", .1 947.93)
110
111    // nested function example
112    func bankVault(passcode : String) -> String {
113        func openBankVault(Void) -> String {
114            return "Vault opened"                                       "Vault opened"
115        }
116        func closeBankVault(Void) -> String {
117            return "Vault closed"                                       "Vault closed"
118        }
119        if passcode == "secret" {
120            return openBankVault()                                      "Vault opened"
121        }
122        else {
123            return closeBankVault()                                     "Vault closed"
124        }
125    }
126
127    println(bankVault("wrongsecret"))                                   "Vault closed"
128    println(bankVault("secret"))                                        "Vault opened"
129
130    println(openBankVault())        ⓘ Use of unresolved identifier 'openBankVault'  (3 times)
131
```

INTO THE VOID

On lines 113 and 116, you'll notice a new Swift keyword: Void. It means exactly what you might think: emptiness. The Void keyword is used mostly as a placeholder when declaring empty parameter lists, and is optional in this case. However, be aware of it because you will be seeing more of it later.

Lines 127 and 128 show the result of calling the bankVault method with an incorrect and correct passcode. What's important to realize is that the openBankVault and closeBankVault functions are "enclosed" by the bankVault function, and are not known outside of that function.

If you were to attempt to call either openBankVault or closeBankVault outside of the bankVault function, you would get an error. That's because those functions are not in *scope*. They are, in effect, hidden by the bankVault function and are unable to be called from the outside. **Figure 4.12** illustrates an attempt to call one of these nested functions.

In general, the obvious benefit of nesting functions within functions is that it prevents the unnecessary exposing of functionality. In Figure 4.12, The bankVault function is the sole gateway to opening and closing the vault, and the functions that perform the work are isolated within that function. Always consider this when designing functions that are intended to work together.

FIGURE 4.13 Using default parameters in a function

DEFAULT PARAMETERS

As you've just seen, Swift functions provide a rich area for utility and experimentation. A lot can be done with functions and their parameters to model real-world problems. Functions provide another interesting feature called *default parameter values*, which allow you to declare functions that have parameters containing a "prefilled" value.

Let's say you want to create a function that writes checks. Your function would take two parameters: a payee (the person or business to whom the check is written) and the amount. Of course, in the real world, you will always want to know these two pieces of information, but for now, think of a function that would assume a default payee and amount in the event the information wasn't passed.

Figure 4.13 shows such a function on lines 130 through 132. The writeCheck function takes two String parameters, the payee and amount, and returns a String that is simply a sentence describing how the check is written.

```
func writeCheck(payee : String = "Unknown", amount : String = "10.00") ->
→ String {
    return "Check payable to " + payee + " for $" + amount
}

writeCheck()
writeCheck(payee : "Donna Soileau")
writeCheck(payee : "John Miller", amount : "45.00")
```

Take note of the declaration of the function on line 130:

```
func writeCheck(payee : String = "Unknown", amount : String = "10.00") ->
→ String
```

What you haven't seen before now is the assignment of the parameters to actual values (in this case, payee is being set to "Unknown" by default and amount is being set to "10.00"). This is how you can write a function to take default parameters—simply assign the parameter name to a value!

So how do you call this function? Lines 134 through 136 show three different ways:

- Line 134 passes no parameters when calling the function.
- Line 135 passes a single parameter.
- Line 136 passes both parameters.

In the case where no parameters are passed, the default values are used to construct the returned String. In the other two cases, the passed parameter values are used in place of the default values, and you can view the results of the calls in the Results sidebar.

Another observation: When calling a function set up to accept default parameters, you must pass the parameter name and a colon as part of that parameter. On line 135, only one parameter is used:

```
writeCheck(payee : "Donna Soileau")
```

And on line 136, both parameter names are used:

```
writeCheck(payee : "John Miller", amount : "45.00")
```

Default parameters give you the flexibility of using a known value instead of taking the extra effort to pass it explicitly. They're not necessarily applicable for every function out there, but they do come in handy at times.

WHAT'S IN A NAME?

As Swift functions go, declaring them is easy, as you've seen. In some cases, however, what really composes the function name is more than just the text following the keyword func.

Each parameter in a Swift function can have an optional *external parameter* preceding the parameter name. External names give additional clarity and description to a function name. Consider another check writing function in **Figure 4.14**, lines 138 through 140.

```
func writeCheck(payer : String, payee : String, amount : Double) -> String {
    return "Check payable from \(payer) to \(payee) for $\(amount)"
}


writeCheck("Dave Johnson", "Coz Fontenot", 1000.0)
```

FIGURE 4.14 A function without external parameter names

```
● ○ ○                    ▣ Chapter 4.playground — Edited
       Chapter 4.playground
⊞  ◀  ▶  ▐ Chapter 4.playground ⟩ No Selection
103
104    // option 1: capture the function in a constant and call it
105    let myTransaction = chooseTransaction("Deposit")          (Function)
106    myTransaction(225.33, account2)                           (.0 "State Bank Business", .1 24,534.96)
107
108    // option 2: call the function result directly
109    chooseTransaction("Withdraw")(63.17, account1)            (.0 "State Bank Personal", .1 947.93)
110
111    // nested function example
112    func bankVault(passcode : String) -> String {
113        func openBankVault(Void) -> String {
114            return "Vault opened"                              "Vault opened"
115        }
116        func closeBankVault(Void) -> String {
117            return "Vault closed"                              "Vault closed"
118        }
119        if passcode == "secret" {
120            return openBankVault()                             "Vault opened"
121        }
122        else {
123            return closeBankVault()                            "Vault closed"
124        }
125    }
126
127    println(bankVault("wrongsecret"))                          "Vault closed"
128    println(bankVault("secret"))                              "Vault opened"
129
130    func writeCheck(payee : String = "Unknown", amount : String = "10.00")
           -> String {
131        return "Check payable to " + payee + " for $" + amount  (3 times)
132    }
133
134    writeCheck()                                              "Check payable to Unknown for $10.00"
135    writeCheck(payee : "Donna Soileau")                       "Check payable to Donna Soileau for $10.00"
136    writeCheck(payee : "John Miller", amount : "45.00")       "Check payable to John Miller for $45.00"
137
138    func writeCheck(payer : String, payee : String, amount : Double) ->
           String {
139        return "Check payable from \(payer) to \(payee) for $\(amount)"  "Check payable from Dave Johnson to Coz Fonten..."
140    }
141
142    writeCheck("Dave Johnson", "Coz Fontenot", 1000.0)        "Check payable from Dave Johnson to Coz Fonten..."
143
```

This function is different from the earlier check writing function on lines 130 through 132 in two ways:

- An additional parameter named payer to indicate who the check is coming from
- No default parameters

On line 142, the new writeCheck function is called with three parameters: two String values and a Double value. From the name of the function, its purpose is clearly to write a check. When writing a check, you need to know several things: who the check is being written for; who is writing the check; and for how much? A good guess is that the Double parameter is the amount, which is a number. But without actually looking at the function declaration itself, how would you know what the two String parameters actually mean? Even if you were to deduce that they are the payer and payee, how do you know which is which, and in which order to pass the parameters?

FIGURE 4.15 A function with external parameter names

```
111    // nested function example
112    func bankVault(passcode : String) -> String {
113        func openBankVault(Void) -> String {
114            return "Vault opened"                          "Vault opened"
115        }
116        func closeBankVault(Void) -> String {
117            return "Vault closed"                          "Vault closed"
118        }
119        if passcode == "secret" {
120            return openBankVault()                         "Vault opened"
121        }
122        else {
123            return closeBankVault()                        "Vault closed"
124        }
125    }
126
127    println(bankVault("wrongsecret"))                     "Vault closed"
128    println(bankVault("secret"))                          "Vault opened"
129
130    func writeCheck(payee : String = "Unknown", amount : String = "10.00")
           -> String {
131        return "Check payable to " + payee + " for $" + amount    (3 times)
132    }
133
134    writeCheck()                                          "Check payable to Unknown for $10.00"
135    writeCheck(payee : "Donna Soileau")                   "Check payable to Donna Soileau for $10.00"
136    writeCheck(payee : "John Miller", amount : "45.00")   "Check payable to John Miller for $45.00"
137
138    func writeCheck(payer : String, payee : String, amount : Double) ->
           String {
139        return "Check payable from \(payer) to \(payee) for $\(amount)"   "Check payable from Dave Johnson to Coz Fonten...
140    }
141
142    writeCheck("Dave Johnson", "Coz Fontenot", 1000.0)    "Check payable from Dave Johnson to Coz Fonten...
143
144    func writeBetterCheck(from payer : String, to payee : String, total
           amount : Double) -> String {
145        return "Check payable from \(payer) to \(payee) for $\(amount)"   "Check payable from Fred Charlie to Ryan Hanks f...
146    }
147
148    writeBetterCheck(from : "Fred Charlie", to: "Ryan Hanks", total :      "Check payable from Fred Charlie to Ryan Hanks f...
           1350.0)
149
```

External parameter names solve this problem by adding an additional name to each parameter that *must* be passed when calling the function, which makes very clear to anyone reading the calling function what the intention is and the purpose of each parameter. **Figure 4.15** illustrates this quite well.

```
func writeBetterCheck(from payer : String, to payee : String, total amount :
→ Double) -> String {
    return "Check payable from \(payer) to \(payee) for $\(amount)"
}
```

```
writeBetterCheck(from : "Fred Charlie", to: "Ryan Hanks", total : 1350.0)
```

On line 144, you declare a function, `writeBetterCheck`, which takes the same number of parameters as the function on line 138. However, each of the parameters in the new function now has its own *external* parameter: `from`, `to`, and `total`. The original parameter names are still there, of course, used inside the function itself to reference the assigned values.

This extra bit of typing pays off on line 148, when the `writeBetterCheck` function is called. Looking at that line of code alone, the order of the parameters and what they indicate is clear: Write a check *from* Fred Charlie *to* Ryan Hanks for a *total* of $1350.

FIGURE 4.16
shorthand external
parameter syntax

```
119    if passcode == "secret" {
120        return openBankVault()                                    "Vault opened"
121    }
122    else {
123        return closeBankVault()                                   "Vault closed"
124    }
125  }
126
127  println(bankVault("wrongsecret"))                                "Vault closed"
128  println(bankVault("secret"))                                     "Vault opened"
129
130  func writeCheck(payee : String = "Unknown", amount : String = "10.00")
131      -> String {
         return "Check payable to " + payee + " for $" + amount     (3 times)
132  }
133
134  writeCheck()                                                     "Check payable to Unknown for $10.00"
135  writeCheck(payee : "Donna Soileau")                              "Check payable to Donna Soileau for $10.00"
136  writeCheck(payee : "John Miller", amount : "45.00")              "Check payable to John Miller for $45.00"
137
138  func writeCheck(payer : String, payee : String, amount : Double) ->
         String {
139      return "Check payable from \(payer) to \(payee) for $\(amount)"   "Check payable from Dave Johnson to Coz Fonten..."
140  }
141
142  writeCheck("Dave Johnson", "Coz Fontenot", 1000.0)               "Check payable from Dave Johnson to Coz Fonten..."
143
144  func writeBetterCheck(from payer : String, to payee : String, total
         amount : Double) -> String {
145      return "Check payable from \(payer) to \(payee) for $\(amount)"   "Check payable from Fred Charlie to Ryan Hanks f..."
146  }
147
148  writeBetterCheck(from : "Fred Charlie", to: "Ryan Hanks", total :     "Check payable from Fred Charlie to Ryan Hanks f..."
         1350.0)
149
150  func writeBestCheck(#from : String, #to : String, #total : Double) ->
         String {
151      return "Check payable from \(from) to \(to) for $\(total)"    "Check payable from Bart Stewart to Alan Lafleur f..."
152  }
153
154  writeBestCheck(from : "Bart Stewart", to: "Alan Lafleur", total :     "Check payable from Bart Stewart to Alan Lafleur f..."
         101.0)
155
```

WHEN IT'S GOOD ENOUGH

External parameter names bring clarity to functions, but they can feel somewhat redundant and clumsy as you search for something to accompany the parameter name. Actually, you may find that in certain cases, the parameter name is descriptive enough to act as the external parameter name. Swift allows you to use the parameter name as an external name, too, with a special syntax: the # character.

Instead of providing an external parameter name, simply prepend the # character to the parameter name, and use that name when calling the new function writeBestCheck, as done on line 150 in **Figure 4.16**. This is known as *shorthand external parameter naming*.

The three parameter names, from, to, and total, all are prepended with #. On line 154, the parameter names are used as external parameter names once again to call the function, and the use of those names clearly shows what the function's purpose and parameter order is: a check written *from* Bart Stewart *to* Alan Lafleur for a *total* of $101.

```
func writeBestCheck(#from : String, #to : String, #total : Double) -> String {
    return "Check payable from \(from) to \(to) for $\(total)"
}


writeBestCheck(from : "Bart Stewart", to: "Alan Lafleur", total : 101.0)
```

FIGURE 4.17 When external parameter names are not necessary

FIGURE 4.17 When external parameter names are not necessary

TO USE OR NOT TO USE?

External parameter names bring clarity to functions, but they also require more typing on the part of the caller who uses your functions. Since they are optional parts of a function's declaration, when should you use them?

In general, if the function in question can benefit from additional clarity of having external parameter names provided for each parameter, by all means use them. The check writing example is such a case. Avoid parameter ambiguity in the cases where it might exist. On the other hand, if you're creating a function that just adds two numbers (see lines 156 through 160 in **Figure 4.17**), external parameter names add little to nothing of value for the caller.

```
func addTwoNumbers(number1 : Double, number2 : Double) -> Double {
    return number1 + number2
}

addTwoNumbers(33.1, 12.2)
```

FIGURE 4.18 Assigning a value to a parameter results in an error.

DON'T CHANGE MY PARAMETERS!

Functions are prohibited from changing the values of parameters passed to them, because parameters are passed as constants and not variables. Consider the function cashCheck on lines 162 through 169 in **Figure 4.18**.

```
func cashCheck(#from : String, #to : String, #total : Double) -> String {
    if to == "Cash" {
        to = from
    }
    return "Check payable from \(from) to \(to) for $\(total) has been cashed"
}

cashCheck(from: "Jason Guillory", to: "Cash", total: 103.00)
```

The function takes the same parameters as our earlier check writing function: who the check is from, who the check is to, and the total. On line 163, the to variable is checked for the value "Cash" and if it is equal, it is reassigned the contents of the variable from. The rationale here is that if you are writing a check to "Cash," you're essentially writing it to yourself.

FIGURE 4.19

A potential work-around to the param-eter change problem

```
                                                                                                              
  136   writeCheck(payee : "John Miller", amount : "45.00")          "Check payable to John Miller for $45.00"
  137
  138   func writeCheck(payer : String, payee : String, amount : Double) ->
            String {
  139     return "Check payable from \(payer) to \(payee) for $\(amount)"   "Check payable from Dave Johnson to Coz Fonten...
  140   }
  141
  142   writeCheck("Dave Johnson", "Coz Fontenot", 1000.0)          "Check payable from Dave Johnson to Coz Fonten...
  143
  144   func writeBetterCheck(from payer : String, to payee : String, total
            amount : Double) -> String {
  145     return "Check payable from \(payer) to \(payee) for $\(amount)"   "Check payable from Fred Charlie to Ryan Hanks f...
  146   }
  147
  148   writeBetterCheck(from : "Fred Charlie", to: "Ryan Hanks", total :    "Check payable from Fred Charlie to Ryan Hanks f...
            1350.0)
  149
  150   func writeBestCheck(#from : String, #to : String, #total : Double) ->
            String {
  151     return "Check payable from \(from) to \(to) for $\(total)"    "Check payable from Bart Stewart to Alan Lafleur f...
  152   }
  153
  154   writeBestCheck(from : "Bart Stewart", to: "Alan Lafleur", total :    "Check payable from Bart Stewart to Alan Lafleur f...
            101.0)
  155
  156   func addTwoNumbers(number1 : Double, number2 : Double) -> Double {
  157     return number1 + number2                                   45.3
  158   }
  159
  160   addTwoNumbers(33.1, 12.2)                                     45.3
  161
  162   func cashCheck(#from : String, #to : String, #total : Double) -> String
            {
  163     var otherTo  = to                                          "Cash"
  164     if to == "Cash" {
  165        otherTo = from                                          "Jason Guillory"
  166     }
  167     return "Check payable from \(from) to \(otherTo) for $\(total) has   "Check payable from Jason Guillory to Jason Guillo...
            been cashed"
  168   }
  169
  170   cashCheck(from: "Jason Guillory", to: "Cash", total: 103.00)   "Check payable from Jason Guillory to Jason Guillo...
  171
```

Notice the error: **Cannot assign to 'let' value 'to'**. Swift is saying that the parameter to is a constant, and since constants cannot change their values once assigned, this is prohibited and results in an error.

To get around this error, you could create a temporary variable, as done in **Figure 4.19**. Here, a new variable named otherTo is declared on line 163 and assigned to the to variable, and then possibly to the from variable assuming the condition on line 164 is met. This is clearly acceptable and works fine for our purposes, but Swift gives you a better way.

With a var declaration on a parameter, you can tell Swift the parameter is intended to be variable and can change within the function. All you need to do is add the keyword before the parameter name (or external parameter name in case you have one of those). **Figure 4.20** shows a second function, cashBetterCheck, which declares the to parameter as a variable parameter. Now the code inside the function can modify the to variable without receiving an error from Swift, and the output is identical to the workaround function above it.

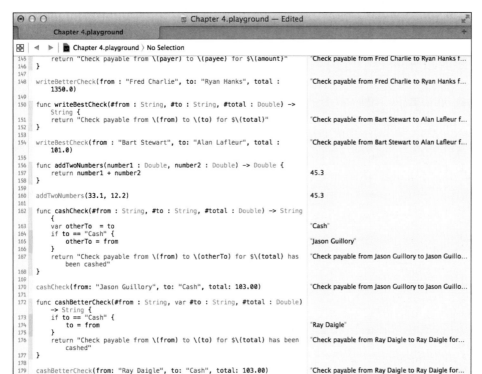

FIGURE 4.20 Using variable parameters to allow modifications

```
func cashBetterCheck(#from : String, var #to : String, #total : Double) ->
→ String {
   if to == "Cash" {
      to = from
   }
      return "Check payable from \(from) to \(to) for $\(total) has been cashed"
}


cashBetterCheck(from: "Ray Daigle", to: "Cash", total: 103.00)
```

Using
...out keyword to
establish a modifiable
parameter

```
158  }
159
160  addTwoNumbers(33.1, 12.2)                                          45.3
161
162  func cashCheck(#from : String, #to : String, #total : Double) -> String
     {
163      var otherTo  = to                                             "Cash"
164      if to == "Cash" {
165          otherTo = from                                            "Jason Guillory"
166      }
167      return "Check payable from \(from) to \(otherTo) for $\(total) has   "Check payable from Jason Guillory to Jason Guillo...
         been cashed"
168  }
169
170  cashCheck(from: "Jason Guillory", to: "Cash", total: 103.00)       "Check payable from Jason Guillory to Jason Guillo...
171
172  func cashBetterCheck(#from : String, var #to : String, #total : Double)
     -> String {
173      if to == "Cash" {
174          to = from                                                 "Ray Daigle"
175      }
176      return "Check payable from \(from) to \(to) for $\(total) has been   "Check payable from Ray Daigle to Ray Daigle for...
         cashed"
177  }
178
179  cashBetterCheck(from: "Ray Daigle", to: "Cash", total: 103.00)     "Check payable from Ray Daigle to Ray Daigle for...
180
181  func cashBestCheck(#from : String, inout #to : String, #total : Double)
     -> String {
182      if to == "Cash" {
183          to = from                                                 "James Perry"
184      }
185      return "Check payable from \(from) to \(to) for $\(total) has been   "Check payable from James Perry to James Perry fo...
         cashed"
186  }
187
188  var payer = "James Perry"                                          "James Perry"
189  var payee = "Cash"                                                 "Cash"
190  println(payee)                                                     "Cash"
191  cashBestCheck(from: payer, to: &payee, total: 103.00)              "Check payable from James Perry to James Perry fo...
192
193  println(payee)                                                     "James Perry"
194
```

THE INS AND OUTS

As you've just seen, a function can be declared to modify the contents of one or more of its passed variables. The modification happens inside the function itself, and the change is not reflected back to the caller.

Sometimes having a function change the value of a passed parameter so that its new value is reflected back to the caller is desirable. For example, in the cashBetterCheck function on lines 172 through 177, having the caller know that the to variable has changed to a new value would be advantageous. Right now, that function's modification of the variable is not reflected back to the caller. Let's see how to do this in **Figure 4.21** using Swift's inout keyword.

```
func cashBestCheck(#from : String, inout #to : String, #total : Double) ->
→ String {
   if to == "Cash" {
      to = from
   }
   return "Check payable from \(from) to \(to) for $\(total) has been cashed"
}
```

```
var payer = "James Perry"
var payee = "Cash"
println(payee)
cashBestCheck(from: payer, to: &payee, total: 103.00)

println(payee)
```

Lines 181 through 186 define the cashBestCheck function, which is virtually identical to the cashBetterCheck function on line 172, except the second parameter to is no longer a variable parameter—the var keyword has been replaced with the inout keyword. This new keyword tells Swift the parameter's value can be expected to change in the function and that the change should be reflected back to the caller. With that exception, everything else is the same between the cashBetterCheck and cashBestCheck functions.

On lines 188 and 189, two variables are declared: payer and payee, with both being assigned String values. This is done because inout parameters must be passed a variable. A constant value will not work, because constants cannot be modified.

On line 190, the payee variable is printed, and the Results sidebar for that line clearly shows the variable's contents as "Cash". This is to make clear that the variable is set to its original value on line 189.

On line 191, we call the cashBestCheck function. Unlike the call to cashBetterCheck on line 179, we are passing variables instead of constants for the to and from parameters. More so, for the second parameter (payee), we are prepending the ampersand character (&) to the variable name. This is a direct result of declaring the parameter in cashBestCheck as an inout parameter. You are in essence telling Swift that this variable is an in-out variable and that you expect it to be modified once control is returned from the called function.

On line 193, the payee variable is again printed. This time, the contents of that variable do not match what was printed on line 189 earlier. Instead, payee is now set to the value "James Perry", which is a direct result of the assignment in the cashBestCheck function on line 183.

BRINGING CLOSURE

Functions are great, and in the earlier code you've written, you can see just how versatile they can be for encapsulating functionality and ideas. Although the many contrived examples you went through may not give you a full appreciation of how useful they can be in every scenario, that will change as you proceed through the book. Functions are going to appear over and over again both here and in your coding, so understand them well. You may want to re-read this chapter to retain all the ins and outs of functions.

We've got a little more to talk about before we close this chapter, however. Our tour of functions would not be complete without talking about another significant and related feature of functions in Swift: *closures.*

In layman's terms, a closure is essentially a block of code, like a function, which "closes in" or "encapsulates" all the "state" around it. All variables and constants declared and defined before a closure are "captured" in that closure. In essence, a closure preserves the state of the program at the point that it is created.

Computer science folk have another word for closures: *lambdas.* In fact, the very notion of the function you have been working with throughout this chapter is actually a special case of a closure—a function is a closure with a name.

So if functions are actually special types of closures, then why use closures? It's a fair question, and the answer can be summed up this way: Closures allow you to write simple and quick code blocks that can be passed around just like functions, but without the overhead of naming them.

In essence, they are anonymous blocks of executable code.

Swift closures have the following structure:

```
{ (parameters) -> return_type in
    statements
}
```

This almost looks like a function, except that the keyword func and the name is missing; the curly braces encompass the entire closure; and the keyword in follows the return type.

Let's see closures in action. **Figure 4.22** shows a closure being defined on lines 196 through 201. The closure is being assigned to a constant named simpleInterestCalculationClosure. The closure takes three parameters: loanAmount, interestRate (both Double types), and years (an Int type). The code computes the future value of a loan over the term and returns it as a Double.

```
// Closures
let simpleInterestCalculationClosure = { (loanAmount : Double, var
→ interestRate : Double, years : Int) -> Double in
    interestRate = interestRate / 100.0
    var interest = Double(years) * interestRate * loanAmount

    return loanAmount + interest
}

func loanCalculator(loanAmount : Double, interestRate : Double, years :
→ Int, calculator : (Double, Double, Int) -> Double) -> Double {
    let totalPayout = calculator(loanAmount, interestRate, years)
    return totalPayout
}

var simple = loanCalculator(10_000, 3.875, 5, simpleInterestCalculationClosure)
```

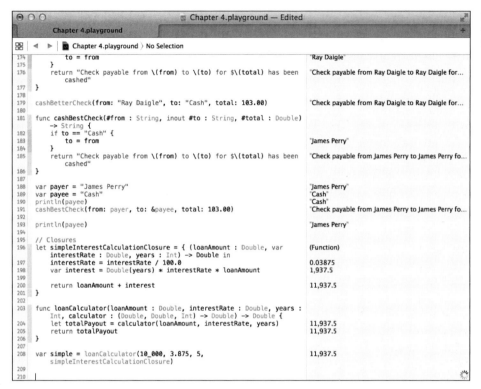

FIGURE 4.22 Using a closure to compute simple interest

The formula for simple interest calculation is:

*futureValue = presentValue * interestRate * years*

Lines 203 through 206 contain the function `loanCalculator`, which takes four parameters: The same three that the closure takes, and an additional parameter, `calculator`, which is a closure that takes two `Double` types and an `Int` type and returns a `Double` type. Not coincidentally, this is the same parameter and return type signature as our previously defined closure.

On line 208, the function is called with four parameters. The fourth parameter is the constant `simpleInterestCalculationClosure`, which will be used by the function to compute the total loan amount.

This example becomes more interesting when you create a second closure to pass to the `loanCalculator` function. Since you've computed simple interest, then write a closure that computes the future value of money using the compound interest formula:

futureValue = presentValue (1 + interestRate)^{years}

FIGURE 4.23 Adding
a second closure that
computes compound
interest

Figure 4.23 shows the compound interest calculation closure defined on lines 210 through 215, which takes the exact same parameters as the simple calculation closure on line 196. On line 217, the loanCalculator function is again called with the same parameters as before, except the compoundInterestCalculationClosure is passed as the fourth parameter. As you can see in the Results sidebar, compound interest yields a higher future value of the loan than simple interest does.

```
let compoundInterestCalculationClosure = { (loanAmount : Double,
→ var interestRate : Double, years : Int) -> Double in
   interestRate = interestRate / 100.0
   var compoundMultiplier = pow(1.0 + interestRate, Double(years))

   return loanAmount * compoundMultiplier
}


var compound = loanCalculator(10_000, 3.875, 5, compoundInterest
→ CalculationClosure)
```

On line 212 you may notice something new: a reference to a function named pow. This is the power function, and is part of Swift's math package. The function takes two Double parameters: the value to be raised and the power to raise it to. It returns the result as a Double value.

SUMMING IT UP

We've spent the entire chapter discussing functions and their use. Toward the end, you learned about closures and how they are essentially nameless functions that can be passed around to do useful work. As I indicated earlier, functions and closures are the foundations on which Swift apps are written. They appear everywhere and are an integral part of the development process. Knowing how they work and when to use them is a skill you will acquire over time.

In fact, there are even more things about functions and closures that I didn't touch on in this chapter. There's no need to overload you on every possible feature they have; we'll cover those extras later in the book. For now, you have enough of the basics to start doing useful programming.

Also, feel free to work with the code in the playground for this chapter. Change it, modify it, add to it, and make a mess of it if you want. That's what playgrounds are for, after all!

STAY CLASSY

With functions and closures covered, we'll turn our attention to the concept of the *class*. If you are familiar with object-oriented programming (OOP), Swift's notion of a class is similar to that of Objective-C and C++. If you're new to the idea of objects and OOP, don't worry, we'll explain all that terminology in the next chapter.

Meanwhile, feel free to take a break and review the notes and code in this chapter, as well as experiment with your playground file. When you're ready, proceed to Chapter 5, and we'll get down and dirty with classes.

CHAPTER 5

Organizing with Classes and Structures

Swift is an object-oriented language, and as such, it is apropos to devote some considerable real estate to the subject. If you are familiar with other object-oriented languages such as Objective-C and C++, the concepts presented here will be very familiar to you. If you are new to the idea of object-oriented programming, don't be alarmed. I'll take you through a tour of the concepts to prepare you for Swift's flavor of OOP (that's the common acronym for object-oriented programming, by the way, and I'll be using it throughout the chapter).

No matter what your current familiarity is with OOP concepts, preparing yourself with a new playground file in Xcode 6 is a good idea. Choose File > New > Playground menu, and save your new playground file as `Chapter 5.playground`. You'll use this playground for all the examples in this chapter, and you can easily go back and refer to it as you need.

Ready? Let's dive in.

OBJECTS ARE EVERYWHERE

OOP is a methodology in software development that involves thinking about problems in terms of *objects*.

Look around you—objects are everywhere. Anything you can pick up and hold, or even touch and feel, could be considered an object.

If you think about an object—any object—you can immediately identify certain *properties* (also called *attributes*) of that object, as well as certain *behaviors*. In OOP parlance, objects have properties and behaviors. This is true in the real world, and it's true in Swift.

Take a moment to glance around the room. Pick out an object on the wall—a door, a window, a mirror, a picture, or a piece of furniture. Let's start with the door, which any room should have (or else you'll be stuck inside). Look at the door and ask yourself: What properties does this door have?

- Dimensions (width, height, and depth)
- Weight
- Color
- State (is it opened or closed?)

These very generic properties could be applied to another item in the room, namely the window. The door and the window share these same properties, which makes them similar but not the same—a door is not a window. This notion of similar properties will come in handy later as we study classes.

Now that you've identified the properties of the door, can you ascertain what its behaviors are? In other words, what is it that the door can do?

- A door can open and close.
- A door can lock or unlock (assuming it has a lock).

Technically, it takes someone (or something) to open or close a door, or even to lock or unlock it, so out of these behaviors comes a number of actions that can be performed on the object.

Let's continue this process a bit further by identifying another object. If you have a window you can look out of, perhaps you can see other objects: cars, people, trees, and so on. Set your sights on a tree if possible, and note its properties:

- Height
- Type (oak, maple, cypress, and so on)
- Foliage state (Does it have leaves or have they all fallen due to the time of year?)

Of course, a tree has many other properties, but we'll keep it simple with these three. What about behaviors of a tree? What can a tree "do?"

- A tree can sway in the breeze.
- A tree can produce seeds.
- A tree can perform photosynthesis.

This process you just went through is an important one when thinking about objects. What you have done is a common task in OOP: *modeling*. Modeling an object entails examining its properties and behaviors, and then coming up with the code to describe that model in whatever programming language you want to use.

In this case, you've modeled two very different objects: a tree and a door. Other than dimensions, one has very little similarity to the other. That's where objects can get interesting.

Now that you have an idea how to model an object, it's time to look at how to express that model in Swift.

SWIFT OBJECTS ARE CLASSY

In Swift, objects are expressed using a special construct called the *class*. Just like in our modeling exercise, a Swift class contains the elements to express the model in code. The word class is an actual keyword and comprises several items:

- A name
- One or more properties
- One or more methods

Every class has a name that uniquely identifies it. A class also has properties, just like the objects you modeled earlier. A class also has methods. A *method* is a formal name for a function that exists inside a class. We explored functions in the previous chapter; now they come back to us in the form of methods, as we'll see shortly.

So to summarize, a Swift class defines the properties that make up the object, as well as the methods that perform the behaviors and act on those properties.

FIGURE 5.1 The Door
object in Swift

```
// Playground - noun: a place where people can play

import Cocoa

var str = "Hello, playground"                          "Hello, playground"

class Door {
    var opened : Bool = false
    var locked : Bool = false
    let width : Int = 32
    let height : Int = 72
    let weight : Int = 10
    let color : String = "Red"

    func open(Void) -> String {
        opened = true;
        return "C-r-r-e-e-a-k-k-k... the door is open!"
    }

    func close(Void) -> String {
        opened = false;
        return "C-r-r-e-e-a-k-k-k... the door is
            closed!"
    }

    func lock(Void) -> String {
        locked = true;
        return "C-l-i-c-c-c-k-k... the door is locked!"
    }

    func unlock(Void) -> String {
        locked = false;
        return "C-l-i-c-c-c-k-k... the door is
            unlocked!"
    }
}
```

KNOCK, KNOCK

As we explore this idea of object modeling in Swift, let's look more closely at the door as an object, which is as good an example as any. **Figure 5.1** shows a definition for a new object you'll call Door.

Get started on the example by typing the following on lines 7 through 34.

```
class Door {
    var opened : Bool = false
    var locked : Bool = false
    let width : Int = 32
    let height : Int = 72
    let weight : Int = 10
    let color : String = "Red"

    func open(Void) -> String {
        opened = true;
        return "C-r-r-e-e-a-k-k-k... the door is open!"
    }
```

```
func close(Void) -> String {
    opened = false;
    return "C-r-r-e-e-a-k-k-k... the door is closed!"
}

func lock(Void) -> String {
    locked = true;
    return "C-l-i-c-c-c-k-k... the door is locked!"
}

func unlock(Void) -> String {
    locked = false;
    return "C-l-i-c-c-c-k-k... the door is unlocked!"
}
}
```

In Swift, an object is defined using the `class` keyword, followed by the name of the class. In this case, Door on line 7. Following that is an opening curly brace and the rest of the definition of the class.

Lines 8 through 13 define the properties of the class. Every property, be it a variable or a constant, has an assigned value. Swift requires that all properties be assigned to some value to avoid ambiguity. Notice that two of the properties are variables: opened and `closed`. These Booleans reflect the door's state, which can change throughout the lifetime of the object; thus they are declared as variables.

The remaining properties, however, are constants. The door's `width`, `height`, `weight`, and `color` are not expected to change once it has been created.

Lines 15 through 33 define the methods for the class. This class has four methods: open, close, lock, and unlock. In the case of the open and `close` methods, they set the opened variable accordingly and return a `String` indicating the state of the door. The `lock` and `unlock` methods perform a similar function.

LET THERE BE OBJECTS!

So now that you have defined a class, how do you use it?

In OOP parlance, the process of turning a class into an object is known as *instantiation*. This is effectively the process of creating a real, live object that can be interacted with. Without the act of instantiating an object, a class is merely just a template, or blueprint to build an object. Just as blueprints don't turn a house into a home until the carpenters arrive and the hammers start swinging, a class alone cannot deliver a ready-to-run object. It requires the instantiation process.

FIGURE 5.2 Instantiating the Door class

```
30        func unlock(Void) -> String {
31            locked = false;
32            return "C-l-i-c-c-c-k-k... the door is
                  unlocked!"
33        }
34    }
35
36    let frontDoor = Door()                          {opened false locked false width 32 height 72 weight 10 colo...
37
```

FIGURE 5.3 Calling
the close and open
methods

```
30        func unlock(Void) -> String {
31            locked = false;
32            return "C-l-i-c-c-c-k-k... the door is
                  unlocked!"
33        }
34    }
35
36    let frontDoor = Door()                          {opened false locked false width 32 height 72 weight 10 colo...
37
38    frontDoor.close()                               "C-r-r-e-e-a-k-k-k... the door is closed!"
39    frontDoor.open()                                "C-r-r-e-e-a-k-k-k... the door is open!"
40
```

Let's see how instantiation works in **Figure 5.2**.

On line 36, an instance of the Door class is created by simply referencing the class's name, followed by open and close parentheses. This is the basic method for creating and initializing an object. The result of the assignment is a newly created object, which is assigned in this case to the frontDoor object. It's that simple!

If you are coming from Objective-C, you may ask "where is the init method defined?" That's a good question, and we'll explore that more in just a bit. For now, this Swift class does not have one.

Along with the creation of the frontDoor object, notice the Results sidebar shows the values of the properties. You'll need to expand the size of your window to see the values for all the properties available in the Door class.

OPENING AND CLOSING THE DOOR

Quiz time! How would you tell the frontDoor object to open and close?

The methods, of course. You just saw in Figure 5.2 how to call a method; lines 38 and 39 in **Figure 5.3** reveal the answer.

```
let frontDoor = Door()

frontDoor.close()
frontDoor.open()
```

Now that the object frontDoor is created, you reference the named constant and the dot notation when calling the open and close methods. The open and close parentheses indicate that the names following the dot are method names.

```
36  let frontDoor = Door()                                          [opened false locked false width 32 height 72 weight 10 colo...
37
38  frontDoor.close()                                                "C-r-r-e-e-a-k-k-k... the door is closed!"
39  frontDoor.open()                                                 "C-r-r-e-e-a-k-k-k... the door is open!"
40
41  frontDoor.lock()                                                 "C-l-i-c-c-c-k-k... the door is locked!"
42  frontDoor.unlock()                                               "C-l-i-c-c-c-k-k... the door is unlocked!"
43
```

FIGURE 5.4 Locking and unlocking the door

DOT NOTATION—IT ISN'T JUST FOR PROPERTIES

Note how the open and close methods are called. They follow the class name you've instantiated (Door) and a dot (.) character. The dot is part of Swift's *dot notation*, and it applies to both accessing properties and calling methods in a class. The dot acts as a syntactical element that delineates an object from its properties or methods. In the case of calling methods, the method name is always followed by open and close parentheses () to be typed after the method name.

Dot notation is a very common element of Swift; you'll see it used over and over again.

LOCKING AND UNLOCKING THE DOOR

In the same way you opened and closed the door with the available methods, you can lock and unlock the door. Type in the following code on lines 41 and 42 (**Figure 5.4**), and notice the Results sidebar.

```
frontDoor.lock()
frontDoor.unlock()
```

Again, just as you closed and opened the door with the appropriate methods, locking and unlocking the door produced similar results in the Results sidebar. Things appear to be working as designed. However, notice a couple of odd things about the Door class.

For instance, ask yourself: Can you lock an open door? Shouldn't a door have to be closed before it's locked? And what if you tell the frontDoor object to close the door when it's already closed (or conversely, tell the frontDoor object to open the door when it's already open). Should a door creak if it's not going to move?

Let's fix these issues right away with some additional logic. **Figure 5.5** shows a new class, NewDoor, along with revised open, close, lock, and unlock methods that handle the various cases, as well as a new object, newFrontDoor.

FIGURE 5.5 Addressing holes in the Door class logic

FIGURE 5.5 Addressing holes in the Door class logic

In the case of the open method, a check is added for the opened property. If it's false (meaning the door is closed), the door is allowed to be closed, otherwise you are reminded that the door is already opened. The inverse logic is applied to the close method on line 62.

```
class NewDoor {
    var opened : Bool = false
    var locked : Bool = false
    let width : Int
    let height : Int
    let weight : Int
    var color : String

    func open(Void) -> String {
        if (opened == false) {
```

```
            opened = true
            return "C-r-r-e-e-a-k-k-k... the door is open!"
        }
        else {
            return "The door is already open!"
        }
    }

    func close(Void) -> String {
        if (opened == true) {
            opened = false
            return "C-r-r-e-e-a-k-k-k... the door is closed!"
        }
        else {
            return "The door is already closed!"
        }
    }

    func lock(Void) -> String {
        if (opened == false) {
            locked = true
            return "C-l-i-c-c-c-k-k... the door is locked!"
        }
        else {
            return "You cannot lock an open door!"
        }
    }

    func unlock(Void) -> String {
        if (opened == false) {
            locked = false
            return "C-l-i-c-c-c-k-k... the door is unlocked!"
        }
        else {
            return "You cannot unlock an open door!"
        }
    }
}
```

FIGURE 5.6 Examining the properties of the newFrontDoor object

```
 93   let newFrontDoor = NewDoor()                              (opened false locked false width 32 height 72 weight 10 colo…
 94
 95   newFrontDoor.close()                                      "The door is already closed!"
 96   newFrontDoor.open()                                       "C-r-r-e-e-a-k-k… the door is open!"
 97
 98   newFrontDoor.lock()                                       "You cannot lock an open door!"
 99   newFrontDoor.unlock()                                     "You cannot unlock an open door!"
100
101   newFrontDoor.locked                                       false
102   newFrontDoor.opened                                       true
103
104   newFrontDoor.width                                        32
105   newFrontDoor.height                                       72
106   newFrontDoor.weight                                       10
107
```

Likewise, the lock and unlock methods are adapted to check for the opened property. If the door is open, you are reminded that you can neither lock nor unlock the door. You can clearly see the Results sidebar showing the altered output based on the additions in the methods. Feel free to experiment with changing the order of the close, open, lock, and unlock methods on lines 95 through 99 in your playground file.

The only hole left in this logic is locking a door that is locked, or unlocking a door that is unlocked. I'll leave that as an exercise for you to solve.

EXAMINING THE PROPERTIES

Up to this point, we've ignored the other properties of the newFrontDoor object. They are accessible, however, by using the dot notation you've used thus far to call the methods.

Lines 101 through 106 in **Figure 5.6** demonstrate how to access the individual properties, with the results showing in the Results sidebar.

```
newFrontDoor.lock()
newFrontDoor.unlock()

newFrontDoor.locked
newFrontDoor.opened

newFrontDoor.width
newFrontDoor.height
newFrontDoor.weight
```

DOOR DIVERSITY

The NewDoor class has proven to be quite clever. Thanks to the added code, the class can open, close, lock, and unlock, and can do so only when appropriate.

However, one thing you cannot currently do is create a door with a different size, weight, or color. Every door object that is created has the same values for the properties. That's because those properties are set to the specific values when the object is instantiated (scroll back to lines 47 through 50 of your playground file as a reminder). Those properties also happen to be constants, meaning that their values cannot change once the object is created, so no matter what door you create, you always get the same size, height, and color. A little boring, isn't it?

FIGURE 5.7 Creating your very own **init** method

How can you change this? You could change the constants to variables by changing the let keywords to var keywords. Doing so would allow you to change the properties using dot notation like so:

```
newFrontDoor.width = 36
newFrontDoor.height = 80
```

This approach would certainly work; however, it feels "wrong" to change a door's dimensions after it has already been instantiated. After all, when you purchase a door at your local hardware store, its size and weight are already determined. These properties should be set at the time the door is created, and remain immutable for the lifetime of the object. So how do you do this?

The answer is a special method known as `init`, which initializes an object. Up to this point, we haven't actually written an `init` method; we've just let Swift do the initialization for us. This method seems like a natural and proper place to allow the user to specify alternate values for these properties.

Swift thinks so, too, and actually allows you to create your own `init` method with your own parameter list. This is a great way to set up an object to your own liking, and that's exactly what is happening in lines 52 through 57 in **Figure 5.7**. Type the `init` method in your playground file.

```
init(width : Int = 32, height : Int = 72, weight : Int = 10, color :
→ String = "Red") {
    self.width = width
    self.height = height
    self.weight = weight
    self.color = color
}
```

FIGURE 5.8 Exercising the new init method with additional parameters

```
100   let newFrontDoor = NewDoor()                                    (opened false locked false width 32 height 72 weight 10 colo...
101
102   newFrontDoor.close()                                           "The door is already closed!"
103   newFrontDoor.open()                                            "C-r-r-e-e-a-k-k... the door is open!"
104
105   newFrontDoor.lock()                                            "You cannot lock an open door!"
106   newFrontDoor.unlock()                                          "You cannot unlock an open door!"
107
108   newFrontDoor.locked                                            false
109   newFrontDoor.opened                                            true
110
111   newFrontDoor.width                                             32
112   newFrontDoor.height                                            72
113   newFrontDoor.weight                                            10
114
115   let newBackDoor = NewDoor(width: 36, height: 80, weight: 20, color: "Green")   (opened false locked false width 36 height 80 weight 20 colo...
116
```

This `init` method takes four parameters corresponding to the four properties on lines 47 through 50. In Figure 5.7, the default values have been removed from those lines. Instead, they are now part of the default parameter values in the `init` method's declaration (remember we discussed default parameters earlier in the book). As a result, you no longer need to initialize the properties on lines 47 through 50. Go ahead and remove these initialization values in your playground file, too.

A new keyword is used on lines 53 through 56: `self`. This keyword is Swift's way of letting an object refer to itself. Using the `self` keyword is particularly important in this example, because the parameter names in the `init` method match exactly to the property names in the class. Without `self`, the following statements would not only be ambiguous, they would cause a Swift compiler error:

```
width = width
height = height
weight = weight
color = color
```

The `self` keyword explicitly points out that it is the property of the instantiated object receiving the assignment.

If you've kept a sharp eye, you may be asking how the properties `width`, `height`, `weight`, and `color`, which are declared as constants with the `let` keyword, can be assigned values if they are constants. You are witnessing an exception to the rule that constants cannot change. Swift allows constant properties of a class to be assigned values at initialization time—but not after. Once the value of an object's constant property has been set in the `init` method, it cannot be changed later.

One other note: The keyword `func` does not precede the init method name.

With the new `init` method in place, you can now create another object from the `NewDoor` class, this time with your very own dimensions.

Line 115 in **Figure 5.8** shows how to instantiate a second NewDoor object with the parameter list defined in your new `init` method. Notice that the parameter names are being used to explicitly show which values go with which parameters. This is a small but important difference between functions and methods. In methods, parameter names are automatically promoted to external parameter names. As a result, you must specify the names for parameters when creating new objects.

```
let newBackDoor = NewDoor(width: 36, height: 80, weight: 20, color: "Green")
```

FIGURE 5.9 Attempting to change the color of the `newBackDoor` object

The `width`, `height`, `weight`, and `color` for the `newBackDoor` object are clear and unambiguous, as shown by the Results sidebar. Notice that the `newFrontDoor` object created on line 100 still retains the default values that now exist in the `init` method's default parameter list.

PAINTING THE DOOR

Let's revisit the properties of the `NewDoor` class. We can assume that once a door is created, its dimensions and weight are fixed, but the color can change. You can paint the door a different color, for example.

Attempting to change the color of the `newBackDoor` object, however, results in an error as shown in **Figure 5.9**.

```
newBackDoor.color = "White"
```

Can you spot the reason for the error? Look back to line 50 in your playground file for the definition of the `color` property in the `NewDoor` class.

```
let color : String
```

Changing the `let` keyword to var removes the error and allow you to change the color of the `newBackDoor` object, or any object of type `NewDoor`. Remember to consider what properties should be constants and which should be variables when creating your classes.

You've just seen how classes are created in Swift. Using just a single, compact class, you modeled both the attributes and behavior of a door. How cool was that!

The `NewDoor` class exercise should also give you an appreciation of just how the modeling process works. When you create a class to model something, you must think about its properties and behaviors, and let them guide your design as well as any constraints.

INHERITANCE

FIGURE 5.10
Illustrating the class
relationship

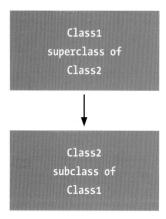

Another important principle of OOP is the idea of *inheritance* (and no, we're not talking about your rich uncle's estate). Inheritance allows an object to obtain the attributes and behaviors of another class while bringing its own unique attributes and behaviors to the mix.

It helps to think of inheritance in terms of genealogy and genetics. As an individual, you are the product of your parents' genetics. You inherited one or more of their traits, including possibly their name, yet you remain a unique individual with your own properties (height, weight, eye color, and so on) as well as behaviors (diet, exercise habits, and so on) Likewise, your children will inherit certain properties and behaviors from you and your parents, yet retain their own.

Inheritance also creates a *hierarchy*. Just as you have parents, your children have you as a parent, and eventually they may become parents. This connection also applies to objects and the classes from which they derive.

A class can derive from another class, known as its *superclass*. Likewise, a class derived from another class is known as a *subclass* of that class. **Figure 5.10** clarifies this relationship.

Inheritance is a neat concept in OOP because it allows you to compartmentalize functionality into a specific class, which can then flow down to subclasses without code duplication.

Recall earlier when you were asked to look around the room you are in to select an object for modeling. We used the door for our class, but if you had chosen a window, how different would that class have been from the Door class you created?

Looking at the Door class in your playground file, you'll come to realize that every property and behavior a door has, a window has. Both open and close; both can lock and unlock; and both have dimensions, weight, and color. But is a window a door? Of course not. So what makes a window different from a door?

Well, for one thing, you would consider walking through an open door, but you likely wouldn't walk through an open window. Also, a door might have a door handle and a door-knob; a window doesn't.

Based on that small difference, how can you use inheritance to model both a door and a window in such a way that they share a common set of properties and behaviors, yet retain their distinctions that make them uniquely what they are?

MODELING THE BASE CLASS

In OOP parlance, the *base class* is considered the most basic class from where all other classes derive. A base class does not inherit from any other class; it's essentially a root, or anchor class. In Swift, any class that does not derive from a superclass is known as a base class.

In thinking about the door/window class, you can create a base class that captures most of what currently exists in the Door class. Then you can create two new subclasses: one for doors and one for windows.

The quickest way to achieve this would be to rename the Door class to something else. Thinking about class names is important, and in this case, you want a name that can fit both a door and a window. Let's choose Portal for the new class name. After all, windows and doors are portals, right?

Select and copy lines 44 through 98 (the NewDoor class), and paste it at the very bottom of your playground file. Once pasted, change the class name from NewDoor to Portal.

Now that you've added the new class Portal, notice that references to the word "door" on lines 136, 139, 146, 149, 156, 159, 166, and 169 seem out of place. The quickest way to handle that is to create a new name property, pass that in the init method, and then use Swift's string interpolation to embed the property name in the string constants. You can see the changes in their entirety in **Figure 5.11**; go ahead and change your playground file accordingly.

```
class Portal {
    var opened : Bool = false
    var locked : Bool = false
    let width : Int
    let height : Int
    let weight : Int
    let name : String
    var color : String

    init(name : String, width : Int = 32, height : Int = 72, weight :
    p Int = 10, color : String = "Red") {
        self.name = name
        self.width = width
        self.height = height
        self.weight = weight
        self.color = color
    }
```

```
func open(Void) -> String {
    if (opened == false) {
        opened = true
        return "C-r-r-e-e-a-k-k-k... the \(name) is open!"
    }
    else {
        return "The \(name) is already open!"
    }
}

func close(Void) -> String {
    if (opened == true) {
        opened = false
        return "C-r-r-e-e-a-k-k-k... the \(name) is closed!"
    }
    else {
        return "The \(name) is already closed!"
    }
}

func lock(Void) -> String {
    if (opened == false) {
        locked = true
        return "C-l-i-c-c-c-k-k... the \(name) is locked!"
    }
    else {
        return "You cannot lock an open \(name)!"
    }
}

func unlock(Void) -> String {
    if (opened == false) {
        locked = false
        return "C-l-i-c-c-c-k-k... the \(name) is unlocked!"
    }
    else {
        return "You cannot unlock an open \(name)!"
    }
}
}
```

FIGURE 5.11 The Portal class adjusted with the new name property

```
118  class Portal {
119      var opened : Bool = false
120      var locked : Bool = false
121      let width : Int
122      let height : Int
123      let weight : Int
124      let name : String
125      var color : String
126
127      init(name : String, width : Int = 32, height : Int = 72, weight : Int =
             10, color : String = "Red") {
128          self.name = name
129          self.width = width
130          self.height = height
131          self.weight = weight
132          self.color = color
133      }
134
135      func open(Void) -> String {
136          if (opened == false) {
137              opened = true
138              return "C-r-r-e-e-a-k-k-k... the \(name) is open!"
139          }
140          else {
141              return "The \(name) is already open!"
142          }
143      }
144
145      func close(Void) -> String {
146          if (opened == true) {
147              opened = false
148              return "C-r-r-e-e-a-k-k-k... the \(name) is closed!"
149          }
150          else {
151              return "The \(name) is already closed!"
152          }
153      }
154
155      func lock(Void) -> String {
156          if (opened == false) {
157              locked = true
158              return "C-l-i-c-c-c-k-k... the \(name) is locked!"
159          }
160          else {
161              return "You cannot lock an open \(name)!"
162          }
163      }
164
165      func unlock(Void) -> String {
166          if (opened == false) {
167              locked = false
168              return "C-l-i-c-c-c-k-k... the \(name) is unlocked!"
169          }
170          else {
171              return "You cannot unlock an open \(name)!"
172          }
173      }
174  }
```

Notice the addition of the name property on line 124, as well as the name parameter in the init method on line 127 and the assignment on line 128. This will allow you to pass an appropriate string to identify the type of object. Also, the word "door" in the string literals has been replaced everywhere with \(name), allowing the printed string to properly identify the object.

The new Portal class looks good so far. Now we'll create the replacement classes to represent the door and window.

FIGURE 5.12
The addition of the new `NiceDoor` and `NiceWindow` classes

```
146    if (opened == true) {
147        opened = false
148        return "C-r-e-e-a-k-k-k... the \(name) is closed!"
149    }
150    else {
151        return "The \(name) is already closed!"
152    }
153  }
154
155  func lock(Void) -> String {
156    if (opened == false) {
157        locked = true
158        return "C-l-i-c-c-k-k... the \(name) is locked!"
159    }
160    else {
161        return "You cannot lock an open \(name)!"
162    }
163  }
164
165  func unlock(Void) -> String {
166    if (opened == false) {
167        locked = false
168        return "C-l-i-c-c-k-k... the \(name) is unlocked!"
169    }
170    else {
171        return "You cannot unlock an open \(name)!"
172    }
173  }
174 }
175
176 class NiceDoor : Portal {
177    init(width : Int = 32, height : Int = 72, weight : Int = 10,
         color : String = "Red") {
178        super.init(name : "door", width: width, height: height,
            weight: weight, color: color)
179    }
180 }
181
182 class NiceWindow : Portal {
183    init(width : Int = 48, height : Int = 48, weight : Int = 5,
         color : String = "Blue") {
184        super.init(name : "window", width: width, height: height,
            weight: weight, color: color)
185    }
186 }
187
```

CREATING THE SUBCLASSES

We'll create two new classes: `NiceDoor` and `NiceWindow`. Both of these classes will be subclasses of the `Portal` class. Take your time and type in lines 176 through 186 in **Figure 5.12** into your playground window.

```
class NiceDoor : Portal {
    init(width : Int = 32, height : Int = 72, weight : Int = 10, color :
    → String = "Red") {
        super.init(name : "door", width: width, height: height, weight:
        → weight, color: color)
    }
}


class NiceWindow : Portal {
    init(width : Int = 48, height : Int = 48, weight : Int = 5, color :
    → String = "Blue") {
        super.init(name : "window", width: width, height: height, weight:
        → weight, color: color)
    }
}
```

On line 176 is the definition of the NewDoor class. Notice that the class name is followed by a colon, and then the name of the superclass, Portal. This is how classes in Swift specify the class they wish to inherit from.

Line 177 shows the definition of the init method for the NiceDoor class. Notice that this method is identical to the init method of the Portal class, even down to the default parameter values for the parameters. The reason for this duplication becomes apparent when you look at line 178 and its special syntax.

There you'll notice a new keyword: super. Somewhat related to the self keyword mentioned earlier, super actually refers to the superclass. In our case, the superclass is the Portal class. What follows the keyword is the familiar dot notation and the name of the method to call in the superclass: init.

It is common and expected practice to call the superclass's init method first, giving the superclass the opportunity to initialize itself. In this case, you're passing named parameters, including the new name parameter. Since this is the NiceDoor class, the string "door" is passed, along with the width, height, weight, and color. Since the superclass, Portal, contains the properties for these values, we need to make sure its init method is called.

Lines 71 through 75 show the definition of the NiceWindow class, which looks almost identical to the NiceDoor class. It too derives from the Portal class, but has width, height, and weight defaults that make sense for a window. The name also reflects this class and gives the string "window" to the superclass's init method.

INSTANTIATING THE SUBCLASS

With the new NiceDoor and NiceWindow classes created, now we'll exercise them. **Figure 5.13** shows the earlier code where the frontDoor object was created—keep that code in place. Also notice that the Results sidebar shows the same results even though we've changed the class hierarchy, and Door is now subclassed from Portal.

```
let sunRoomDoor = NiceDoor()

sunRoomDoor.close()
sunRoomDoor.open()

sunRoomDoor.lock()
sunRoomDoor.unlock()

sunRoomDoor.locked
sunRoomDoor.opened

sunRoomDoor.width
sunRoomDoor.height
sunRoomDoor.weight
```

FIGURE 5.13 Instantiating the NiceDoor and NiceWindow classes

```
179        }
180    }
181
182    class NiceWindow : Portal {
183        init(width : Int = 48, height : Int = 48, weight : Int = 5,
                color : String = "Blue") {
184            super.init(name : "window", width: width, height: height,
                    weight: weight, color: color)
185        }
186    }
187
188    let sunRoomDoor = NiceDoor()                        {{opened false locked false width 32 height 72 weight 10 na...
189
190    sunRoomDoor.close()                                 "The door is already closed!"
191    sunRoomDoor.open()                                  "C-r-r-e-e-a-k-k-k... the door is open!"
192
193    sunRoomDoor.lock()                                  "You cannot lock an open door!"
194    sunRoomDoor.unlock()                                "You cannot unlock an open door!"
195
196    sunRoomDoor.locked                                  false
197    sunRoomDoor.opened                                  true
198
199    sunRoomDoor.width                                   32
200    sunRoomDoor.height                                  72
201    sunRoomDoor.weight                                  10
202
203
204    let bayWindow = NiceWindow()                        {{opened false locked false width 48 height 48 weight 5 name...
205
206    bayWindow.close()                                   "The window is already closed!"
207    bayWindow.open()                                    "C-r-r-e-e-a-k-k-k... the window is open!"
208
209    bayWindow.lock()                                    "You cannot lock an open window!"
210    bayWindow.unlock()                                  "You cannot unlock an open window!"
211
212    bayWindow.locked                                    false
213    bayWindow.opened                                    true
214
215    bayWindow.width                                     48
216    bayWindow.height                                    48
217    bayWindow.weight                                    5
218
```

```
let bayWindow = NiceWindow()

bayWindow.close()
bayWindow.open()

bayWindow.lock()
bayWindow.unlock()

bayWindow.locked
bayWindow.opened

bayWindow.width
bayWindow.height
bayWindow.weight
```

Type in lines 188 through 217 in Figure 5.13, which create two new objects: sunRoomDoor and bayWindow. These objects are instantiated from the NiceDoor and NiceWindow class, respectively, and those in turn are subclassed from Portal. The Results sidebar shows the objects being manipulated, which confirms that the code in the Portal superclass is being exercised appropriately.

FIGURE 5.14 The new
CombinationDoor class

```
219  class CombinationDoor : NiceDoor {
220      var combinationCode : String?
221
222      override func lock(Void) -> String {
223          return "This method is not valid for a combination door!"
224      }
225
226      override func unlock(Void) -> String {
227          return "This method is not valid for a combination door!"
228      }
229
230      func lock(combinationCode : String) -> String {
231          if (opened == false) {
232              if (locked == true) {
233                  return "The \(name) is already locked!"
234              }
235              self.combinationCode = combinationCode
236              locked = true
237              return "C-l-i-c-c-c-k-k... the \(name) is locked!"
238          }
239          else {
240              return "You cannot lock an open \(name)!"
241          }
242      }
243
244      func unlock(combinationCode : String) -> String {
245          if (opened == false) {
246              if (locked == false)
247              {
248                  return "The \(name) is already unlocked!"
249              }
250              else
251              {
252                  if (self.combinationCode != combinationCode) {
253                      return "Wrong code.... the \(name) is still locked!"
254                  }
255              }
256              locked = false
257              return "C-l-i-c-c-c-k-k... the \(name) is unlocked!"
258          }
259          else {
260              return "You cannot unlock an open \(name)!"
261          }
262      }
263  }
264
265  let securityDoor = CombinationDoor()
```

SECURING THE DOOR

The NiceDoor class can be instantiated to provide a door object that will unlock and lock the door intelligently, but what if you want to add a combination lock? Before such a door can be unlocked, a security code needs to be entered. If the code is wrong, unlocking the door fails. If the code is correct, the door is unlocked, and all is well.

This secure door class will require a secret combination code to unlock the door. The combination can be any series of numbers or letters, but for our purposes, we'll define the secret combination with four numbers: 6809. The user of the class will be able to instantiate the object with a personal combination. Then, upon invoking the unlock method on the class, it will either return that the door is unlocked (because the user passed the correct code), or it will indicate that the door remains locked due to an incorrect code.

You could add this functionality into the existing NiceDoor class, but how much fun would that be? Instead, create a new class, CombinationDoor, which will be a subclass of NiceDoor. The CombinationDoor class will inherit all the properties and methods of Nice-Door and add the combination lock ability.

Figure 5.14 shows the newly created class on lines 219 through 263.

```swift
class CombinationDoor : NiceDoor {
    var combinationCode : String?

    override func lock(Void) -> String {
        return "This method is not valid for a combination door!"
    }

    override func unlock(Void) -> String {
        return "This method is not valid for a combination door!"
    }

    func lock(combinationCode : String) -> String {
        if (opened == false) {
            if (locked == true) {
                return "The \(name) is already locked!"
            }
            self.combinationCode = combinationCode
            locked = true
            return "C-l-i-c-c-c-k-k... the \(name) is locked!"
        }
        else {
            return "You cannot lock an open \(name)!"
        }
    }

    func unlock(combinationCode : String) -> String {
        if (opened == false) {
            if (locked == false)
            {
                return "The \(name) is already unlocked!"
            }
            else
            {
                if (self.combinationCode != combinationCode) {
                    return "Wrong code.... the \(name) is still locked!"
                }
            }
            locked = false
            return "C-l-i-c-c-c-k-k... the \(name) is unlocked!"
        }
```

```
        else {
            return "You cannot unlock an open \(name)!"
        }
    }
}
```

```
let securityDoor = CombinationDoor()
```

The new class has a new property, `combinationCode`, defined on line 220. This is an optional `String` property. Remember optionals? We discussed them very early in the book. They are normal types that can have `nil` as a value. In this case, there is no explicit initialization, so the `combinationCode` is presumed to be `nil`. Defining this property means that you can defer its initialization to an actual value until later. Combined with the state of the door being closed at initialization time (see line 119), this is a sensible setting.

Now turn your attention to the `lock` and `unlock` methods starting on line 222. A security door with a combination lock like this one just cannot unlock when told—it first has to verify that the security code passed to the method by the user matches its internal code. Only if they are the same does the door unlock. Therefore, creating new methods in the `CombinationDoor` subclass is necessary to disallow wanton unlocking; otherwise, the superclass's implementation would happily unlock the door when told, no matter what the `combinationCode` was set to.

The ability to create a method of the same name in a subclass is the `override` keyword. Swift requires that a subclass that redefines a similarly named method in any superclass use this keyword to indicate the intent to override that method. We do not intend on calling the superclass's implementation of these methods, either.

Lines 230 through 262 hold the new `lock` and `unlock` methods. They are the same in name as their superclass counterparts, but also take a `String` parameter. In the case of the `lock` method, a combination code is passed and saved in the property `combinationCode`, and the door is locked. Notice that you are duplicating the same logic in the superclass to determine if the door is closed before you attempt to lock it. This is necessary because you are not calling the superclass's implementation of the method.

The `unlock` method is a little larger than the `lock` method due to the extra logic that must be evaluated. It too takes a `String` parameter: the combination code to use when unlocking. On line 252, a check is made between the property `combinationCode` and the passed code. If the passed combination code is incorrect, a message is returned indicating that the code is wrong, and the door remains locked.

If the combination code is correct, the `unlock` method sets the `locked` property to `false`, and returns the message that the door is unlocked.

On line 265 a shiny new security door object is instantiated. By default it's closed and unlocked, ready for you to interact with it.

So far, you've created the new `CombinationDoor` class and have instantiated the `securityDoor` object from it. You've followed the code and understand how the methods inside your new superclass override the same named methods above. Now it's time to unlock the door!

FIGURE 5.15 Testing the CombinationDoor class

```
265   let securityDoor = CombinationDoor()                                    {{...}} nil}
266
267   // show values of properties
268   securityDoor.width                                                      32
269   securityDoor.height                                                     72
270   securityDoor.weight                                                     10
271   println(securityDoor.color)                                            "Red"
272   println(securityDoor.combinationCode)                                  "nil"
273
274   // unlock the door without providing a combination
275   securityDoor.unlock()                                                  "This method is not valid for a combination d...
276
277   // lock the door without providing a combination
278   securityDoor.lock()                                                    "This method is not valid for a combination d...
279
280   // unlock the door with a combination
281   securityDoor.unlock("6809")                                            "The door is already unlocked!"
282
283   // lock the door with a combination
284   securityDoor.lock("6809")                                              "C-l-i-c-c-c-k-k... the door is locked!"
285
286   // unlock the door with the wrong combination
287   securityDoor.unlock("3344")                                            "Wrong code.... the door is still locked!"
288
289   // unlock the door with the right combination
290   securityDoor.unlock("6809")                                            "C-l-i-c-c-c-k-k... the door is unlocked!"
291
```

USING THE RIGHT COMBINATION

With the securityDoor object created on line 265, let's see how the new locking and unlocking works. Lines 268 through 290 are intended to flex and demonstrate the CombinationDoor and its superclasses. We'll go over them one by one.

Lines 268 through 272 of **Figure 5.15** show the values of the properties, including the combinationCode property, which is set to nil as discussed earlier. On line 275, you attempt to unlock the door only to learn in the Results sidebar that this method no longer works. The same message appears on line 278 when the lock method is invoked.

Next, on line 281, the unlock method with the combination parameter is used, but the Results sidebar indicates that the door is already unlocked; this is a good sign, and shows that the logic behind the door code is working.

The door is successfully locked on line 284 with a security code of 6809. With this door locked, an attempt is made to unlock it on line 287 with a different security code—that attempt fails, and the door remains locked. Finally, on line 290 the unlock method is again called with the right combination, and the door unlocks.

```
// show values of properties
securityDoor.width
securityDoor.height
securityDoor.weight
println(securityDoor.color)
println(securityDoor.combinationCode)

// unlock the door without providing a combination
securityDoor.unlock()

// lock the door without providing a combination
securityDoor.lock()

// unlock the door with a combination
securityDoor.unlock("6809")
```

```
286     // unlock the door with the wrong combination
287     securityDoor.unlock("3344")
288
289     // unlock the door with the wrong combination
290     securityDoor.unlock("6809")
291
292     class Tractor {
293         let horsePower : Int
294         let color : String
295
296         init(horsePower : Int, color : String) {
297             self.horsePower = horsePower
298             self.color = color
299         }
300
301         convenience init(horsePower : Int) {
302             self.init(horsePower: horsePower, color: "Green")
303         }
304
305         convenience init() {
306             self.init(horsePower: 42, color: "Green")
307         }
308     }
309
```

'Wrong code.... the door is still locked!'

'C–I–i–c–c–k–k... the door is unlocked!'

FIGURE 5.16
An example of conve-
nience initializers in
the Tractor class

```
// lock the door with a combination
securityDoor.lock("6809")
```

```
// unlock the door with the wrong combination
securityDoor.unlock("3344")
```

```
// unlock the door with the right combination
securityDoor.unlock("6809")
```

Now that you've spent some time going over the ins and outs of classes, subclasses, and inheritance, let's spend a little time diving deeper into the convenience initializers.

CONVENIENCE INITIALIZERS

So far, I've touched lightly on the init method, which is the method that is called when a class is instantiated in Swift. You've seen several init methods already for the classes that we explored in this chapter. In the case of the Door class, no explicit init method was needed because the properties for that class were assigned default values inside the class itself. Both the NewDoor and NiceDoor classes had init methods along with parameters that had default values assigned to them.

Sometimes, when designing a class, you may want to have a mix of different init methods. For instance, one init method might assume some defaults, while another might require the passing of additional parameters. Ultimately, these initializers all funnel to a single init method known as the *designated initializer*. This is typically the init method with the most parameters.

Swift has a special designation for these types of initialization methods. They are known as *convenience initializers*.

Let's explore the concept of convenience initializers, by looking at tractors, which come in various sizes for different jobs. I've created a Tractor class defined on lines 292 through 308 in **Figure 5.16**. Type in the code, and let's take a look.

```
class Tractor {
    let horsePower : Int
    let color : String

    init(horsePower : Int, color : String) {
        self.horsePower = horsePower
        self.color = color
    }

    convenience init(horsePower : Int) {
        self.init(horsePower: horsePower, color: "Green")
    }

    convenience init() {
        self.init(horsePower: 42, color: "Green")
    }
}
```

The Tractor class looks somewhat similar to the other classes you've studied in this chapter. It has properties at the top, followed by a number of methods. The properties are the horsepower (an Int), and a color (a String).

On line 296 is the *designated initializer*. It is the init method that contains the most parameters. Each parameter represents one property in the class, and lines 297 and 298 contain the assignments for those properties. If you wanted to instantiate an object of this class, you could call this method with the three parameters of your choosing.

Line 301 contains a second init method, prefaced with the keyword convenience. This is a convenience initializer. It's convenient because you can save some typing when instantiating an object from this method. Note that it contains one fewer parameter than the designated initializer: The color parameter is not passed, but assumed to be the value "Green".

This convenience initializer calls self.init on line 302. The initializer being called here is the designated initializer defined on line 296, which sets the two available properties.

Another convenience initializer is defined on line 305. This init method takes no parameters. Instead, it assumes that the tractor being created is a 42-horsepower tractor with green paint. If that's the kind of tractor you want, you can save yourself some typing by instantiating a Tractor object with this initializer.

Let's create a few tractors, shall we?

```
let myBigTractor = Tractor()
let myBiggerTractor = Tractor(horsePower: 71)
let myYardTractor = Tractor(horsePower: 16, color : "Orange")
```

```
292   class Tractor {
293       let horsePower : Int
294       let color : String
295
296       init(horsePower : Int, color : String) {
297           self.horsePower = horsePower
298           self.color = color
299       }
300
301       convenience init(horsePower : Int) {
302           self.init(horsePower: horsePower, color: "Green")
303       }
304
305       convenience init() {
306           self.init(horsePower: 42, color: "Green")
307       }
308   }
309
310   let myBigTractor = Tractor()                                    {horsePower 42 color "Green"}
311   let myBiggerTractor = Tractor(horsePower: 71)                   {horsePower 71 color "Green"}
312   let myYardTractor = Tractor(horsePower: 16, color : "Orange")   {horsePower 16 color "Orange"}
313
314
```

FIGURE 5.17 Creating tractors with the Tractor class

Line 310 of **Figure 5.17** calls the convenience initializer that sets up all the parameters for us. We can expect a 42-horsepower tractor in the standard green color, and the Results sidebar verifies this.

Likewise on line 311, we are calling one of the convenience initializers that sets the tractor color to green automatically. Finally on line 312, the third tractor is called with the designated initializer, forcing you to pass all the parameters explicitly.

Convenience initializers are certainly convenient. You can create a number of them to aid in the creation of an object, and they all funnel into the designated initializer, which is ultimately responsible for initializing all the properties of the object.

There's more to discuss regarding initializers, but I'll save that for a later time. Instead, let's turn our attention to several other useful Swift language features used for data organization: enumerations and structures.

ENUMERATIONS

Enumerations allow you to specify a group of related names with the intent of referencing those names in your coding. Enumerations are often used in conjunction with classes, but are useful anywhere. Their roots are in the C language, but are much more flexible and powerful in Swift. Enumerations have the following basic form:

```
enum enumerationName {
    // constant definitions
}
```

Since tractors have been on the agenda for the last few examples, here's an example of using an enumeration to represent the different types of fuel for any number of vehicles:

```
enum FuelType {
    case Gasoline
    case Diesel
    case Biodiesel
    case Electric
    case NaturalGas
}
```

FIGURE 5.18

Creating and using an enumeration

```
310    let myBigTractor = Tractor()                              {horsePower 42 color "Green"}
311    let myBiggerTractor = Tractor(horsePower: 71)             {horsePower 71 color "Green"}
312    let myYardTractor = Tractor(horsePower: 16, color : "Orange")   {horsePower 16 color "Orange"}
313
314    // enumerations
315    enum FuelType : String {
316        case Gasoline = "89 octane"
317        case Diesel = "sulphur free"
318        case Biodiesel = "vegetable oil"
319        case Electric = "30 amps"
320        case NaturalGas = "coalbed methane"
321    }
322
323    var engine : FuelType = .Gasoline                         (Enum Value)
324
325    var vehicleName : String
326
327    switch engine {
328        case .Gasoline:
329            vehicleName = "Ford F-150"                        "Ford F-150"
330
331        case .Diesel:
332            vehicleName = "Ford F-250"
333
334        case .Biodiesel:
335            vehicleName = "Custom Van"
336
337        case .Electric:
338            vehicleName = "Toyota Prius"
339
340        case .NaturalGas:
341            vehicleName = "Utility Truck"
342    }
343
```

In this code snippet, the case keyword is used to define each enumeration member. The member becomes associated with the enumeration name (FuelType) and accessible via dot notation, as you'll see shortly.

For added convenience, multiple enumeration members can be placed on a single line like so:

```
enum FuelType {
    case Gasoline, Diesel, Biodiesel, Electric, NaturalGas
}
```

And simple mappings in enumerations can be achieved with a feature known as *raw values*:

```
enum FuelType : String {
    case Gasoline = "89 octane"
    case Diesel = "sulphur free"
    case Biodiesel = "vegetable oil"
    case Electric = "30 amps"
    case NaturalGas = "coalbed methane"
}
```

These values can then be extracted using rawValue:

```
let fuelCharacteristic = FuelType.Gasoline.rawValue
```

That's pretty robust for a seemingly simple construct!

Once an enumeration is defined, any of its members can be assigned to a variable and used in your code quite naturally. **Figure 5.18** shows this technique.

```
// enumerations
enum FuelType : String {
    case Gasoline = "89 octane"
    case Diesel = "sulphur free"
    case Biodiesel = "vegetable oil"
    case Electric = "30 amps"
    case NaturalGas = "coalbed methane"
}

var engine : FuelType = .Gasoline

var vehicleName : String

switch engine {
    case .Gasoline:
        vehicleName = "Ford F-150"

    case .Diesel:
        vehicleName = "Ford F-250"

    case .Biodiesel:
        vehicleName = "Custom Van"

    case .Electric:
        vehicleName = "Toyota Prius"

    case .NaturalGas:
        vehicleName = "Utility Truck"
}
```

The enumeration defined on lines 315 through 321 shows the different fuel types. On line 323, a variable engine is declared as an enumeration and assigned the value Gasoline. Note that the dot preceding the value is a shorthanded dot notation. Because you are being explicit about declaring the variable as a type of FuelType, Swift assumes that Gasoline is part of that enumeration, so an explicit reference is not needed. You could have typed the following:

```
var engine : FuelType = FuelType.Gasoline
```

And it would have worked as well, but the extra typing is unnecessary.

On lines 325 through 340, a switch statement is used to traverse all the possibilities in the FuelType enumeration, with a type of vehicle being printed depending on the value of the engine variable.

FIGURE 5.19 Creating a Vehicle struct and initializing it

```
337        case .Electric:
338            vehicleName = "Toyota Prius"
339
340        case .NaturalGas:
341            vehicleName = "Utility Truck"
342    }
343
344    println("Vehicle \(vehicleName) takes \(engine.rawValue)")        "Vehicle Ford F-150 takes 89 octane"
345
346    enum TransmissionType {
347            case Manual4Gear
348            case Manual5Gear
349            case Automatic
350    }
351
352    struct Vehicle {
353        var fuel : FuelType
354        var transmission : TransmissionType
355    }
356
357    var dieselAutomatic = Vehicle(fuel: .Diesel, transmission: .Automatic)     {(Enum Value), (Enum Value)}
358    var gasoline4Speed = Vehicle(fuel: .Gasoline, transmission: .Manual4Gear)  {(Enum Value), (Enum Value)}
359
```

If you're familiar with enumerations in C, you know that internally the compiler assigns a number to each enumeration value, and that any reference to that enumeration value actually decomposes into a number. This is not so in Swift. Enumeration values remain their actual label names internally.

STRUCTURAL INTEGRITY

Classes are pretty powerful constructs in Swift for representing objects of various kinds, but the language also offers choices for organizing data in similar ways: *structures*.

If you're familiar with C or one of its variants, you'll recognize structures immediately. They are organizational constructs for holding data, and they look and feel like classes in several ways, including how they are created:

```
struct structureName {
    // variable and constant definitions
}
```

Lines 346 to 358 of **Figure 5.19** combine an enumeration and a structure together. The Vehicle structure, defined on lines 352 through 355, has two members to represent the type of fuel and type of transmission. Lines 357 and 358 demonstrate how to create variables representing the structure.

```
println("Vehicle \(vehicleName) takes \(engine.rawValue)")


enum TransmissionType {
        case Manual4Gear
        case Manual5Gear
        case Automatic
}


struct Vehicle {
    var fuel : FuelType
```

```
361   // ****************************              {copyVar 20}
362   // value type vs reference type              "10"
363   // ****************************              "20"
364
365   // In Swift, structures are value types
366   struct Structure {
367       var copyVar : Int = 10
368   }
369
370   var struct1 = Structure() // struct1 created
371   var struct2 = struct1 // struct2 is a copy of struct1    {copyVar 10}
372   struct2.copyVar = 20 // change struct2's copyVar          {copyVar 10}
373   println("\(struct1.copyVar)") // struct1's copyVar        {copyVar 20}
374   println("\(struct2.copyVar)") // struct2's copyVar        "20"
375                                                             "20"
376
377   // In Swift, classes are reference types
378   class Class {
379       var copyVar : Int = 10
380   }
381
382   var class1 = Class() // class1 instantiated               24.0
383   var class2 = class1 // class2 is a reference to class1
384   class2.copyVar = 20 // change class2's copyVar
385   println("\(class1.copyVar)") // class1's copyVar
386   println("\(class2.copyVar)") // class2's copyVar          {base 4.0, height 12.0}
387                                                             "24.0"
```

FIGURE 5.20 Value versus reference types illustrated by structures and classes

```
    var transmission : TransmissionType
}

var dieselAutomatic = Vehicle(fuel: .Diesel, transmission: .Automatic)
var gasoline4Speed = Vehicle(fuel: .Gasoline, transmission: .Manual4Gear)
```

In the C language, structures are very useful for organizing and aggregating related data because there are no such things as classes. In Swift, structures take on that same behavior, but can also include methods. This makes structures almost the same as classes, but with some notable differences.

Whereas classes can establish hierarchy through inheritance, structures have no notion of subclassing. Also, structures are copied in their entirety when being assigned from one variable to the next; classes are *referenced* and not copied between variables.

VALUE TYPES VS. REFERENCE TYPES

A very subtle but important distinction between classes and structures is how they behave when assigned to a variable or constant. Classes in Swift are known as *reference types*. No matter how many variables or constants are assigned to a particular object, they all point to the same object. Each variable or constant holds a reference, and not a copy, of that object.

Structures are completely different. When a structure is assigned to a variable or constant, a *copy* of that structure is made at that point. The same thing happens if a structure is passed as a parameter to a function. This copy behavior makes structures *value types*.

This behavior can be illustrated in your playground by examining the contents of a class or a structure after it has been assigned. Type in the following code, which lands at lines 361 through 386 in **Figure 5.20**.

```
// ****************************
// value type vs reference type
// ****************************
```

```
// In Swift, structures are value types
struct Structure {
    var copyVar : Int = 10
}

var struct1 = Structure() // struct1 created
var struct2 = struct1 // struct2 is a copy of struct1
struct2.copyVar = 20 // change struct2's copyVar
println("\(struct1.copyVar)") // struct1's copyVar
println("\(struct2.copyVar)") // struct2's copyVar


// In Swift, classes are reference types
class Class {
        var copyVar : Int = 10
}

var class1 = Class() // class1 instantiated
var class2 = class1 // class2 is a reference to class1
class2.copyVar = 20 // change class2's copyVar
println("\(class1.copyVar)") // class1's copyVar
println("\(class2.copyVar)") // class2's copyVar
```

On line 366, a simple structure, Structure, with one member, copyVar, is defined. The copyVar member is assigned the value 10 by default. On line 370, a variable named struct1 is assigned an instance of Structure. In the Results sidebar, the value of copyVar is shown as 10, as you would expect.

On line 371, a second variable, struct2, is assigned to the struct1 variable that was just created. At this point struct1 is copied and assigned to struct2; as a copy, any change to struct2's copyVar will be independent and not affect struct1's copyVar. This is tested on line 372, where copyVar of struct2 is assigned the value 20.

With that assignment made, both struct1 and struct2's copyVar contents are printed. As you would expect from a copy type, copyVar of struct1 remains the initial value, 10, whereas copyVar of struct2 is 20. The values are different, proving that struct1 and struct2 are not references to the same structure—they are completely different, independent copies.

Contrast that behavior to the contrived Class class on line 378. This class looks identical to the structure example with the same variable copyVar, except it is marked as a class.

Just like in the structure example, a new class is instantiated on line 382 and assigned to class1. On the next line, a variable class2 is assigned to the new class1 variable. At this point a *reference* is made from class2 to class1, which means that both variables are referencing, or pointing to, the exact same object in memory.

To demonstrate this, class2's copyVar is set to 20 on line 384, and then both copyVar variables from class1 and class2 are printed on lines 385 and 386. According to the Results sidebar, they are both set to 20, proving that both class1 and class2 point to the same object. Any modification of variables in class1 will immediately affect class2.

This behavior is important to understand, and should guide your use of classes versus structures. Any type of language construct that is copyable should be thought of as "expensive to use" compared with a referenced construct. For that reason, structures should be relegated to uses where small aggregations of data are tightly related, like this example:

```
struct Triangle {
   var base : Double
   var height : Double

   func area() -> Double {
      return (0.5 * base) * height
   }
}
```

Here, the structure is organized around the idea of a triangle's measurements of base and height, and a single function that computes the area. Although a class would also work here, a structure fits better for this type of compact representation. Classes are more appropriate for larger, more disparate data organized with a number of different methods.

LOOKING BACK, LOOKING AHEAD

From classes to structures and enumerations, you've covered quite a lot of territory in this chapter. Although we have yet to explore a few intricacies of these Swift constructs, that will come. For now, you have enough of an understanding to begin to exploit these concepts.

I encourage you to practice modeling various types of objects around you and define them in terms of classes. What are their properties? What are their behaviors? What types of objects are similar? Can they inherit properties and behaviors from other objects?

Now turn the page and move forward into the next chapter. There, you'll expand your existing Swift knowledge with several additional class-related concepts: protocols and extensions.

CHAPTER 6

Formalizing with Protocols and Extensions

Congratulations on completing a set of milestone topics in the last chapter: classes, structures, and enumerations—your Swift journey through this book is halfway finished! Yet, you've scratched only the surface of what Swift's object-oriented capabilities are. There's still plenty to explore in this area, and for now, our focus will remain on concepts related to classes and structures.

Two significant features of the Swift language expand the utility and flexibility of classes as well as structures: protocols and extensions. That material will carry us through this chapter.

FOLLOWING PROTOCOL

Dinner fork versus salad fork. Saying "please" and "yes sir" or "yes ma'am." These are behavior examples we learn to apply in certain situations (in this case, eating at a table, or addressing someone). Such behaviors are usually taught by a parent and become mannerisms. Essentially, when we employ such behaviors, we are following existing protocols or modes of conduct.

The idea of protocol also extends to Swift, specifically with respect to classes and structures. Protocols enforce a "code of conduct" on classes and structures, making them promise to implement certain methods or properties. This enforcement is mandatory, but only if the class or structure decides to opt-in, or *adopt* the protocol.

To illustrate how to use a protocol in Swift, think back to the Portal class in the previous chapter (you might want to review the playground file for that chapter). The Portal class was created when we realized that the Door class and the Window class shared a common ability to both lock and unlock. It demonstrated class hierarchy and inheritance principles that are central to OOP.

CLASS OR PROTOCOL?

Inheritance made sense for doors and windows, but what about other unrelated objects that can also be locked and unlocked? A car and a house can both be locked and unlocked, but constructing a class hierarchy that could encapsulate the properties and behaviors of both objects would be unwieldy. They're different enough to make inheritance too much of a reach. That's where protocols come into play.

As you can see on lines 8 through 11 in **Figure 6.1**, a protocol definition looks a lot like a class definition. The basic form of a protocol is:

```
protocol ProtocolName {
    // protocol members
}
```

FIGURE 6.1
Demonstrating Swift's
protocol feature

Start up Xcode, and create a new playground named **Chapter 6**. Type the following code into your playground file on line 7 (Figure 6.1):

```
// protocol for locking/unlocking
protocol LockUnlockProtocol {
    func lock(Void) -> String
    func unlock(Void) -> String
}

class House : LockUnlockProtocol {
    func lock(Void) -> String {
        return "Click!"
    }

    func unlock(Void) -> String {
        return "Clack!"
    }
1}
```

```
class Vehicle : LockUnlockProtocol {
    func lock(Void) -> String {
        return "Beep-Beep!"
    }

    func unlock(Void) -> String {
        return "Beep!"
    }
}

let myHouse = House()
myHouse.lock()
myHouse.unlock()

let myCar = Vehicle()
myCar.lock()
myCar.unlock()
```

On lines 9 and 10, two functions are declared: lock and unlock. Both take no parameters and return a String type. What might look strange is that the body of the function is missing, but that's the point of a protocol. It lists the method signatures a class must adopt.

To clarify, look at line 13. This is a regular class declaration, but notice what follows the colon: the name of the protocol. This looks a lot like inheritance as you saw in the last chapter, but in this case, a protocol follows, not a superclass name.

Lines 14 and 18 show the definition of the lock and unlock methods in the House class. Those same methods exist in the Vehicle class on lines 24 and 28, except the result returned is different (locking a house sounds different than locking a vehicle).

Lines 33 through 39 show the declaration of constants of type House and Vehicle, and the subsequent calls to lock and unlock both via the methods dictated by the LockUnlockProtocol.

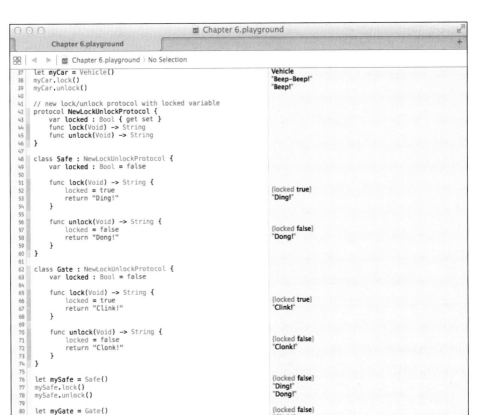

FIGURE 6.2 Adding a variable to a protocol definition

MORE THAN JUST METHODS

Swift protocols can work with more than just methods. Variable declarations can even be dictated to the adopters of protocols. Recall in Chapter 5 that a variable, locked, was used to track the lock status? This makes a great candidate for enhancing the previous example.

Type the following code starting on line 41 (**Figure 6.2**):

```swift
// new lock/unlock protocol with locked variable
protocol NewLockUnlockProtocol {
    var locked : Bool { get set }
    func lock(Void) -> String
    func unlock(Void) -> String
}


class Safe : NewLockUnlockProtocol {
    var locked : Bool = false
```

```
        func lock(Void) -> String {
            locked = true
            return "Ding!"
        }

        func unlock(Void) -> String {
            locked = false
            return "Dong!"
        }
    }

    class Gate : NewLockUnlockProtocol {
        var locked : Bool = false

        func lock(Void) -> String {
            locked = true
            return "Clink!"
        }

        func unlock(Void) -> String {
            locked = false
            return "Clonk!"
        }
    }

    let mySafe = Safe()
    mySafe.lock()
    mySafe.unlock()

    let myGate = Gate()
    myGate.lock()
    myGate.unlock()
```

A new protocol NewLockUnlockProtocol is created on lines 42 through 46. It's nearly identical to the previous protocol except for the addition of line 43:

```
var locked : Bool { get set }
```

```
80   let myGate = Gate()                                                        {locked false}
81   myGate.lock()                                                              "Clink!"
82   myGate.unlock()                                                            "Clonk!"
83
84   // a structure adopting multiple protocols
85   protocol AreaComputationProtocol {
86       func computeArea(Void) -> Double
87   }
88
89   protocol PerimeterComputationProtocol {
90       func computePerimeter(Void) -> Double
91   }
92
93   struct Rectangle : AreaComputationProtocol, PerimeterComputationProtocol
         {
94       var width, height : Double
95
96       func computeArea(Void) -> Double {
97           return width * height                                              (2 times)
98       }
99
100      func computePerimeter(Void) -> Double {
101          return width * 2 + height * 2                                       (2 times)
102      }
103  }
104
105  var square = Rectangle(width : 3, height : 3)                              {width 3.0, height 3.0}
106  var rectangle = Rectangle(width : 4, height : 6)                           {width 4.0, height 6.0}
107
108  square.computeArea()                                                       9.0
109  square.computePerimeter()                                                  12.0
110
111  rectangle.computeArea()                                                    24.0
112  rectangle.computePerimeter()                                               20.0
113
```

FIGURE 6.3 Adopting multiple protocols

Within the context of a protocol, a variable can be designated as mandatory by adding the familiar var keyword, the name of the variable, and the type following a colon. What is new is the { get set } that follows the type.

Both get and set are special qualifiers that force the protocol adopter to consider the mutability of the variable. With both get and set present, the resulting locked declaration in any adopting class or structure must declare it with the var keyword, indicating mutability. With only get present, the adopting class or structure can be declared with either the let or var keyword.

ADOPTING MULTIPLE PROTOCOLS

Swift allows a class or structure to adopt more than one protocol; this flexibility allows you to refactor your work into separate protocols for better organization. Take for instance, the task of finding the area of a geometric shape as well as the perimeter. The area is the measurement of the space within the bounds of the shape, while the perimeter is the measurement of the length of all the sides.

If we consider the computation of the area and perimeter as methods declared in separate protocols, they can be adopted by a variety of structures that represent different shapes. Type the following code starting on line 84 (**Figure 6.3**).

```
// a structure adopting multiple protocols
protocol AreaComputationProtocol {
    func computeArea(Void) -> Double
}
```

```
protocol PerimeterComputationProtocol {
    func computePerimeter(Void) -> Double
}

struct Rectangle : AreaComputationProtocol, PerimeterComputationProtocol {
    var width, height : Double

    func computeArea(Void) -> Double {
        return width * height
    }

    func computePerimeter(Void) -> Double {
        return width * 2 + height * 2
    }
}

var square = Rectangle(width : 3, height : 3)
var rectangle = Rectangle(width : 4, height : 6)

square.computeArea()
square.computePerimeter()

rectangle.computeArea()
rectangle.computePerimeter()
```

Lines 85 through 91 show the two new protocols, each requiring the creation of a single function. On line 93, the Rectangle structure shows the multiple adoption syntax. Each protocol is separated by a comma. Since both protocols are specified, the methods and variables of both must be adopted. In this case, only the functions computeArea and computePerimeter are necessary for adoption by the Rectangle structure.

Lines 105 and 106 show the declaration of two variables: One is a square (which is a special case of a rectangle), and the other is a rectangle. Both create an instance of the Rectangle structure with the width and height parameters; the Results sidebar confirms their creation.

```
111   rectangle.computeArea()                                        24.0
112   rectangle.computePerimeter()                                   20.0
113
114   // protocol inheritance
115   protocol TriangleProtocol : AreaComputationProtocol,
          PerimeterComputationProtocol {
116       var a : Double { get set }
117       var b : Double { get set }
118       var c : Double { get set }
119       var base : Double { get set }
120       var height : Double { get set }
121   }
122
123   struct Triangle : TriangleProtocol {
124       var a, b, c : Double
125       var height, base : Double
126
127       func computeArea(Void) -> Double {
128           return (base * height) / 2                              60.0
129       }
130
131       func computePerimeter(Void) -> Double {
132           return a + b + c                                        15.0
133       }
134   }
135
136   var triangle1 = Triangle(a : 4, b : 5, c : 6, height : 12, base : 10)    (a 4.0, b 5.0, c 6.0, height 12.0, base 10.0)
137
138   triangle1.computeArea()                                        60.0
139   triangle1.computePerimeter()                                   15.0
140
```

FIGURE 6.4
Demonstrating
protocol inheritance

PROTOCOLS CAN INHERIT, TOO

It may come as a surprise, but just like classes can inherit from each other, protocols can as well. Protocol inheritance allows you to build on basic protocols and extend them with either new method or variable requirements.

Type the following code beginning on line 114 (**Figure 6.4**):

```
// protocol inheritance
protocol TriangleProtocol : AreaComputationProtocol,
PerimeterComputationProtocol {
    var a : Double { get set }
    var b : Double { get set }
    var c : Double { get set }
    var base : Double { get set }
    var height : Double { get set }
}

struct Triangle : TriangleProtocol {
    var a, b, c : Double
    var height, base : Double

    func computeArea(Void) -> Double {
        return (base * height) / 2
    }
```

```
    func computePerimeter(Void) -> Double {
        return a + b + c
    }
}

var triangle1 = Triangle(a : 4, b : 5, c : 6, height : 12, base : 10)

triangle1.computeArea()
triangle1.computePerimeter()
```

Line 115 shows the TriangleProtocol definition, followed by the names of the two protocols it inherits: AreaComputationProtocol and PerimeterComputationProtocol. In addition to adopting these two protocols, TriangleProtocol also enforces the addition of five helpful variables for computing both the area and the perimeter of a triangle. Note that each variable has both the get and set qualifiers specified.

On line 123, a new structure, Triangle, is defined that adheres to the TriangleProtocol. By adhering to that protocol, the Triangle structure must also adhere to AreaComputationProtocol and PerimeterComputationProtocol. Those methods are defined on lines 127 through 133. Lines 124 and 125 create the additional variables, which are required by the TriangleProtocol definition.

Line 136 creates an instance of the Triangle structure, aptly named triangle1, along with the initialization of the parameters. Lines 138 and 139 show the result of calling the computation methods, and you can verify the results in the Results sidebar.

DELEGATION

One specific use for Swift's protocols is an important programming design pattern called *delegation*. Delegation allows one class or structure to concede work or even decision making to another class or structure. When you delegate a task to someone, you expect that person to do the task and report back the status to you; it's very much the same idea in Swift. Other classes can be delegates, performing work on behalf of your class, and protocols are perfect for this. Delegation can also be used to query, or ask, another class or structure whether or not something is permissible.

FIGURE 6.5 Using a protocol for delegation

Begin typing the following code on line 141 (**Figure 6.5**). This snippet demonstrates delegation by modeling a vending machine, which takes a coin and vends an item:

```
// delegation via protocol
protocol VendingMachineProtocol {
    var coinInserted : Bool {get set}
    func shouldVend(Void) -> Bool
}

class Vendor : VendingMachineProtocol {
    var coinInserted : Bool = false
```

```swift
    func shouldVend(Void) -> Bool {
        if coinInserted == true {
            coinInserted = false
            return true
        }
        return false
    }
}


class ColaMachine {
    var vendor : VendingMachineProtocol

    init(vendor : VendingMachineProtocol) {
        self.vendor = vendor
    }

    func insertCoin(Void) {
        vendor.coinInserted = true
    }

    func pressColaButton(Void) -> String {
        if vendor.shouldVend() == true {
            return "Here's a Cola!"
        }
        else {
            return "You must insert a coin!"
        }
    }

    func pressRootBeerButton(Void) -> String {
        if vendor.shouldVend() == true {
            return "Here's a Root Beer!"
        }
        else {
            return "You must insert a coin!"
        }
    }
}
```

```
var vendingMachine = ColaMachine(vendor : Vendor())

vendingMachine.pressColaButton()
vendingMachine.insertCoin()
vendingMachine.pressColaButton()
vendingMachine.pressColaButton()
```

Lines 142 through 145 define the protocol, VendingMachineProtocol, with a Bool variable and a method. The variable is set to true to indicate a coin is inserted, or false if not. The method returns a Bool indicating whether or not an item should be vended.

Lines 147 through 157 define a new class, Vendor, which adheres to the VendingMachineProtocol. It creates the coinInserted variable that the protocol dictates, as well as the shouldVend method. The logic is simple: If a coin has been inserted, clear the coinInserted variable and return true, indicating that an item should be vended; otherwise, no coin has been inserted—return false to prevent a item from vending.

Lines 159 through 187 define the ColaMachine class, which holds an object that adheres to the VendingMachineProtocol protocol. The init method on line 162 takes that object and assigns it to the self.vendor variable on line 163. This vendor object will act on behalf of our class to determine whether it is appropriate to vend an item.

A convenient method, insertCoin, is defined on lines 166 through 168, and simply sets the vendor object's coinInserted variable to true when called.

Two other methods, pressColaButton and pressRootBeerButton, call the vendor's delegate method shouldVend to determine whether to return a vended item (a cola or a root beer) or to remind the user gently to insert a coin.

Finally, a new vendingMachine variable is created on line 189, and its methods called on lines 191 through 194 to demonstrate that the class works as expected. Figure 6.5 shows the results in the Results sidebar.

EXTENDING WITH EXTENSIONS

In the previous chapter, you were introduced to subclassing as a means of extending a Swift class through inheritance. Inheritance via subclassing is a time-tested way of extending an existing class, and it works well for modeling and solving problems in object-oriented languages.

However, alternatives to subclassing in Swift still allow you to extend the functionality of a class without inheritance. Such an approach can be useful when you want to extend, and not fundamentally create, a new class structure. Subclassing is also limited to classes and does not work on structures.

FIGURE 6.6 Extending
the ColaMachine class
with an extension

```
191  vendingMachine.pressColaButton()                              "You must insert a coin!"
192  vendingMachine.insertCoin()                                   {{coinInserted true}}
193  vendingMachine.pressColaButton()                              "Here's a Cola!"
194  vendingMachine.pressColaButton()                              "You must insert a coin!"
195  |
196  // extensions
197  extension ColaMachine {
198      func pressDietColaButton(Void) -> String {
199          if vendor.shouldVend() == true {
200              return "Here's a Diet Cola!"                       "Here's a Diet Cola!"
201          }
202          else {
203              return "You must insert a coin!"
204          }
205      }
206  }
207
208  var newVendingMachine = ColaMachine(vendor: Vendor())         {{coinInserted false}}
209
210  vendingMachine.insertCoin()                                   {{coinInserted true}}
211  vendingMachine.pressDietColaButton()                          "Here's a Diet Cola!"
212
```

On the other hand, *extensions* allow you to expand and extend the behavior and functionality of classes, structures, and even basic types, in a rather non-invasive and straightforward manner. Swift's extensions are analogous to Objective-C categories but are much more powerful.

In true Swift form, the basic form of an extension looks similar to a class or protocol declaration:

```
extension className {
    // extension methods
}
```

In the case of an extension, the keyword is followed by the name of the class or structure that will be extended. Let's start by extending the class you just worked with: the ColaMachine class. Right now, the class contains methods to vend colas and root beers. Let's extend the class to also vend diet colas. Type the following code starting on line 195 (**Figure 6.6**):

```
// extensions
extension ColaMachine {
    func pressDietColaButton(Void) -> String {
        if vendor.shouldVend() == true {
            return "Here's a Diet Cola!"
        }
        else {
            return "You must insert a coin!"
        }
    }
}

var newVendingMachine = ColaMachine(vendor : Vendor())

vendingMachine.insertCoin()
vendingMachine.pressDietColaButton()
```

```
208   var newVendingMachine = ColaMachine(vendor: Vendor())              {{coinInserted false}}
209
210   vendingMachine.insertCoin()                                        {{coinInserted true}}
211   vendingMachine.pressDietColaButton()                               "Here's a Diet Cola!"
212
213   // extending Int to handle memory size designations
214   extension Int {
215       var kb : Int { return self * 1_024 }                           4,096
216       var mb : Int { return self * 1_024 * 1_024 }                   8,388,608
217       var gb : Int { return self * 1_024 * 1_024 * 1_024 }           2,147,483,648
218   }
219
220   var x : Int = 4.kb                                                  4,096
221   var y = 8.mb                                                        8,388,608
222   var z = 2.gb                                                        2,147,483,648
223   |
```

FIGURE 6.7 Using extensions to extend the Int type

Line 197 in Figure 6.6 shows the start of the extension of the ColaMachine class. Following that is the new method, pressDietColaButton, on lines 198 through 205, which mirrors similar methods in the definition of the ColaMachine class earlier in the playground.

A new vending machine object is instantiated on line 208, and the new extension method is called on lines 210 and 211. The Results sidebar shows the results of that code.

You may be asking, "why create an extension when we could have simply added the function to the ColaMachine class?" In this case, you could have certainly done that, but as you build your apps in Swift, you'll find yourself relying on third-party classes, and you may not necessarily have access to the source code. Using extensions is a great way to add features to a class defined elsewhere, even when the class's source code is not available.

EXTENDING BASIC TYPES

Bringing additional functionality to classes via extensions is one thing, but extending types is something entirely different. Swift's extensions allow you to enhance standard types such as Double and String to make them more powerful and easier to use.

MEGABYTES AND GIGABYTES

Let's start out by extending the most common of the basic Swift types: the ubiquitous integer (Int). Type the following code starting on line 213 to convert an Int to kilobytes (kb), megabytes (mb), or gigabytes (gb) (**Figure 6.7**):

```
// extending Int to handle memory size designations
extension Int {
    var kb : Int { return self * 1_024 }
    var mb : Int { return self * 1_024 * 1_024 }
    var gb : Int { return self * 1_024 * 1_024 * 1_024 }
}

var x : Int = 4.kb
var y = 8.mb
var z = 2.gb
```

FIGURE 6.8 Using
extensions on the
Double type

```
220   var x : Int = 4.kb                                              4,096
221   var y = 8.mb                                                    8,388,608
222   var z = 2.gb                                                    2,147,483,648
223
224   // extending Double to handle temperature conversions
225   extension Double {
226       var F : Double { return self }                              80.4
227       var C : Double { return (((self - 32.0) * 5.0) / 9.0) }     26.8888888888889
228       var K : Double { return (((self - 32.0) / 1.8) +            300.038888888889
              273.15) }
229   }
230
231   var temperatureF = 80.4.F                                       80.4
232   var temperatureC = temperatureF.C                               26.8888888888889
233   var temperatureK = temperatureF.K                               300.038888888889
234
235   |
```

This extension demonstrates a feature known as *computed properties*. Unlike classes, extensions prevent the addition of regular (or stored) properties, but computed properties are very much allowed. Computed properties are just that: Their values are derived from computations and take on the form:

var *propertyName* : *type* { *code* }

On lines 215 through 217, the extension to the Int type takes care of conversions for kilobytes, megabytes, and gigabytes by performing simple math on the value of the type, represented by the keyword self.

The declared variables on lines 220 through 222 are assigned values appended with the now familiar dot notation and the appropriate symbol (kb, mb, or gb).

WHAT'S THE TEMPERATURE?

Let's extend the Double type to handle computations for three types of temperature units: F for degrees Fahrenheit, C for degrees Celsius, and K for degrees Kelvin. Type the following code starting on line 224 (**Figure 6.8**):

```
// extending Double to handle temperature conversions
extension Double {
    var F : Double { return self }
    var C : Double { return (((self - 32.0) * 5.0) / 9.0) }
    var K : Double { return (((self - 32.0) / 1.8) + 273.15) }
}

var temperatureF = 80.4.F
var temperatureC = temperatureF.C
var temperatureK = temperatureF.K
```

This looks a lot like the Int extensions we just discussed. Computed properties are once again used to extend the Double type.

In Figure 6.8, the variables lines 231 through 233 are assigned values appended with the recurring dot notation and the symbol F, C, or K. The results can be confirmed by looking at the Results sidebar in Figure 6.8.

Computed properties are quite handy in giving new functionality and utility to even the most elementary types, but there's a bonus: Extensions can extend a type with functions, too!

```
231    var temperatureF = 80.4.F                                    80.4
232    var temperatureC = temperatureF.C                            26.8888888888889
233    var temperatureK = temperatureF.K                            300.038888888889
234
235    // extending String with functions
236    extension String {
237        func prependString(value : String) -> String {
238            return value + self                                  "prefixx"
239        }
240
241        func appendString(value : String) -> String {
242            return self + value                                  "ypostfix"
243        }
244    }
245
246    "x".prependString("prefix")                                  "prefixx"
247    "y".appendString("postfix")                                  "ypostfix"
248
```

FIGURE 6.9 Using methods to extend the String type

BEFORE OR AFTER?

Since we've been picking on Int and Double, let's show the String type a little love. Type the following code starting on line 235 to use extensions and add two methods: prepend and append (**Figure 6.9**):

```
// extending String with functions
extension String {
    func prependString(value : String) -> String {
        return value + self
    }

    func appendString(value : String) -> String {
        return self + value
    }
}

"x".prependString("prefix")
"y".appendString("postfix")
```

Lines 237 through 243 define two methods that create a new string by combining a literal string such as "prefix" with the passed-in String object. Again, the self keyword is used to reference the value. In the case of the prepend method, self is being added to the passed value parameter. For the append method, self comes before value.

Lines 246 and 247 demonstrate using the new methods. In both cases, the "x" or "y" string literal calls the method, which itself takes a single parameter, with the results appearing in the Results sidebar.

IT'S MUTATING!

Up to this point, each of the extension examples return some variant of self: Depending on the type, there's self appended with a string, self prepended with a string, self multiplied by a number, and so on. The result can be captured in a constant or variable, as is done on lines 231 through 233 in Figure 6.9.

FIGURE 6.10 Using a mutating method on the Int class

```
246   "x".prependString("prefix")                              "prefixx"
247   "y".appendString("postfix")                              "ypostfix"
248
249   // extensions with mutating instance methods
250   extension Int {
251       mutating func triple() {
252           self = self * 3                                  9
253       }
254   }
255
256   var trip = 3                                             3
257   trip.triple()                                            9
258
259   extension String {
260       mutating func decorate() {
261           self = "*** " + self + " ***"                    "*** decorate this ***"
262       }
263   }
264
265   var testString = "decorate this"                         "decorate this"
266   testString.decorate()                                    "*** decorate this ***"
267   |
268
```

What if you want to change the value of self instead of simply returning some variation of it? Swift allows this by specifying a method as *mutating*. A mutating method in an extension allows the actual object to be changed.

Type the following code starting on line 249 to create such a mutating method on the Int type (**Figure 6.10**):

```
// extensions with mutating instance methods
extension Int {
    mutating func triple() {
        self = self * 3
    }
}


var trip = 3
trip.triple()


extension String {
    mutating func decorate() {
        self = "*** " + self + " ***"
    }
}


var testString = "decorate this"
testString.decorate()
```

On line 251, the mutating keyword is used before the function definition. This keyword is required when creating a mutating method; if it is omitted, the Swift compiler will throw an error on line 252 when it attempts to assign a value to self.

FIGURE 6.11 Using a closure in an extension (using the Timeline view)

The `triple` function simply takes the value and multiplies it by three. This is done on line 252, where `self` is assigned to itself times three. This is the essence of a mutating method: `self` appears on the left side of the equal sign, indicating that it will be modified.

On line 256, a variable named `trip` is created and assigned the value 3. Following that is a call to the `triple` method, which triples the value. The Results sidebar shows the value changing from 3 to 9.

Likewise, on line 260, a mutating function is defined for the `String` type. Line 261 sets `self` to be bounded by asterisks in the `decorate` method. Lines 265 and 266 demonstrate the creation of a string variable that calls the `decorate` method. Once again, the Results sidebar reveals that the method indeed works.

Remember, mutating methods are all about change—modifying the actual value of the extended class. They cannot work on constants since by definition, a constant is immutable, and attempting to call a mutating method on a constant will result in a Swift compiler error.

USING CLOSURES IN EXTENSIONS

Closures are blocks of code that can be passed around just like variables in Swift. You can pass a closure as a parameter to an extension on the `Int` type to make a useful repeating feature. Type the following code starting on line 268 (**Figure 6.11**):

```
// extension with a closure as a parameter
extension Int {
    func repeat(work: () -> ()) {
        for _ in 0..<self {
            work()
        }
    }
}


5.repeat({
    println("repeat this string")
})
```

FIGURE 6.12 Clicking the circle shows the Timeline pane in your playground

Line 269 shows that this is clearly an extension on the Int type. For repeatable tasks, an integer is the right type choice (a Double wouldn't work well since you cannot repeat something 3.153 times, for example).

In line 270, you're using a function named repeat to extend Int, but the parameter is interesting:

```
work: () -> ()
```

This is the simplest form of a closure declaration, a block of code that takes nothing as a parameter and returns nothing as a result. The name of the parameter is work.

In lines 271 through 273, a simple for-in loop iterates over the closure, which is called the number of times equal to the value of self. What may be new to you is the underscore (_) in the place where you might expect a variable. This is a great feature of the Swift language; essentially, it's a "don't care" symbol that tells Swift to disregard any use of a variable. In this case, we don't need to use a variable to iterate through the loop, because the loop variable is not used anywhere in the for-in loop.

The code on lines 277 through 279 uses the repeat method on the integer literal 5. The println("repeat this string") statement is embedded in the passed closure, which shows the results in the Timeline pane.

Remember, to view the Timeline pane, click the round circle next to the output in the Results sidebar (**Figure 6.12**). You may need to hover over a line of code or click a specific line to get this circle to appear.

SUMMARY

It's been another whirlwind chapter hasn't it? You've taken in a lot, so feel free to go back and review all the code examples. And of course take some time to experiment with your playground file to get a good grounding on the concepts.

Now is also a good time for a break as you leave this section and start the next one. Although we still have more features of the Swift language to cover, next you'll start learning how to write an app or two. Delving into writing a full-fledged program is a great way to learn Swift. And there's no better way to start than learning the ins and outs of Xcode—Apple's incredible development environment.

SECTION II
Developing with Swift

Welcome to the second half of the book! Over the last six chapters, you spent time learning important aspects of the Swift language. Even though you didn't explore every aspect of the language, you did cover the basics as well as some of Swift's more intermediate features. Now it's time for you to begin to build upon your newly gained knowledge.

Since you've made it this far, you should now consider yourself a graduate of sorts—no more playgrounds or simple examples for you in the next few chapters. You're moving on to full-fledged development and debugging of Swift applications using Xcode.

- Chapter 7, Working with Xcode
- Chapter 8, Making a Better App
- Chapter 9, Going Mobile with Swift
- Chapter 10, Advancing Ahead

CHAPTER 7

Working with Xcode

As Apple's hallmark software development platform for Mac and iOS app creation, Xcode is the tool that virtually every Swift developer needs to know and use in order to make the most out of the language. Up to now, you have had very light interaction with Xcode—specifically when creating your playgrounds. But Xcode is so much more, as you'll soon learn. It can do a lot to help you hone your Swift skills and make the best apps possible.

Xcode is an *integrated development environment* (IDE). Essentially, it's a system of integrated components that make writing, debugging, and testing software easier. The major components of any modern IDE are:

- Compiler—Turns your human-readable source code into processor-specific executable code that can run on your computer
- Debugger—Helps you find problems in your code when things aren't working correctly
- Editor—Lets you edit your code
- Project manager—Helps you keep your software project's tens (or even hundreds) of files organized
- Test subsystem—Facilitates testing (an always-important aspect of software development)
- Profiling and analyzing tools—Helps you inspect your code while it's running to determine how well it performs, uses resources, and so on

Xcode contains all these components and more. We'll touch on most of these throughout the remainder of the book. But first a little history lesson.

XCODE'S PEDIGREE

As of the time of this writing, Xcode is in its sixth major release. That's quite an achievement for a single IDE. Since it has always been an Apple product, Xcode has exclusively focused on building software for its products using the Objective-C programming language, as well as C and C++.

Xcode 1.0 was released in the fall of 2003. Based on Apple's earlier IDE, Project Builder, Xcode 1.0 was Apple's foray into a single development platform that would become the basis for its growing line of Macintosh computers.

It wasn't until Xcode 3.1 that support for iPhone OS (now iOS) came into being. By that time, additional debugging and inspection tools were made available, embodied in a powerful application known as Instruments. It was also the version that heralded a powerful compiler technology that is ubiquitous in Xcode today: the LLVM compiler system.

Now with Xcode 6, support for the Swift language is bolted in, along with continued support for Objective-C. You can expect Apple to continue to develop and enhance Xcode for some time going forward.

CREATING YOUR FIRST SWIFT PROJECT

FIGURE 7.1 Xcode 6's File menu

FIGURE 7.2 Select a new project template in Xcode.

Let's start by taking a tour of Xcode. If you haven't already launched Xcode 6, go ahead and do so now. Choose File > New > Project as shown in **Figure 7.1**.

Previously, you used the Playground menu item to create a new playground. This time, you're creating a new project.

What is an Xcode project? It's a file package that contains references to all the code source files and resources that make up an application. The project file essentially manages all these files for you and makes certain that the Swift compiler does the right thing with them.

After clicking the Project menu item, a new Xcode window appears along with a drop-down sheet. Here you are prompted to select a project template (**Figure 7.2**).

Two major groups are available for project creation: iOS and OS X. If you are writing an iOS app, you would normally select an item from the first group.

FIGURE 7.3 Project options for the new project

FIGURE 7.4 The project save dialog. Navigate to a location on your Mac to save the project.

Choose OS X as the project template. Specifically, select the Application item, select Cocoa Application in the template chooser, and then click Next. In the dialog that appears, you can set the project's options (**Figure 7.3**).

If your organization name is different than what appears in **Figure 7.3**, you can simply ignore it for now. More importantly, ensure the Product Name is set to `MyFirstSwiftApp` and the Language is set to Swift and not Objective-C. You can also leave the remaining options deselected. Click Next.

Another dialog appears, prompting you to save the project. **Figure 7.4** shows where your project will be saved. You can choose any convenient location. Feel free to leave the Create Git Repository option selected (if it is already); however, we won't be worrying about source control. Once you have selected a place to save the project, click Create.

Congratulations! You've taken your first step toward creating your first Swift app on your Mac.

DIVING DOWN

Now that you've created your project, you're ready to dive into the details. The project window may seem daunting and intimidating at first. Don't worry. I'll show you the ins and outs of this window and how you can use it to manage your Swift development.

The project window is composed of five major areas, four of which you see now:

- The **toolbar**, which runs along the top, is where you can quickly see the name of your project file and obtain the status of any compilations or other work going in Xcode.

- The **navigator area** falls along the left side of the window. It arranges all the files in your project in a hierarchal fashion, allowing you to organize and browse according to your liking. You'll refer to the navigator area quite a bit when working with your project.

FIGURE 7.5 Setting up the target

- On the right side of the project window is the **utilities area**. This area is automatically populated with information about the currently selected file in the navigator area. It's also a place where you can set information about various resources that compose your application.

- The **debug area** rests at the bottom of the project window. It is currently hidden from your view, but we'll look at it soon. As you might expect, this is where you interact with the debugger to fix issues in your code.

- The **editor area** is where you will spend most of your time interacting with Xcode. You'll edit your source code in this area. It is also the largest and centermost area of the project window, allowing you to focus on your code.

At the moment, the editor area doesn't contain source code, but instead shows the General panel related to your application. You can ignore many of these settings for the purposes of learning Swift, but you should understand the correlation between the navigator area and this pane.

In the navigator area, the topmost selected item is the name of your project. When this is selected, the editor area shows the content shown in **Figure 7.5**. A subpane of the editor area shows your project, MyFirstSwiftApp, as well as two targets. A *target* in Xcode is a destination of sorts. It's an entity that is expected to be "built" or "made." Your application, MyFirstSwiftApp, is a target and is currently selected. A second target, in our case MyFirstSwiftAppTests, is automatically created for an application project such as this. It allows you to write tests that help fortify and strengthen your code.

```
1   //
2   //  AppDelegate.swift
3   //  MyFirstSwiftApp
4   //
5   //  Created by Boisy Pitre on 9/28/14.
6   //  Copyright (c) 2014 MyCompany. All rights reserved.
7   //
8
9   import Cocoa
10
11  @NSApplicationMain
12  class AppDelegate: NSObject, NSApplicationDelegate {
13
14      @IBOutlet weak var window: NSWindow!
15
16
17      func applicationDidFinishLaunching(aNotification: NSNotification) {
18          // Insert code here to initialize your application
19      }
20
21      func applicationWillTerminate(aNotification: NSNotification) {
22          // Insert code here to tear down your application
23      }
24
25
26  }
27
28
```

MyFirstSwiftApp
2 targets, OS X SDK 10.10

▼ MyFirstSwiftApp
    AppDelegate.swift
    Images.xcassets
    MainMenu.xib
  ▶ Supporting Files
▶ MyFirstSwiftAppTests
▶ Products

FIGURE 7.6 Selecting the App-Delegate.swift source file from the navigator area

FIGURE 7.7 The AppDelegate.swift code in the editor area

INTERACTING WITH THE PROJECT WINDOW

Go to the navigator area on the left side of the window (Figure 7.5), and locate the file named AppDelegate.swift. Xcode expects all Swift source files to have the .swift extension, so this should become familiar to you over time.

In the navigator area, single-click the AppDelegate.swift source file (**Figure 7.6**). Doing so will show the code in **Figure 7.7**.

The code in Figure 7.7 should look somewhat familiar to you. It has comments on lines 1 through 7 and a class definition starting at line 12. The rest looks strange and new. Not to worry; I'll explain it to you shortly.

What you are looking at is the entry point to a Mac OS X application written in Swift, specifically the method `applicationDidFinishLaunching`, which is a member function of the `AppDelegate` class. This is the first method in your code that will be called after the application has started up.

The comment in the method directs you to insert code to initialize your application. A second method, `applicationWillTerminate`, is called when the application is terminating.

Both of these methods are wrapped in the `AppDelegate` class, which is the class that OS X applications are expected to implement (and indeed, this class is automatically created for you).

Also note that the editor area provides visual clues about your source code: Comments are colored in green and Swift keywords are in blue. This coloring gives you immediate, at-a-glance cues as to how your source code is composed. The colors are actually configurable by going to the Xcode > Preferences menu and selecting the Fonts & Colors toolbar button. (I'll leave that as an exercise for you to play with.)

For clarity, let's review the code in the AppDelegate.swift file line by line.

The comments in lines 1 through 7 indicate the vintage of the file as well as the author and company to whom it belongs.

Line 9 shows the `import` statement:

```
import Cocoa
```

The `import` keyword tells the Swift compiler to import other software components into your project. In this case, that component is Cocoa. Cocoa is the name of Apple's vast framework of classes that make up the OS X experience. You'll be learning a bit about these frameworks throughout the remainder of the book.

Line 11 is a special attribute type that tells the Swift compiler to generate code specifically for starting the application. You can safely ignore it.

Line 12 is a now-familiar class definition. Named `AppDelegate`, it inherits from a base class named `NSObject`. This is a historical class that has its roots in Objective-C. This is followed by `NSApplicationDelegate`, which is a protocol.

```
class AppDelegate: NSObject, NSApplicationDelegate {
```

Line 14 should look somewhat familiar. It's a declaration for a variable named `window` of type `NSWindow`. The strange-looking preface, `@IBOutlet weak`, is a special attribute that identifies this variable as an outlet to a UI element (we'll see this a bit later). The exclamation mark following the type `NSWindow` is a special character related to optionals (remember those were discussed in the beginning of the book). We'll get into the actual meaning of the (!) operator later. For now, just ignore it.

```
@IBOutlet weak var window: NSWindow!
```

As mentioned earlier, lines 17 through 23 are the member methods of the `AppDelegate` class defined by the Cocoa framework. In both cases, the methods are passed the following parameter:

```
aNotification: NSNotification
```

Notifications are special objects used to pass information between classes in Cocoa; a notification is an instantiated object of the `NSNotification` class passed into both methods when they are called.

That completes the tour of the AppDelegate.swift source file. It's short, sweet, and automatically generated by Xcode when it creates an app. Think of it as a boilerplate, or template for you to start your project.

FIGURE 7.8
The window of your
first Swift application

IT'S ALIVE!

You may find it difficult to believe, but even with this minimal source file, you actually have a runnable application. This is one of Xcode's many great features: You can get off the ground running with minimal effort. To convince you of just how neat this is, choose Product > Run to start the compilation process. In short order, you'll see a window like the one in **Figure 7.8**.

You just ran your first app. The window appears with the name of the app, MyFirstSwift-App, advertised in the window title bar. It's something to show for your minimal work, but as a blank window, it's not that impressive. That's because you haven't done anything to the project as of yet, but we'll get to that soon enough.

As a running app, `MyFirstSwiftApp` takes a prominent position in your Dock with a rather generic icon. You can also move the window around and resize it by clicking and dragging the lower-right corner of the window. That's a lot of functionality you get "for free."

This is cool, but ultimately a means to an end—you want to build something useful; after all, that's what learning Swift is all about.

Next we'll make some alterations, so go ahead and quit the app by pressing Command-Q.

PIQUING YOUR INTEREST

An empty window isn't something that gets you excited, but what can you put there? That depends on what you want to build.

An earlier chapter touched on interest rate calculations. The idea worked OK in the REPL, but the user interface wasn't the best. Who wants to type code to get the answer when they can point and click?

A simple interest calculator is a perfect fit for your first real Swift app, and the user interface should be simple to craft. We'll do a quick inventory of the user interface elements you need to make this app work; but first, the core problem you're trying to solve is computing simple interest on a loan.

FIGURE 7.9 Selecting `MainMenu.xib` from the navigator area

To do that, you need to think about the inputs (what the user will type in) and the outputs (what the calculation will yield).

- Inputs—Simple interest requires three: a loan amount, a period of time (or term), and an interest rate.

- Outputs—The result of the calculation is a single output, namely the total amount of the loan over the term at the given interest rate.

If you take a quick inventory of how the user interface (or UI as we'll call it from now on) looks, you'll need three input fields and an output field. You'll also need a button the user can click to perform the calculation.

Now that you know what you need, you can start building; but first, let's address the screen real-estate issue of Xcode.

MAKING ROOM

Xcode gives you all the tools you need to create your user interface; in fact, it already created the window for you as you saw when you ran the app. That window is hiding in a file named `MainMenu.xib`. Locate that file in the navigator area (it's under the group folder named `MyFirstSwiftApp`), and single-click it.

The editor area changes to look something like **Figure 7.9**.

The AppDelegate.swift code goes away, and the editor area's contents change to an inner pane and what looks like a partial window. Just above the window is the menu bar for the app. By clicking the `MainMenu.xib` file, the editor area changed to accommodate the view of the window. The editor area is context sensitive, showing the content you want to edit.

If you're working on a Mac with a smaller screen, you may not be able to see the entire editor area. To help maximize your screen real estate while working with large content, Xcode gives you some options.

FIGURE 7.10 Xcode allows you to collapse areas to maximize your workspace.

FIGURE 7.11 The Push Button UI element

FIGURE 7.12 The window with the Push Button UI element placed

In the upper-right corner of the Xcode window are three buttons (**Figure 7.10**) you can click to reclaim areas of the Xcode window. These buttons expand or collapse various areas of the Xcode window. Be aware that the area you collapse might be needed for subsequent work, so use these carefully.

You can also click the double arrow (shown in Figure 7.10) to put Xcode into full screen mode and utilize the entire area of your monitor.

Whichever method you choose, have the entire window visible in the Xcode editor area and ensure that the utilities area on the right of the Xcode window is still visible—you will need access to it shortly.

BUILDING THE UI

Now the fun begins! You can start building your application's window with the appropriate UI elements. Start by looking at the lower-right corner of the Xcode window (the utilities area). There you'll see a table of UI elements you can scroll through. This is the "palette" of goodies you can use in your apps.

BUTTON UP!

Let's start with the Push Button (**Figure 7.11**). Locate it, and drag it onto the window in the editor area.

When dragging the button in the area inside of the app window, Xcode places helpful perforated guidelines indicating when the button is centered on the window, as well as appropriate edge boundaries that conform to Apple's user interface guidelines. Don't worry about being too exact with placement—just position the button in the bottom of your app window (**Figure 7.12**).

FIGURE 7.13 Using the search field to locate a specific UI element (in this case, "label")

FIGURE 7.14 The window populated with the labels

LABELS, LABELS, LABELS

Labels are special noneditable text fields used to hold textual information. For this app, they'll precede the editable text fields, which will come shortly.

To find the Label UI element, you can scroll through the element library in the utilities area until you find "Label," but a quicker way is to use the search field. Doing so gets you right to that element (**Figure 7.13**).

Two types of labels are available: single line and multi-line. The latter is convenient if you need labels to span multiple lines for larger descriptions. For this app, a single-line label is all that's needed.

Drag the label from the utilities area into the window in the editor area. Notice the placement in **Figure 7.14**. Again, don't worry about getting it exactly right; just place it in the general area. Double-click the "Label" text to highlight it and type the following to replace the text:

Loan Amount:

The label field's width automatically expands to accommodate the additional text.

Drag two more labels to the window, and position them underneath each other. Again, refer to Figure 7.14 for general placement, and be sure to use Xcode's perforated guides to line things up. Give the additional two labels the following text:

Loan Term:

Interest Rate:

Next we'll bring the editable text fields into view.

FIGURE 7.15 The text field in the UI element library

FIGURE 7.16 The window now has a button, three labels, and three text fields.

INPUT'S THE KEY

By now you should be getting the rhythm of the UI element library: Find the appropriate type of control in the list and drag it to the window. This is part of the process of building a user interface. There's one more set of elements to bring into the window: text fields.

A text field is similar to a label, but it is editable. Text fields are where your user interacts with the app. In this case, you need three, corresponding to the three labels you just created.

Using the search field below the UI element library, search for "field" (**Figure 7.15**). Once you've located the element, drag it into the window, aligning the text field to the right of the label. Repeat the process two more times, aligning the text field with the labels as in **Figure 7.16**.

Note that the text fields are "taller" than their companion labels. As you place them on the window, Xcode will suggest a proper vertical spacing. In doing so, you should read just the labels' vertical spacing so they line up horizontally with their corresponding text field.

TIDYING UP

You're almost finished with the user interface and will soon move on to the fun stuff—coding the logic in Swift. However, you have a few more things to do before moving onto the next phase.

RENAME THE BUTTON TITLE

The name of the button is "Button," which obviously isn't intuitive. Double-click the button, and rename it to **Calculate**.

FIGURE 7.17 The Attributes inspector pane

FIGURE 7.18 The app's window is complete and ready to go,

ADD A RESULT LABEL

The app needs to communicate the result of the calculation, and this is best done using a label. Drag a new label from the UI element library over to the window, and insert it between the interest rate text field and the button. Double-click this label, and set its name to **RESULT**.

To make it stand out, click the Attributes inspector icon in the utilities area, and change the Font from System Regular to System 17 to increase its size (**Figure 7.17**). Also, click the second icon from the left in the Alignment set so that the label is centered in the text field.

OPTIMIZE THE WINDOW SIZE

The default window size is a little large for our app. Take this opportunity to reposition the UI elements so that the real estate is better utilized. Then click the lower-right corner of the window and drag inward until an optimal size is reached. **Figure 7.18** shows the desired final result. Again, don't worry about getting your window exactly right—just go through the exercise to understand the process.

TAKE IT FOR A QUICK SPIN

Now that the window is set up properly, choose Product > Run to run the application. You should be able to interact with the three text fields and click the Calculate button. Of course, nothing happens of interest because there's Swift code to write! That's coming next.

FIGURE 7.19 The new file template in Xcode

FIGURE 7.20 The file creation dialog

CLASS TIME

Recall back in Chapter 5 where Swift's class concept was introduced. The idea behind the class is to create reusable models of real-world and even abstract concepts. It also helps organize your code logically. A huge benefit is that a Swift class can be easily added into one or more of your projects, providing you with instant functionality.

Creating a Swift class to handle interest calculations is a good approach here. So how do you do this? Up to now, you've used a playground to write your class code. Here, playgrounds aren't applicable. Instead, you must create a class file.

Choose File > New > File. The new file template dialog appears (**Figure 7.19**).

Here you have the opportunity to create many different file types. The file types are grouped by platform (iOS and OS X). Since this is an OS X app, and you're creating a Swift class, select the Source option on the left, click Swift File on the right, and click Next. You'll be prompted to save the newly created file via the file save dialog in **Figure 7.20**.

You can select the targets the file will be associated with. `MyFirstSwiftApp` is already selected; go ahead and select the `MyFirstSwiftAppTests` target as well.

Xcode creates the file and gives it the extension .swift. It also adds the file in the navigator area. The editor area is updated to show the contents of the file, which contains a set of comments and an import statement. Below that line is where you can start building your class.

You wrote a simple interest calculation closure in Chapter 4. For this new class, `SimpleInterest`, you'll promote that to a method. Type in the following lines of code at the end of the newly created class file.

```
class SimpleInterest {
    func calculate(loanAmount : Double, var interestRate : Double, years :
    → Int) -> Double {
        interestRate = interestRate / 100.0
```

```
        var interest = Double(years) * interestRate * loanAmount

        return loanAmount + interest
    }
}
```

This should look familiar to you: a method that takes a loan amount, an interest rate, and a term (in years), and returns the value of the loan after the term.

Now turn your attention to the AppDelegate.swift file by clicking its name in the navigator area. Just below line 9 (the import Cocoa statement), replace subsequent lines with the following code:

```
@NSApplicationMain
class AppDelegate: NSObject, NSApplicationDelegate {

    @IBOutlet weak var window : NSWindow!

    @IBOutlet weak var loanAmountField : NSTextField!
    @IBOutlet weak var interestRateField : NSTextField!
    @IBOutlet weak var yearsField : NSTextField!
    @IBOutlet weak var resultsField : NSTextField!

    var simpleInterestCalculator : SimpleInterest = SimpleInterest()

    func applicationDidFinishLaunching(aNotification: NSNotification) {
        // Insert code here to initialize your application
    }

    func applicationWillTerminate(aNotification: NSNotification) {
        // Insert code here to tear down your application
    }

    @IBAction func buttonClicked(sender : NSButton) {
        var result : Double

        result = simpleInterestCalculator.calculate(loanAmountField.
        → doubleValue, interestRate: interestRateField.doubleValue, years:
        → yearsField.integerValue)

        self.resultsField.stringValue = result.description
    }
}
```

FIGURE 7.21 The code
as it appears in the edi-
tor area of Xcode

```
1   //
2   //  AppDelegate.swift
3   //  MyFirstSwiftApp
4   //
5   //  Created by Boisy Pitre on 9/28/14.
6   //  Copyright (c) 2014 MyCompany. All rights reserved.
7   //
8
9   import Cocoa
10
11  @NSApplicationMain
12  class AppDelegate: NSObject, NSApplicationDelegate {
13
14      @IBOutlet weak var window : NSWindow!
15
16      @IBOutlet weak var loanAmountField : NSTextField!
17      @IBOutlet weak var interestRateField : NSTextField!
18      @IBOutlet weak var yearsField : NSTextField!
19      @IBOutlet weak var resultsField : NSTextField!
20
21      var simpleInterestCalculator : SimpleInterest = SimpleInterest()
22
23      func applicationDidFinishLaunching(aNotification: NSNotification) {
24          // Insert code here to initialize your application
25      }
26
27      func applicationWillTerminate(aNotification: NSNotification) {
28          // Insert code here to tear down your application
29      }
30
31      @IBAction func buttonClicked(sender : NSButton) {
32          var result : Double
33
34          result = simpleInterestCalculator.calculate(loanAmountField.doubleValue, interestRate: interestRateField.doubleValue,
                years: yearsField.integerValue)
35
36          self.resultsField.stringValue = result.description
37      }
38  }
39
```

Let's go through the code line by line, referring to the line numbers in **Figure 7.21**.

We discussed lines 9 through 14 earlier, but deferred the discussion on the exclamation mark (!) at the end of line 14. Now four additional variables declared on lines 16 through 19 also have the exclamation mark appended.

So what is this exclamation mark? It is known as an *implicitly unwrapped optional* and is used when, among other things, you are declaring a variable. So what's an implicitly unwrapped optional?

Remember we discussed optionals in Chapter 1. An optional is a special type that indicates a variable can either hold a value or be nil. Accessing a variable whose value is nil is not something the Swift runtime is fond of, so as a Swift programmer, you must always be cognizant of your variables' values, especially when they *could* be nil.

Declaring a variable as an implicitly unwrapped optional is effectively telling the Swift compiler that you are promising this variable will never be accessed when its value is nil. It is a contract you are making with the compiler, and you are obliged to keep it. If you don't, and the variable is accessed while nil, a runtime error will occur, and your app will stop.

We have more to talk about regarding optionals, especially the idea of *unwrapping* them, but we'll save that for a little later. For now, let's continue stepping through the code.

Still looking at lines 16 through 19, these variables are marked with @IBOutlet. This special keyword is an advertisement to the compiler that the variables are *outlets* to actual user interface elements. You'll notice by the names of these four variables that they correspond to the text fields and labels you created earlier on the window. We'll "hook these up" in just a bit.

On line 21 is a variable declaration for an object of type SimpleInterest. This, of course, is the SimpleInterest class you created a short while ago. The object is instantiated right there on the line so that it's ready to use.

You may be surprised that the two methods on lines 23 and 27 haven't changed—they're still empty. It's not a problem because the code on lines 31 through 37 is where everything happens.

The *action method*, `buttonClicked`, is a special method that is called upon the user interacting with a UI element. Recall that you created a Calculate button on the window—this is the method that will be called when that button is clicked.

Action methods are prefaced with the `@IBAction` keyword, which is a big hint to you and the Swift compiler.

The method takes as a parameter the sender, or caller. This is a reference to the `NSButton` object that is clicked. Even though you don't reference that parameter in this method, you still need to have it present in the parameter list.

This method also doesn't have a return type, implying that it returns nothing.

What it does do is declare a `Double` variable named `result` and assign it to the return of the `simpleInterestCalculator` object's `calculate` method, passing in three parameters: `loanAmountField.doubleValue`, `interestRateField.doubleValue`, and `yearsField.integerValue`.

These three parameters reference the `NSTextField` objects you created earlier on the window. Since the contents of these text fields will return strings, you use the `doubleValue` and `integerValue` methods on them to provide numeric types that are necessary to do the math in the `SimpleInterest` class.

The result of the calculation is a `Double`, but it must be converted to a `String` to be assigned to the `resultsField`:

```
self.resultsField.stringValue = result.description
```

The `description` method is a special method available on a Swift class. It allows that class to return a `String` representation of its data. Here, the `Double` variable result is returning the `String` representation of its number, the result of the simple interest calculation. The resulting string is assigned to the contents of the results field.

Run the app by choosing Product > Run, and type in some values in each of the fields. Click the Calculate button. Did anything happen? Did you get a result?

HOOKING IT UP

Clicking the Calculate button ended up in disappointment—nothing happened. That's because you still have some additional work to do.

The `@IBOutlet` and `@IBAction` tags are cues to both the compiler and to you, the developer. When you see these tags in the editor area, you'll also notice a small circle just to the left of the corresponding line number. That hollow circle is an indicator whether your outlets and actions are *connected*.

Connecting your outlets and actions to the user interface is a critical step in making the app complete and working. It's what ties the user interface to the code you write. Without these connections, the user interface doesn't have the "backing" it needs to perform the work.

FIGURE 7.22 The sub-pane associated with the XIB file

FIGURE 7.23 Click the Document outline button to hide or show more detail about the interface.

FIGURE 7.24 The connection dialog prior to connections being made

You can hook up outlets and actions in several ways in Xcode. Here's one way you'll use: In the navigator area, click the `MainMenu.xib` file. The editor area shows the window with the fields you assembled earlier. To the left of the window is a subpane showing several sections: Placeholders, Objects, and MyFirstSwiftApp. Select the object named App Delegate (**Figure 7.22**). Note that you may have to click the icon highlighted in **Figure 7.23** to show the document outline area in full.

The App Delegate object here is an instantiated reference to the source code in AppDelegate.swift that you just reviewed. Inside the XIB file is a stored, serialized instance of this object that will be automatically created and instantiated by the runtime environment when the app is launched. As such, all of this object's outlets and actions are available for connecting to the UI.

Right-click App Delegate. A HUD window (known as a heads-up display window because of its transparent property) appears (**Figure 7.24**). You can see the list of outlets and actions for the app delegate. Two are already connected: `window` (which connects to the window object) and `delegate`. You need to connect the rest:

- `interestRateField`—Outlet to the interest rate text field
- `loanAmountField`—Outlet to the loan amount text field
- `yearsField`—Outlet to the loan term text field
- `resultsField`—Outlet to the result text field
- `buttonClicked`—Action to the Calculate button

FIGURE 7.25 The act of connecting an outlet to its corresponding UI element

FIGURE 7.26 Your first Swift app running correctly!

Single-click the circle on the right of the HUD window for each outlet and action, and begin dragging. A line appears. Drag the line to the appropriate UI element on the window, and the connection will be made (**Figure 7.25**).

Once all four outlets and the actions have been connected, rerun the app. This time, input the values in **Figure 7.26**, and click the Calculate button. If everything is hooked up correctly, you'll see the result field change to 13125.0, or $13,125. If you don't get the correct answer, or no answer at all, double-check that you have made the proper outlet and action connections.

YOU MADE AN APP!

Sure it's simple, but it works. You wrote your very own Swift app. And it was easy. As you saw, Xcode's environment made it a cinch to create the basic skeleton of the app. All you needed to do was add some UI elements, write code to perform actions, capture values from those elements, and connect the code and the elements together. That's the basic idea behind any application.

There's still more Swift to learn, and more that can be done with your new app. You'll do that, and more, in the next chapter.

CHAPTER 8

Making a Better App

You may have heard the saying: "The last 20 percent of a task takes 80 percent of the effort." That axiom certainly rings true for software development. Often times as a developer, you'll expend most of your energy on getting the final touches of your application just right. It's what makes the difference between a good app and a great app.

IT'S THE LITTLE THINGS

The simple interest calculator you began working on in the last chapter is an example of such a process. Although it is definitely functional, it could use some additional tender loving care. Let's dive into making this nice little app better, and at the same time, dive deeper into Swift.

SHOW ME THE MONEY

In the simple interest app, the result is not shown as a dollar amount, which is an obvious deficiency. The default representation of a Double using the description method is to show the number in plain decimal representation. This is fine in most cases, but for applications that deal with money, it's a bit bland.

How can you spice this up? One idea would be to build a string that prefaces the number with a dollar sign ($), but what about the numbers after the decimal place? Representing change in cents is customary, with two numbers following the decimal point. We'll have to think about how to do that.

Also, if the amount is greater than $999.99, adding a comma for the thousands place would be nice (for example, $11,311.33 instead of $11313.33).

Beyond that, we're only thinking in terms of U.S. dollars (assuming you're in the U.S. of course). What if this app will be used in other countries with other currencies? Their format for money can be entirely different, even using commas instead of decimal points.

As you can see, solving this problem can get out of hand fairly quickly, depending on how accurately you want to convey the visual representation of a financial amount.

You're in luck, because Cocoa provides something known as a *formatter*. A formatter is a special class that understands how to format data in a specific way. There are date formatters and number formatters, for instance, and you can even create your own formatters for reuse in your apps.

The class NSNumberFormatter is what we're interested in. It is actually a subclass of NSFormatter, which is the base class for all formatter classes. NSNumberFormatter can accommodate a handsome number of numeric formats, including currency, which is perfect for this application. Not only that, it handles formatting in a number of different localizations, so users in the United Kingdom or Spain, for example, will see the result formatted in a style customary for their locale.

How do you use this class? More importantly, how can you easily integrate it into the existing code? Recall Swift's extension language feature that was discussed in Chapter 6. Extensions would make an excellent candidate for extending the Double type, and that's exactly what is done in the following code.

Be sure that Xcode is running and your MyFirstSwiftApp project is loaded, and then type in the highlighted code into the AppDelegate.swift source file:

```
import Cocoa

extension Double {
    var dollars: String {
        var formatter : NSNumberFormatter = NSNumberFormatter()
        var result : String? // declare result as an optional String
        formatter.numberStyle = NSNumberFormatterStyle.CurrencyStyle
        result = formatter.stringFromNumber(self)
        if (result == nil) {
            return "FORMAT FAILURE!"
        }
        return result!  // unwrap the optional
    }
}


@NSApplicationMain
class AppDelegate: NSObject, NSApplicationDelegate {

    @IBOutlet weak var window: NSWindow!

    @IBOutlet weak var loanAmountField: NSTextField!
    @IBOutlet weak var interestRateField: NSTextField!
    @IBOutlet weak var yearsField: NSTextField!
    @IBOutlet weak var resultsField: NSTextField!

    var simpleInterestCalculator : SimpleInterest = SimpleInterest()

    func applicationDidFinishLaunching(aNotification: NSNotification) {
        // Insert code here to initialize your application
    }

    func applicationWillTerminate(aNotification: NSNotification) {
        // Insert code here to tear down your application
    }

    @IBAction func buttonClicked(sender : NSButton) {
        var result : Double
```

As you use Xcode, understand how to discover the cornucopia of classes and methods Swift offers. The NSNumberFormatter you used in the example is just one of the many, many classes the Cocoa frameworks grant you access to.

One of Xcode's great features is context-sensitive help right in the editor area. To see this in action, hold down the Option key on your keyboard and hover the mouse pointer over the word NSNumberFormatter on line 13. The pointer changes to a question mark, and a dotted line underscores the word. Click, and a popover appears like the one in **Figure 8.2**.

Declaration	class NSNumberFormatter : NSFormatter
Description	Instances of NSNumberFormatter format the textual representation of cells that contain NSNumber objects and convert textual representations of numeric values into NSNumber objects. The representation encompasses integers, floats, and doubles; floats and doubles can be formatted to a specified decimal position. NSNumberFormatter objects can also impose ranges on the numeric values cells can accept.
Availability	OS X (10.10 and later)
Declared In	Foundation
Reference	NSNumberFormatter Class Reference

FIGURE 8.2 Context-sensitive help in Xcode

The contents of the window provide the name of the class as well as a clickable link to its superclass, which gives information on that as well. A description and compatibility information is also provided, as well as a link to more complete class documentation. Once you're finished viewing the help information, click outside the help window to dismiss it.

Commit this Option-click keyboard shortcut to memory—you'll find it comes in handy as you learn Swift and Cocoa.

Another handy feature is to hold down the Command key while hovering the mouse pointer over your source code. Using the NSNumberFormatter again, try this trick. The pointer changes to a hand, and a solid underline appears under the word. Click, and this time the editor area's content changes to show you the Swift class file for the NSNumber-Formatter class. Here you are getting the direct scoop on all the variables and methods available to you. This, combined with the documentation available in Xcode, gives you a very comprehensive view of Cocoa frameworks available in Swift.

When you're finished, click the folder icon in the navigator area toolbar to switch back to the standard editing view.

FORMATTING: A DIFFERENT TECHNIQUE

While the result looks great, you still have two text fields that could use some face lifting, too: the loan amount and interest rate.

Like the result field, the loan amount is a monetary figure, and we should represent the contents of that field as such. The same goes for the interest rate field. Having the user type $20,000 for the loan amount, for example, as well as 6.25% for the interest rate would clarify the meanings of these fields.

FIGURE 8.3 Bringing the window back into Xcode's editor area

FIGURE 8.4
The NSNumberFormatter object in Xcode's object library

Instead of doing this in code, however, you're going to use Xcode to facilitate the process. You will still use your new friend, NSNumberFormatter, to perform the job, just in a different way.

Make sure that the window appears in the editor area of Xcode by selecting MainMenu.xib in the navigator area (you may have to click the folder icon in the navigator area toolbar), and then select MyFirstSwiftApp (**Figure 8.3**). This sets the stage for the work you'll do next.

Now, turn your attention to the right side of the Xcode window and down to the object library. Make sure the Object button is selected in the object library toolbar, as shown in Figure 8.4. Scroll or use the search field to locate the NSNumberFormatter object. This is the same object you used earlier in the code, except that here it is available to use within Xcode and right in your window (**Figure 8.4**).

FIGURE 8.5 The attributes inspector of the newly created NSNumberFormatter for the Loan Amount text field

FIGURE 8.6 The attributes inspector of the newly created NSNumberFormatter for the Interest Rate text field

FIGURE 8.7 The interest calculator application with properly formatted input

Using your mouse or trackpad, click and drag the NSNumberFormatter object from the object library and into the text field to the right of the Loan Amount label. When you do this, the utility area on the upper right side automatically switches tabs to show the attributes inspector. This is where you can set the attributes of the NSNumberFormatter object you just created by dragging onto the text field. Set the Style pop-up menu to Currency (**Figure 8.5**).

Perform the same action again for the interest rate: Drag the NSNumberFormatter object from the object library to the text field to the right of the Interest Rate label. This time in the Attributes inspector, choose Percent from the Style pop-up menu (**Figure 8.6**).

Now build and run the application. When the application's window appears, type in a number for the loan amount, and fill in the rest of the fields.

If you're noticing an annoying beep when you try to move away from the loan amount text field to enter other data, that's expected. The formatter object is complaining that you aren't entering the data in adherence to the currency format. To get around this, type a dollar sign as the first character of the loan amount. A small bonus: If you didn't type the comma as the thousands separator, the formatter automatically inserts it for you.

The same annoying beep occurs when you move to the interest rate field. Just a number won't do—you'll need to append a percent symbol (%) for the formatter to accept your input.

Figure 8.7 shows what everything looks like just prior to clicking the Calculate button. Make sure the text field contents in your app match what's here, and then click the Calculate button.

The end result looks nice, but isn't it a pain to type in that dollar sign and percentage character? Not only that, but your users probably won't be inclined to type them either, and they will remain puzzled as the app constantly beeps at what seems to be perfectly valid numbers. Sure, you could add some cue, such as an additional label, to prod the user to type in the numbers with the appropriate designators, but that will clutter your window and impede the flow of your app. Plus, it looks strange. There has to be a way for your users to have their cake and eat it too.

FIGURE 8.8 The object tree shows all your objects in relation to each other.

FIGURE 8.9 The Lenient option allows the number formatter to be flexible in how input is typed by your users.

As it turns out, there is. With *input leniency*, your users benefit from the formatter redoing their input to conform to appropriate formatting rules, and they can input the data the way they feel most comfortable.

Quit the app, and then turn on leniency by navigating to the number formatter for both fields in the object tree to the left of the editor area (**Figure 8.8**). This tree is a very convenient and informative view of how all the objects in your `MainMenu.xib` file relate to each other. Finding the formatters here is easy because they fall right underneath the text fields to which they are attached.

Figure 8.9 shows that the Lenient option is selected. Make sure it is also selected for both the loan amount and interest rate formatters.

Tell Xcode to run your program again. This time, type any plain number in both the loan amount and interest rate text fields. Not only are the numbers accepted, but they automatically change to accommodate the formatting rules you've chosen for each field.

As a bonus, the formatters deny any invalid input that doesn't adhere to the formatting rules. For example, you can type an alphabetic character in the text field, but you are not allowed to proceed until it is erased because a valid number cannot be attained. The same annoying beep you heard earlier will be repeated as a reminder.

COMPOUNDING

Given the current state of the interest calculation app, adding compound interest calculation wouldn't be a stretch. After all, the parameters are the same.

In Chapter 4, you reviewed the compound interest calculation. Here it is again:

$$futureValue = presentValue(1 + interestRate)^{years}$$

FIGURE 8.10 Right-clicking in the navigator area to add a new file to Xcode

FIGURE 8.11 Select the Swift file under the OS X Source section.

FIGURE 8.12 Saving the new file

Adding a compound interest class seems like the quickest and easiest way to bring the functionality into your app; doing so requires adding a new Swift file. In the last chapter, you chose File > New > File to create a new Swift source file. That will certainly work, but a slightly quicker method will create the file and put it in the right place in your project.

To begin, go to Xcode's navigation area, and look for the folder named MyFirstSwiftApp. Right-click that folder and choose New File from the shortcut menu (**Figure 8.10**).

In the file template dialog (**Figure 8.11**), select Swift File under the OS X Source section, and click Next.

In the New File dialog (**Figure 8.12**), name the file **CompoundInterest**, select the MyFirstSwiftAppTests checkbox in the Targets area at the bottom. Click Create. The new file appears in the navigator area. Type the following code below the `import Foundation` statement:

```
class CompoundInterest {
    func calculate(loanAmount : Double, var interestRate : Double, years : Int)
-> Double {
        interestRate = interestRate / 100.0
        var compoundMultiplier = pow(1.0 + interestRate, Double(years))

        return loanAmount * compoundMultiplier
    }
}
```

The compound interest rate calculation formula used here is the same that was used in Chapter 4. The method takes the same parameters and returns the same type (Double) as the simple interest calculation method in the `SimpleInterest.swift` class file.

With this new class file created and part of your Xcode project, turn your attention to the user interface. In the navigation area, click the `MainMenu.xib` file, and make sure the window is in view in the editor area.

HOOKING THINGS UP

Currently, you have a single button the user clicks to calculate the simple interest. Since you're giving the user an option to calculate compound interest as well, why not create a second button for that calculation?

You could drag a new `NSButton` object from the object library on the lower-right corner of the Xcode window, but there's a slightly quicker way. Single-click the Calculate button to select it, and then press Command-D to duplicate it. Align the new button under the current one, double-click it to rename it, and enter *Calculate Compound*. Double-click the top button, and rename it to *Calculate Simple*.

You may need to adjust the window size slightly to accommodate the new button, as well as re-center the buttons on the screen. When you're finished, the window should look something like **Figure 8.13**.

FIGURE 8.13 The app window with the new button added and both buttons renamed

```
                     return result!  // unwrap the optional
21           }
22       }
23
24       @NSApplicationMain
25       class AppDelegate: NSObject, NSApplicationDelegate {
26
27           @IBOutlet weak var window: NSWindow!
28
29           @IBOutlet weak var loanAmountField: NSTextField!
30           @IBOutlet weak var interestRateField: NSTextField!
31           @IBOutlet weak var yearsField: NSTextField!
32           @IBOutlet weak var resultsField: NSTextField!
33
34           var simpleInterestCalculator : SimpleInterest = SimpleInterest()
35           var compoundInterestCalculator : CompoundInterest = CompoundInterest()
36
37           func applicationDidFinishLaunching(aNotification: NSNotification?) {
38               // Insert code here to initialize your application
39           }
40
41           func applicationWillTerminate(aNotification: NSNotification?) {
42               // Insert code here to tear down your application
43           }
44
45           @IBAction func buttonClicked(sender : NSButton) {
46               var result : Double
47
48               result = simpleInterestCalculator.calculate(loanAmountField.doubleValue, interestRate: interestRateField.doubleValue,
                         years: yearsField.integerValue)
49
50               self.resultsField.stringValue = result.dollars
51           }
52
53           @IBAction func compoundButtonClicked(sender : NSButton) {
54               var result : Double
55
56               result = compoundInterestCalculator.calculate(loanAmountField.doubleValue, interestRate: interestRateField.doubleValue,
                         years: yearsField.integerValue)
57
58               self.resultsField.stringValue = result.dollars
59           }
60       }
61
```

FIGURE 8.14 The contents of the file after adding the new method

With the window up to snuff, next you'll tie the new button with the compound interest class you just created.

Before proceeding, let's review how the current button is connected. Recall that in the last chapter you created a method in the AppDelegate.swift file named buttonClicked. It had a single parameter (an NSButton object reference), did not have a return value, and was tagged with the special @IBAction keyword.

An easy option would be to copy the method and rename it, and then hook up your new button to that. Here are the steps:

Start by copying the code. Select the AppDelegate.swift file in the Xcode navigator area, and then drag to select lines 44 through 50. Choose Edit > Copy to copy the selected code to the copy buffer. Click line 51 in the editor area, press Return once, and choose Edit > Paste to paste the copied code to that location (**Figure 8.14**).

Now, you need to do some renaming. Double-click the buttonClicked method name on line 52, and rename it to compoundButtonClicked. Highlight the text simpleInterestCalculator on line 55, and rename it to compoundInterestCalculator.

Move the cursor just below line 34 (where the simpleInterestCalculator object is declared), and type this line:

```
var compoundInterestCalculator : CompoundInterest = CompoundInterest()
```

With these changes you have successfully created the code necessary to integrate the new compound interest calculator into the application. The only thing left is to tie the action of the compound button calculator to the appropriate action method.

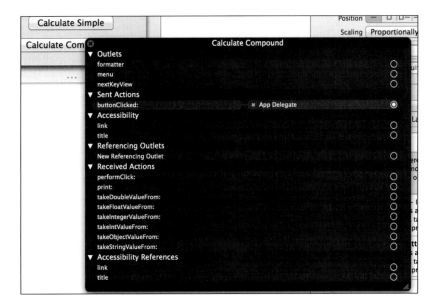

FIGURE 8.15 Break the Calculate Compound Interest button action.

FIGURE 8.16 Connect the selector of the new button to the compound-ButtonClicked method.

To do that, select MainMenu.xib in the navigator area, and bring up the window. Right-click the Calculate Compound button to bring up the connections heads-up display, and then break the existing connection between the buttonClicked method and the App Delegate by clicking the ✖ button (**Figure 8.15**).

This connection must be broken because it came along "for the ride" when you duplicated the button earlier. When clicked, the new button should call the compoundButtonClicked method instead.

Click the circle to the far right of the selector row in the heads-up window, then drag the generated line over to the App Delegate icon just to the left of the editor area. In the new heads-up window that appears, select the compoundButtonClicked method (**Figure 8.16**). This now binds the new button to the proper action method.

TESTING YOUR WORK

Now you'll put your app through its paces with some real-world data. Run the app in Xcode, and input the following values:

- Loan Amount: $25,000
- Loan Term: 10
- Interest Rate: 8%

Click the Calculate Simple button to calculate simple interest.

If you didn't receive an answer in the result area, be sure to recheck your work and your connections.

If you did get an answer, it should be $45,000. Is it?

I'll wager that instead, you're seeing $25,200. That means everything is wired right, but the calculation is wrong. What's going on?

You've encountered a bug. Don't fret—it happens to even the best of us. Bugs are a fact of life in software development, even with languages as easy to use as Swift. However, you don't have to live with it. Apple has imbued Xcode with a powerful debugging tool that helps you find bugs and terminate them on the spot.

WHEN THINGS GO WRONG

Tracking down bugs can be both frustrating and instructive at the same time. There's nothing quite as exhilarating as finding and fixing a particularly tricky problem in your code. It gives you the satisfaction of knowing that you can troubleshoot problems, and it builds your confidence going forward.

When I encounter a bug, I ask the following questions:

1. What are the symptoms?
2. What changed since the last time it worked (assuming it did work before)?
3. Where should I begin looking to find the root cause?

    Let's go over and answer each of these questions for this particular bug:

    - Question 1: In this app, the symptom is obvious: The calculation for simple interest is providing an incorrect result.

    - Question 2: The simple interest app worked in the last chapter. What changed? You've added NSNumberFormatter objects to the loan amount and interest rate text fields. This certainly warrants some investigation.

    - Question 3: Since the result of the calculation is wrong, the first place to start hunting for the bug is in the calculation method in the SimpleInterest.swift file.

WHERE'S THE BUG?

The answers to our questions should lead you to the SimpleInterest.swift file since that is the location of the calculation method. Go to the navigator area in Xcode and select that file so it appears in the editor area.

Looking over the calculate method, everything seems to be in order. The variable interestRate is divided by 100 to yield a number between 0 and 1; it's then multiplied by the loanAmount and the years (cast as a Double from an Int). This is indeed the calculation for simple interest.

Nothing obvious stands out. The formula looks correct, yet the result is wrong. What to do? This sounds like a job for the debugger.

```
       MyFirstSwiftApp ⟩   MyFirstSwiftApp ⟩   SimpleInterest.swift ⟩ No Selection
1    //
2    //   SimpleInterest.swift
3    //   MyFirstSwiftApp
4    //
5    //   Created by Boisy Pitre on 10/2/14.
6    //   Copyright (c) 2014 MyCompany. All rights reserved.
7    //
8
9    import Foundation
10
11   class SimpleInterest {
12       func calculate(loanAmount : Double, var interestRate : Double, years : Int) -> Double {
13           interestRate = interestRate / 100.0
14           var interest = Double(years) * interestRate * loanAmount
15
16           return loanAmount + interest
17       }
18   }
19   |
```

FIGURE 8.17 Setting a breakpoint in the calculate method

AT THE BREAKING POINT

Intuitively, you understand that code is executed in a linear fashion. After one line of code is executed, the next one is, and the next one, and so on. There are exceptions of course: Threads allow multiple lines of code in the same app to execute on different processor cores at the same time, but we're not concerned with that level of detail here. Analyzing the calculate method in a linear fashion is enough for us.

If there were some way to "break into" the code as it is executing and inspect the variables, you could verify the proper operation of the calculate method and thereby rule it in or out as the problem. And there is just such a way to do that. It's called the *breakpoint*.

Breakpoints are stopping points you can place anywhere in the executable areas of your source code. When Xcode runs your application, it stops when it encounters a breakpoint, affording you the opportunity to inspect the environment: variables, constants, and something called the stack trace.

So where should you set this breakpoint? And how do you do it?

The area directly to the left of your source code in the editor area— where the line numbers appear—is known as the *gutter*. Clicking a line in that gutter creates a breakpoint—a blue arrow (**Figure 8.17**).

For this particular debugging session, click line number 13 in the gutter area to set the breakpoint at the first executable line of the calculate method.

The breakpoint is now set, which means that when you run the program again, it will stop when it encounters this location in the execution path.

Run the app again in Xcode. The app starts, and the window appears. Type in the following values for the fields again:

- Loan Amount: $25,000
- Loan Term: 10
- Interest Rate: 8%

FIGURE 8.18 The breakpoint is encountered.

Again, you know the answer should be $45,000, but instead, you're getting $25,200. Click the button to calculate simple interest. As soon as you do, Xcode appears in the forefront of your screen as in **Figure 8.18**. The breakpoint has been encountered, and line 13 is highlighted. Your app is literally frozen in a state where you can inspect all its values.

In addition to Xcode taking over, a new area appears at the bottom. This is the debug area, and it is composed of a split pane. The left pane shows what appears to be the variable names in the `calculate` method along with their values. The right pane shows an (`lldb`) prompt, which is the command-line interface to Apple's debugger known as LLDB.

The prompt area allows you to type commands directly in the LLDB debugger. You won't be using the command line version of the debugger in this book, but if you're interested, the Xcode help has documentation on this powerful way to interact with the debugger.

Instead, you'll concentrate on the left pane. Notice that the `loanAmount`, `interestRate`, and `years` variables are displayed prominently along with their values. You can see clearly that the values correspond to what you typed earlier in the text fields of the application.

You can instruct Xcode to "step over" the current line, which has not executed yet. Stepping over a line causes its code to run and lands the execution point on the following line. The debug toolbar icons are located just above the debug area. To step over line 13, click the fourth icon from the left (**Figure 8.19**). It is shaped like a triangle, indicating that you are stepping *over* a line.

FIGURE 8.19 The debug toolbar allows you to execute control over the Xcode debug process. The Step Over icon is highlighted.

FIGURE 8.20 The updated variables view after stepping over line 13. Note that the `interestRate` value has changed from what it was in Figure 8.18.

When you click the icon, the green arrow indicator moves to line 14, indicating that it will be executed next. Meanwhile, the code on line 13 (to modify the `interestRate` variable) has executed. You can see that the value in the debug area has changed from .08 to .0008 due to the division by 100.0 (**Figure 8.20**).

This change of the `interestRate` value is certainly interesting. It went from .08 to .0008, and as you can see on line 14, will be used to calculate the `interest` variable. Remembering back to your math days, .08 is 8%, but .0008 is .08%. You should be asking for a calculation on an 8% interest rate, not .08%.

If you do the math on line 14 to compute the amount of interest with .0008 as the interest rate, you get:

Interest = 10 years × .0008 × $25,000 = $200

And adding the original loan amount of $25,000 to the $200 of interest gives you $25,200, which is what the app is currently showing.

Now consider the formula using the .08 rate:

Interest = 10 years × .08 × $25,000 = $20,000

Adding $20,000 of interest to $25,000 gives you $45,000, which is the right answer. The bug seems to be identified, but let's continue to be sure.

So why did this same method work in the previous chapter? What is different about the application then compared to now?

`NSNumberFormatter` is certainly new. Considering what `NSNumberFormatter`'s percent style does (transforms a number into a percent), it appears that the 8 you typed into the text field was actually transformed into 0.08. This is confirmed in Figure 8.18 where the debug area shows the `interestRate` variable to be 0.08 and not 8.

Prior to adding the formatter, the value of the text field was passed verbatim to the `calculate` method, and that's why the division by 100.0 was necessary. Now, with the `NSNumberFormatter` doing its job, the division isn't needed anymore.

The solution to fixing this bug? Simply remove line 13 from the `SimpleInterest.swift` class. In this case, however, turn line 13 into a comment by placing the `//` characters at the beginning of the line. This preserves the breakpoint.

FIGURE 8.21 The interestRate variable reflects the correct number, 0.08.

FIGURE 8.22 The Continue program execution button resumes execution of your app.

FIGURE 8.23 The application showing the correct value for simple interest

FIGURE 8.24 The correct compound interest calculation

Run the application again after commenting out line 13, and use the same input values as before. When the breakpoint is encountered, control will be at line 14 (since line 13 is a comment). Note in the debug area that the value of interestRate is now 0.08, which is what is needed for the calculation result to be accurate.

Step over line 14 by clicking the Step Over icon in the debug toolbar, and look in the debug area for the interest variable. It should be set to 20000, or $20,000 (**Figure 8.21**).

At this point, you should be confident that the application will supply the correct result. Since you are still in the debugger and control is stopped, you can instruct Xcode to let the program continue to run unimpeded. Do so by clicking the Continue program execution button on the debug toolbar (**Figure 8.22**).

With the application running at full speed, the result now appears, and you should see a working and accurate simple interest calculation application like the one in **Figure 8.23**.

THE CONFOUNDING COMPOUND

You could declare victory here, but the truth is your work is not complete. There is the compound interest calculation. Is it correct also? A quick examination of the source code in the CompoundInterest.swift file shows that the same assumption is made about the interestRate variable on line 13. It too is being divided by 100.

It's a safe bet that you will need to strike that statement as well to ensure that the compound interest calculator is accurate. Go ahead and comment out that line, and then run the same numbers on the compound interest calculator. You should get the same answer shown in **Figure 8.24**, which is the correct one. You may encounter one of the breakpoints set earlier in your debugging session. If you do, you can click the breakpoint icon and drag it out of the gutter to remove it, and then click the Continue program execution button in the debug toolbar to continue.

THE VALUE OF TESTING

Bugs, such as this one, are sometimes easy to spot and sometimes not so easy. In this case, we obviously needed to check the calculation, but what led us down this path was that the application worked in Chapter 7. Adding the NSNumberFormatter to the text fields broke the calculation, and you were astute enough to notice that the value didn't seem correct.

This demonstrates the fragility of software development and underscores the need for verifiable testing to catch problems like the one you just solved. In testing parlance, the bug you fixed was known as a *regression*. A regression is a failure of something that once worked, and it is one of the worst bugs to deal with. Regressions can sneak up on you because you are lulled into a false sense of security that something that was working one or two versions ago is still working correctly.

THE UNIT TEST

Many different types of tests and testing methodologies are available in software development, but the unit test in particular can be useful. A *unit test* is a very specific, targeted test that verifies one piece of functionality. A unit test can be written to cover one particular method in a class, and there can be many different unit tests for one class. Taken as a whole, a set of unit tests can be used to verify the functionality of a fundamental block of code and ensure that it is working correctly.

Apple emphasizes the use of unit testing right in Xcode. In fact, when you created the Xcode project for your first Swift application, you may have noticed the MyFirstSwiftAppTests target right below your application target (**Figure 8.25**).

The navigator area has a group folder named MyFirstSwiftAppTests and underneath that, a Swift source code file named MyFirstSwiftAppTests.swift. Without you even asking for it, Xcode created all the infrastructure you need to develop tests for your application.

FIGURE 8.25 The MyFirstSwiftAppTests target is a unit test target automatically created by Xcode.

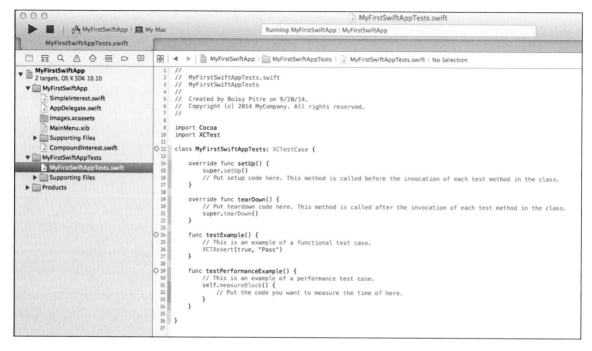

FIGURE 8.26 The unit test file, ready for you to make changes

CRAFTING A TEST

Often when creating unit tests, you'll find yourself asking the question: "What tests do I need to write?" The answer to this question depends on the functionality of your application and the pieces and parts that make up the app.

If you examine the interest calculator app, the calculation methods themselves are obviously candidates for unit tests. Testing the accuracy of the calculation method can give you confidence that it is not only correct, but will remain correct if you decide to change it or tweak it later.

Let's start by looking at the MyFirstSwiftAppTests.swift source file. Locate the source file in the navigator area of Xcode, and then single-click the file. The editor area changes to show the contents of that file (**Figure 8.26**).

Notice that this is a Swift source file, and it contains a Swift class named MyFirstSwiftAppTests. It is a subclass of the XCTestCase class, which is a special unit test class that provides a number of helpful features in performing tests.

Next, notice that a number of methods already exist in the class. The first two—setUp and tearDown—are special methods called when starting and stopping the test class, respectively. These methods provide entry points for you to create objects that may be needed during the testing process.

Two additional methods—testExample and testPerformanceExample—are example test methods you can use as a starting point for your own tests.

In the unit test framework, any method that begins with the word "test" is a test method, and it will be called when the unit test runs. You can have one such method, or many. How you structure your unit tests is all up to you.

Given that the interest application has two classes, one for simple interest and one for compound interest, creating two test methods probably makes sense. These two methods will test the veracity of the calculate methods, ensuring that they are always returning accurate values.

Replace lines 12 through 41 in the MyFirstSwiftAppTests.swift file with the following code:

```
class MyFirstSwiftAppTests: XCTestCase {

    var mySimpleInterestCalculator : SimpleInterest = SimpleInterest()
    var myCompoundInterestCalculator : CompoundInterest = CompoundInterest()

    override func setUp() {
        super.setUp()
        // Put setup code here. This method is called before the invocation of
        → each test method in the class.
    }

    override func tearDown() {
        // Put teardown code here. This method is called after the invocation
        → of each test method in the class.
        super.tearDown()
    }

    func testSimpleInterest() {
        // This is an example of a functional test case.
        var result : Double
        result = mySimpleInterestCalculator.calculate(25_000, interestRate:
        → 0.08, years: 10)
        XCTAssertEqualWithAccuracy(result, 45000, 0.1, "Unexpected result:
        → \(result)")
    }
```

```
func testCompoundInterest() {
    // This is an example of a functional test case.
    var result : Double
    result = myCompoundInterestCalculator.calculate(25_000, interestRate:
    → 0.08, years: 10)
    XCTAssertEqualWithAccuracy(result, 53973.12, 0.1, "Unexpected result:
    →\(result)")
}

}
```

The two methods, testSimpleInterest and testCompoundInterest, test the simple and compound interest calculations, respectively. The test involves using the calculate method of each class to verify that the passed loan amount, loan term, and interest rate yield an expected answer.

Two objects, mySimpleInterestCalculator and myCompoundInterestCalculator, are instantiated at the top of the MyFirstSwiftAppTests class on lines 14 and 15. These objects are then used in the respective test methods at lines 30 and 37 to test interest calculation on a 10-year loan for $25,000 at 8% interest—the same values you used earlier to test the app.

For each test method, a variable named result of type Double is defined and assigned to the return value of the calculate method for the respective object. To verify the test passed, a call to the XCTAssertEqualWithAccuracy function is made. This function takes four parameters: the variable to evaluate, the value that the variable should be, an accuracy factor, and a String that is shown only if the test fails. When dealing with Float or Double types, this particular test function is useful since floating point numbers aren't always exact due to how they are represented in memory. Here, you are indicating that the passed variable and the result can be equal to within 0.1, or 10 cents.

With the source file modified, run the test by choosing Product > Test. The tests run, and the navigator area changes its content to show the results of the two tests. Switch to the test navigator view in the navigator area by clicking the Test Navigator icon (the green diamond-shaped icon). You should see green checkmarks next to the names of each method. You'll also see the same green checkmarks in the gutter next to the source code (**Figure 8.27**).

FIGURE 8.27 The view of the code when the tests have passed

```
34  func testCompoundInterest() {
35      // This is an example of a functional test case.
36      var result : Double
37      result = myCompoundInterestCalculator.calculate(25_000, interestRate: 0.08, years: 10)
38      XCTAssertEqualWithAccuracy(result, 53973.12 + 1|, 0.5, "Unexpected result: \(result)")
39  }
40
41  }
42
```
XCTAssertEqualWithAccuracy failed: ("53973.1249318197") is not equal to ("53974.12") +/- ("0.5") - Unexpected result: 53973.1249318197

FIGURE 8.28 The result of a failed test

WHEN TESTS FAIL

So far the tests pass, but what happens when a failure occurs? Forcing a failure is simple enough—simply change the second parameter in one of the XCTAssertEqualWithAccuracy methods to a completely different value. Try this by changing the value 53973.12 on line 38 to 53973.12 + 1 and rerun the tests. The test fails, and the green checkmark for that method turns into a red X. The test error message is also printed to highlight the details of the error in **Figure 8.28**.

Now that you know how to invoke a failure, you can fix the problem by simply deleting the + 1, and the test will pass again.

One irony of this particular set of unit tests is that it would not have caught the bug you fixed earlier in the chapter; that bug wasn't caused by the calculate method itself, but the interestRate variable passed into it from the NSNumberFormatter. As the old adage goes: garbage in, garbage out.

FIGURE 8.29 The folder icon shows your project's files in the navigator area.

FIGURE 8.30 Selecting the target and Build Phases tab

FIGURE 8.31 Selecting the `MyFirstSwiftAppTests` as a dependency

TESTS THAT ALWAYS RUN

Unit tests are only good when you actually run them. So far, you have used the Product > Test menu to invoke the tests each time. What if instead the tests ran every time you actually ran your app? This way, any changes you make to your program can immediately benefit from retesting. Even though you may think the change is harmless and won't introduce bugs, always run your tests prior to building. Here's how to tell Xcode to do this for you automatically:

Select the folder icon in the navigation area, and then click the `MyFirstSwiftApp` project entry at the top (**Figure 8.29**).

In the editor area, click the `MyFirstSwiftApp` target, and then click the Build Phases tab. Click the disclosure triangle next to the Target Dependencies entry, and then click the Add (+) icon to add a dependency (**Figure 8.30**).

A dialog appears showing `MyFirstSwiftAppTests` as a potential dependency. Select it, then click the Add button (**Figure 8.31**).

Now you have added the test as a dependency of your application. So every time you build your app, the unit tests build and execute first. If any of the tests fail, your app will not be built, forcing you to address the failed tests before moving on.

WRAPPING UP

Over the last two chapters, you've managed to take the Swift knowledge you've acquired and write a full-fledged application. Not only that, you also managed to use Xcode's debugging environment to find and fix a bug, as well as write several unit tests to ensure your calculations would always work correctly. That's a lot of work and a big accomplishment!

Take a well deserved coffee break, and gear up for the next chapter!

CHAPTER 9

Going Mobile with Swift

In the last chapter, you spent some time perfecting your first Swift application for your Mac. Although you were not creating the most complex or demanding app, it was a useful exercise for getting your feet wet with Xcode, and even doing some nominal debugging.

In this chapter, we'll continue with the theme of app development and the Swift language, but this time you'll move away from the desktop and onto the other major Apple platform: iOS. That's right! You'll get some first-hand experience writing a Swift app for the premier mobile platform.

If you don't have an iPhone or iPad, that won't be a problem. You will be playing exclusively in Apple's great iOS simulator environment, so you won't need the actual hardware.

IN YOUR POCKET VS. ON YOUR DESK

The beauty of Swift is that it is agnostic to the platform you're on which you are developing. Whether it's an app for a notebook or desktop running Mac OS X, or the latest iPhone or iPad running iOS, Swift just works.

The differences between OS X and iOS are centered around the particular user interfaces (UIs) and the frameworks used to construct those UIs. As you saw with the interest calculator app in the previous chapters, OS X apps have free rein of the desktop; they are window-based apps that can co-exist peacefully on the same screen as other apps.

In the mobile case, screen real estate is limited, and the UI changes from a keyboard and trackpad (or mouse) to a touch screen with virtual keyboards that come and go as needed.

Apple's Cocoa framework on OS X is known as Cocoa Touch on iOS, aptly named because of the more intimate, touch-based interaction iPhones and iPads are known for.

In this chapter, you will be introduced to an iOS-based app, written in Swift, that takes into account the differences between the two environments. As usual, we'll introduce some more Swift language features for you to study and contemplate. So get yourself a "cup of joe" or your favorite beverage, and settle into some more fun!

HOW'S YOUR MEMORY?

The OS X Swift app you perfected in the last chapter was a bit on the "serious" side. Loan interest calculators are certainly important in the banking business, but they are not most people's idea of fun.

For this next app, you'll use Swift to write something a little more playful.

In 1978, Milton Bradley released Simon, a handheld electronic game. Simon contained four large, back-lit buttons (the button colors were red, green, yellow, and blue). Simon was a round device, and the four buttons were arranged concentrically.

Simon tested the player's ability to memorize patterns. It would light one of the four buttons at random; the player would then press that button to confirm. After a slight pause, that same button would light up again, followed by another button. The player would press the two buttons in the same order. With that round properly completed, Simon would play the sequence again along with an additional button.

The game would continue to progress in this manner, with a new button highlighted at the end of each round. A good player could follow 20 or more lighting sequences, but when the player pressed a button out of order, the game was over.

A game like this makes a perfect candidate to explore a touch-based interactive experience on the iPhone. With Swift in your corner, this will not only be a fun game to write, but an educational one, too!

THINKING ABOUT GAMEPLAY

When considering how a game like Simon is played, several elements should guide your understanding of how to develop this in Swift. Let's go through those now.

- Game elements: This particular type of game has four buttons: red, green, yellow, and blue. Each button is both an input device (can be touched by the user) and an output device (can brighten, or light up). The code will need to process touches as well as brighten and dim each button.

- Randomness: The description of the game includes an element of randomness. The computer decides the order in which to light up the buttons. As the game designer and developer, you will need to employ some type of random number generator to come up with a different sequence for each turn.

- Playability: To make the game interesting, it has to be challenging, perhaps offering different levels of mastery. For this version, the speed at which the computer lights up each button sequentially would certainly affect the degree of difficulty. If each button lights up for a quarter of a second, that would allow the user enough time to observe and learn the pattern. On the other hand, if the button only lit up for one tenth of a second, before the next one, the game would be harder to play.

- What it means to "lose": The game has a very specific lose condition: The player presses the wrong button when mimicking the sequence. When this happens, the player should receive some stimulus that indicates the game is lost: a message on the screen or some type of sound.

- What it means to "win": Winning the game would constitute reaching some terminal number of presses without a single error. If that number is too high, winning the game might be nearly impossible. If it is too low, the game will be too easy to defeat.

- Play flow: A game like this is fairly easy to envision from start to finish. The player launches the game, plays it until either winning or losing, and in either case, a message appears either congratulating or admonishing the player. Once the message is dismissed, the game restarts from the beginning.

DESIGNING THE UI

A game such as this is fairly easy to design from a UI perspective. The screen has four colored buttons, which are touchable elements. To make the game easy to play, the buttons should cover as much of the screen area as possible.

The button arrangement should also facilitate easy and fun gameplay. The easiest way to do that is to arrange them in a 2 x 2 grid so that as the user watches the order of the buttons light up, everything is in one easy field of view. **Figure 9.1** shows the potential layout of the buttons.

For simplicity, this design will be created on the iPhone; iPads can still run the game, although not in its native resolution.

FIGURE 9.1 How the game might look in its simplest form

FIGURE 9.2
The buttons on an
iPhone 5s

The iPhone aspect ratio is such that the screen is taller than it is wide. This leaves room along the bottom (or top) of the screen for other potential game information. **Figure 9.2** shows how the buttons would look on an iPhone 5s.

Finally, how about a name? Every game or app needs a good name, and this one is no exception. For the fun of it, let's call this game "FollowMe" since the object of the game is to follow the order in which the buttons light up.

CREATING THE PROJECT

You've been through this step before—launching Xcode and creating a new project. This time, however, there's a twist: You won't be creating an OS X application but an iOS one.

With Xcode running, choose File > New > Project. For this project, select Application under iOS. The type of application you'll create is a Single View Application (**Figure 9.3**).

Other application templates are available, including one specifically named Game. Although FollowMe is a game, it's very simple in design and will work just fine as a Single View Application.

Once you've selected the Single View Application template, click Next. In the subsequent window, set the Product Name to **FollowMe**, and ensure the settings mimic **Figure 9.4**.

Click Next to continue to the Save dialog, and then click Create. You'll see the Xcode window for the new project as in **Figure 9.5**.

FIGURE 9.3 Selecting the Single View Application template

FIGURE 9.4 Setting the Product Name

FIGURE 9.5 Your new Xcode project is ready for you to begin work.

BUILDING THE USER INTERFACE

FIGURE 9.6 The editor area showing the view of the storyboard

Now that you have a project, you need to start building the UI. By default, iOS apps have a slightly different method for working with views than what you experienced with the Mac OS X app earlier. Xcode provides a convenient technology named *storyboarding* that allows you to build your app in a view-by-view approach, similar to how animators would create a series of scenes in a film.

Locate the storyboard file named Main.storyboard in the navigator area on the left side of the Xcode window, and single-click it. The editor area appears showing the main view of the storyboard (**Figure 9.6**).

This single view is where you'll begin to build the content for the game. If the size of the view looks a little wider than that of an iPhone, that's because it is. It's a 600 x 600 point view, and is intended to be a generic view space. Xcode 6 defaults to a sizing feature known as Auto Layout. It conveniently adapts the content dynamically to the view irrespective of aspect ratio, and lets designers focus more on the content and less on the layout.

Auto Layout can be complex and can take some time to learn. Although it is an important part of developing for iOS, you'll get some minimal exposure to it shortly.

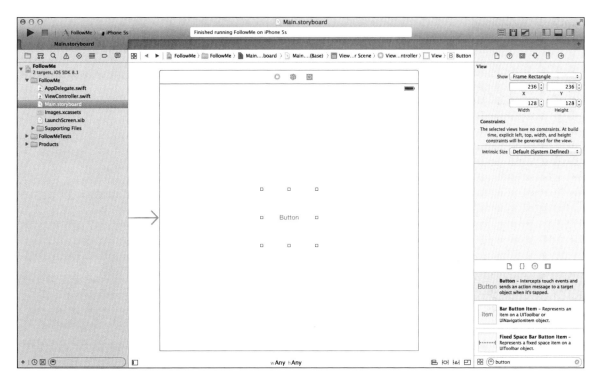

FIGURE 9.7 Creating the first button

CREATING THE BUTTONS

Given how the game will work, Cocoa Touch's `UIButton` object is the best choice for the user interface object. `UIButton` objects can have their background color modified, and they also accept touch input as a bonus.

Start by locating the Button object in the object library. Drag a single button into the view, and then navigate to the Size inspector at the top of the utility area to change the size to 128 x 128 (**Figure 9.7**). You can ignore the X and Y position of the button for now.

INSPECTORS

In Xcode's utility area (on the right side of the window), you'll find a row of icons along the top. These are inspector icons, and they can change depending on the type of file you have selected in Xcode. If you hover your mouse over each inspector icon, the name will appear in a help tag.

Once you have changed the button's size, click the Attributes inspector icon located along the top of the utility area. In the title field, erase the "Button" text. This button will have no text in it. Scroll down in the Attributes inspector and locate the View section. Change the Background of the button to red by clicking the color and selecting the Color Palettes tab of the Colors window that appears (**Figure 9.8**).

Now you'll create the remaining three buttons. The simplest way to do this is to select the red button and choose Edit > Duplicate three times to create three more buttons. Change the colors of the duplicated buttons to yellow, blue, and green, and then position the buttons in a grid pattern as in **Figure 9.9**.

Now, select all four buttons. You can do this by selecting the first button and Command-clicking the remaining three buttons. With all four buttons selected, choose Editor > Embed In > View. With this new view in place, click the view and drag to center it both vertically and horizontally inside of the outer view. This embeds all four buttons into a container view. The purpose of this is to make setting constraints easier.

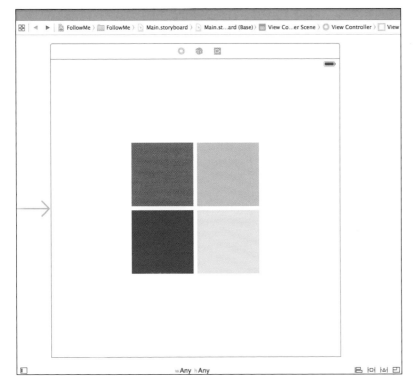

FIGURE 9.9 All four buttons created and positioned

FIGURE 9.10 The iPhone 5s simulator is selected in Xcode.

FIGURE 9.11 FollowMe running the iPhone 5s simulator

RUNNING IN THE SIMULATOR

With the buttons in place and now inside of a container view, it's time to see how the app will look when it runs. Xcode 6 conveniently lets you run your app in a simulator, which mimics the screen size and aspect ratio of a number of iOS devices. For the purposes of developing this app, use the iPhone 5s for now. You can select it in the upper-left corner of the Xcode window (**Figure 9.10**).

You can now run the app in the simulator by choosing Product > Run, which builds the app and launches the chosen iOS simulator. **Figure 9.11** shows the app running.

Something looks awry, doesn't it? The buttons seem to be off-center and falling off the edge of the screen. This is due to the difference in size between the view in the editor area (600 x 600) and the iPhone 5s' screen width. To solve this, we'll dive into Auto Layout.

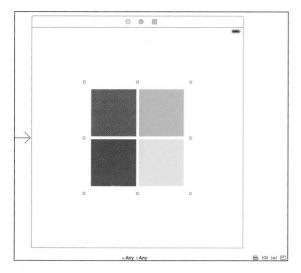

FIGURE 9.12 Selecting the container view

FIGURE 9.13 Setting the horizontal and vertical center constraints

SETTING CONSTRAINTS

Apple's numerous hardware offerings for iOS include iPhones and iPads of various sizes and aspect ratios. Developing user interfaces to accommodate these different screen resolutions and sizes is made much simpler using Auto Layout, and you'll use this technology in your app.

Constraints are relationships between objects that enforce position and sizing behaviors, among other things. For instance, if you rotate your iPhone, your UI should adapt appropriately. Whether your app is running on an iPhone 6 with a larger screen or an iPhone 4, with a properly configured set of constraints, things will look optimal.

For this app, the important constraint is that the buttons remain centered on the screen, irrespective of what device they appear on. This is achieved by setting the constraints on the container view itself, which holds the four buttons.

Quit the simulator and return to the view in Xcode. There, select the container view by clicking just outside any of the four buttons. The container view will show as selected in **Figure 9.12**.

With the container view selected, navigate to the area just to the lower-right side of the editor area where the constraint setting icons are located. Click the Align constraint icon (the leftmost icon), and select both the Horizontal Center in Container and Vertical Center in Container options in the pop-up window (**Figure 9.13**). Add the two constraints by clicking the "Add 2 Constraints" button.

Once the constraints have been set, the lines in **Figure 9.14** appear.

Now that the constraints have been set, run the app in the simulator again. This time the buttons remain centered. You can simulate rotation of the iPhone 5s in the simulator by holding down the Command key while pressing the Left and Right Arrow keys on the Mac. In all orientations, the buttons should align properly in the center (**Figure 9.15**).

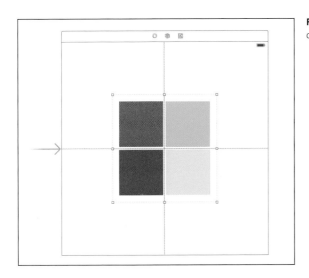

FIGURE 9.14 The view after the constraints have been set

Vertical

Horizontal

FIGURE 9.15 The constraints now allow for preservation of the buttons' locations during rotation.

When you're finished, quit the simulator, and return to Xcode.

At this point, the user interface is nearly good enough; you'll come back to a few settings in a bit, but it's time to delve into the code that controls gameplay. But before getting to that, the next sections discuss an important design pattern you will encounter here and should understand as you become adept at Swift.

THE MODEL-VIEW-CONTROLLER

In software development, *design patterns* are useful and common practices programmers use over and over to solve a common set of problems. Many such design patterns exist and are used in different situations, but the *model-view-controller* (MVC) in particular is pervasive in iOS and Mac app development.

As the name implies, this design pattern is composed of three distinct parts:

- **Model** represents the data and the code that manipulates and processes that data. Examples include the variables, constants, and functions that deal with the logic of games such as FollowMe.

- **View** is the visible set of objects. In FollowMe, these would be the buttons that appear on the screen.

- **Controller** is the object that orchestrates and facilitates communication between the model and the view. As FollowMe is played, the controller becomes the conduit through which both the view and the model are updated.

The advantage of the MVC design pattern is that it allows you to think about your app in terms of what data and functionality it is modeling, what it is showing the user, and how coordination happens between the two. This *separation of concerns* provides opportunity to factor your code such that components can be reused in other applications and projects.

Depending on the complexity of the app, the model, view, and controller may be composed of separate classes, or they may be combined into a single class. For FollowMe, the model and controller will be combined into a single source file; the divisions will be noted in the source code.

CODING THE GAME

Ready for some more Swift?

Locate and single-click the `ViewController.swift` file in Xcode's navigator area; the contents appear in the editor area. Delete the code in the editor area except for the comments and blank line (lines 1 through 8), and then type the following code:

SMART EDITING

As you type, the Swift compiler works in the background to find errors. Hence, you may see errors appear and disappear while typing. This is normal, so just continue typing until all the code is in place. Also, Xcode's editor may try to help you by putting ending curly braces in position when you type opening ones. It may take some getting used to such a smart editor, so be aware as you input the code.

```swift
import UIKit

class ViewController: UIViewController, UIAlertViewDelegate {
    enum ButtonColor : Int {
        case Red = 1
        case Green = 2
        case Blue = 3
        case Yellow = 4
    }

    enum WhoseTurn {
        case Human
        case Computer
    }

    // view related objects and variables
    @IBOutlet weak var redButton : UIButton!
    @IBOutlet weak var greenButton : UIButton!
    @IBOutlet weak var blueButton : UIButton!
    @IBOutlet weak var yellowButton : UIButton!
```

```swift
// model related objects and variables
let winningNumber : Int = 25
var currentPlayer : WhoseTurn = .Computer
var inputs = [ButtonColor]()
var indexOfNextButtonToTouch : Int = 0
var highlightSquareTime = 0.5



override func viewDidLoad() {
    // Do any additional setup after loading the view, typically from a nib.
}

override func didReceiveMemoryWarning() {
    super.didReceiveMemoryWarning()
    // Dispose of any resources that can be recreated.
}

override func viewDidAppear(animated: Bool) {
    startNewGame()
}

func buttonByColor(color : ButtonColor) -> UIButton {
    switch color {
    case .Red:
        return redButton
    case .Green:
        return greenButton
    case .Blue:
        return blueButton
    case .Yellow:
        return yellowButton
    }
}

func playSequence(index: Int, highlightTime: Double) {
    currentPlayer = .Computer
```

```swift
        if index == inputs.count {
            currentPlayer = .Human
            return
        }

        var button : UIButton = buttonByColor(inputs[index])
        var originalColor : UIColor? = button.backgroundColor
        var highlightColor : UIColor = UIColor.whiteColor()

        UIView.animateWithDuration(highlightTime,
            delay: 0.0,
            options: .CurveLinear & .AllowUserInteraction & .BeginFromCurrentState,
            animations: {
                button.backgroundColor = highlightColor
            }, completion: { finished in
                button.backgroundColor = originalColor
                var newIndex : Int = index + 1
                self.playSequence(newIndex, highlightTime: highlightTime)
            })
}

@IBAction func buttonTouched(sender : UIButton) {
    // determine which button was touched by looking at its tag
    var buttonTag : Int = sender.tag

    if let colorTouched = ButtonColor(rawValue: buttonTag) {
        if currentPlayer == .Computer {
            // ignore touches as long as this flag is set to true
            return
        }

        if colorTouched == inputs[indexOfNextButtonToTouch] {
            // the player touched the correct button...
            indexOfNextButtonToTouch++
```

```
                // determine if there are any more buttons left in this round
                if indexOfNextButtonToTouch == inputs.count {
                    // the player has won this round
                    if advanceGame() == false {
                        playerWins()
                    }
                    indexOfNextButtonToTouch = 0
                }
                else {
                    // there are more buttons left in this round... keep going
                }
            }
            else {
                // the player touched the wrong button
                playerLoses()
                indexOfNextButtonToTouch = 0
            }
        }
    }

    func alertView(alertView: UIAlertView, clickedButtonAtIndex
    → buttonIndex: Int) {
        startNewGame()
    }

    func playerWins(Void) {
        var winner : UIAlertView = UIAlertView(title: "You won!", message:
        → "Congratulations!", delegate: self, cancelButtonTitle: nil,
        → otherButtonTitles: "Awesome!")
        winner.show()
    }

    func playerLoses(Void) {
        var winner : UIAlertView = UIAlertView(title: "You lost!", message:
        → "Sorry!", delegate: self, cancelButtonTitle: nil, otherButtonTitles:
        → "Try again!")
        winner.show()
    }
```

```swift
func randomButton(Void) -> ButtonColor {
    var v : Int = Int(arc4random_uniform(UInt32(4))) + 1
    var result = ButtonColor(rawValue: v)
    return result!
}

func startNewGame(Void) -> Void {
    // randomize the input array
    inputs = [ButtonColor]()
    advanceGame()
}

func advanceGame(Void) -> Bool {
    var result : Bool = true

    if inputs.count == winningNumber {
        result = false
    }
    else {
        // add a new random number to the input list
        inputs += [randomButton()]

        // play the button sequence
        playSequence(0, highlightTime: highlightSquareTime)
    }

    return result
}
}
```

Now that you've typed in the code, let's walk through it so you understand how the program works.

THE CLASS

Since this class will deal with UI elements, importing the UIKit frameworks is important:

```
import UIKit
```

Just like the original contents of the file, the class remains named ViewController, which is a subclass of the UIViewController class. In addition, a protocol, UIAlertViewDelegate, has been added. This class must conform to this particular protocol due to alert dialogs used later in the code.

```
class ViewController: UIViewController, UIAlertViewDelegate {
```

ENUMERATIONS

The ButtonColor enumeration exists to represent all four button colors in the game: red, green, blue, and yellow.

This particular enumeration is based on the Int type, and each enumeration member is set to a unique raw value of the Int type. The reason for this will become apparent a little later.

```
enum ButtonColor : Int {
    case Red = 1
    case Green = 2
    case Blue = 3
    case Yellow = 4
}
```

Since the game is played by both the computer (who decides which buttons to highlight) and the player (a human), you need a way in the game to determine whose turn it is to play. This enumeration captures that:

```
enum WhoseTurn {
    case Human
    case Computer
}
```

Note that these two enumerations are declared inside the ViewController class; therefore, they would not be known, or accessible, outside of that class.

THE VIEW OBJECTS

Next is the declaration of the variables and constants needed for the game. All four views (UIButton objects) exist in the Main.storyboard file. The class needs a reference to those so that it can manipulate them during the game. The @IBOutlet weak keywords are a hint that you need to connect these variables to their represented objects in the storyboard. You'll do that later.

```
// view-related objects and variables
@IBOutlet weak var redButton : UIButton!
@IBOutlet weak var greenButton : UIButton!
@IBOutlet weak var blueButton : UIButton!
@IBOutlet weak var yellowButton : UIButton!
```

THE MODEL OBJECTS

Objects and variables related to the model are defined in this section. Unlike a pure model-view-controller separation where each entity gets its own class, the controller class ViewController encompasses these model objects, which represent the data associated with the playing of the game.

The winningNumber variable is an Int that represents the victory condition: the number of consecutive button highlights the user must successfully mimic. The current value, 25, is considered somewhat difficult; you can set this number lower to make the game easier to win.

```
// model-related objects and variables
let winningNumber : Int = 25
```

To keep track of whose turn it is, the currentPlayer is declared as a variable of the WhoseTurn enumeration type. Its default value is set to Computer.

```
var currentPlayer : WhoseTurn = .Computer
```

The progression of the game is built on "rounds." Each round consists of the computer highlighting buttons in the previous round, along with a new random button. The player must touch the buttons in the same order. This ordering is dictated by the inputs variable, which is declared as an array of ButtonColor objects:

```
var inputs = [ButtonColor]()
```

As the player touches the buttons, the computer keeps track of the next button's index in the inputs array. This variable keeps track of that index:

```
var indexOfNextButtonToTouch : Int = 0
```

One aspect of the game that can affect the degree of difficulty is the time the computer takes to highlight the button. This variable, set to one-half of one second, controls this time. Larger numbers slow the highlight progression and make the game easier; smaller numbers increase the game's speed, making the game harder:

```
var highlightSquareTime = 0.5
```

OVERRIDABLE METHODS

Working within the context of Cocoa Touch's `UIViewController` class, you will find several methods recommended to override. One such method is `viewDidLoad`, which is called when the view is loaded and about to appear on the iOS screen. For purposes of this app, we'll leave this method alone.

```
override func viewDidLoad() {
    // Do any additional setup after loading the view, typically from a nib.
}
```

Another method provided to the `UIViewController` class is `didReceiveMemoryWarning`, which is called by iOS when memory is running low on the device. Apps that receive this usually try to free resources, unload images, or take other actions to relieve memory pressure. For this app, we'll simply let the method call its superclass's implementation.

```
override func didReceiveMemoryWarning() {
    super.didReceiveMemoryWarning()
    // Dispose of any resources that can be recreated.
}
```

The `viewDidAppear` method is called after the view is loaded, but just prior to appearing on the screen. This is a perfect place for you to call the `startNewGame` method, which will begin the gameplay.

```
override func viewDidAppear(animated : Bool) {
    startNewGame()
}
```

GAME METHODS

One handy method you need during the game is `buttonByColor`, which takes a `ButtonColor` type and returns the corresponding `UIButton` on the screen. This is helpful to map color names with the buttons in the view they represent. The `switch/case` construct is used to scan through the various supported button colors, returning the appropriate `UIButton` reference.

```
func buttonByColor(color : ButtonColor) -> UIButton {
    switch color {
    case .Red:
        return redButton
    case .Green:
        return greenButton
    case .Blue:
        return blueButton
```

```
        case .Yellow:
            return yellowButton
    }
}
```

The following method is at the heart of the game and drives the highlighting of the button sequence by the computer. Two parameters are passed: an index into the `inputs` array, which will be used to identify the button to highlight, and a highlight time.

Because this is a fairly sophisticated method, exploring it in-depth is worth the time so you can understand exactly how it works, so let's dive in:

```
func playSequence(index : Int, highlightTime : Double) {
```

Upon entering the method, the `currentPlayer` variable is set to indicate the computer is the current player, since it is the one in control of the game board at this juncture.

```
        currentPlayer = .Computer
```

The following `if` statement performs a special check to see if the index value passed is equal to the number of elements in the `inputs` array. If this is true and the two values are equal, it's the human's turn to play, and the method immediately returns to the caller.

```
        if index == inputs.count {
            currentPlayer = .Human
            return
        }
```

Three variables are declared next. The first, `button`, is set to the `UIButton` reference of the current input. The `buttonByColor` method reviewed earlier is used here to find the actual `UIButton` based on the `ButtonColor` stored in the array.

The second variable, `originalColor`, captures the background color of the button just retrieved. This saves the color so that it can be restored later. Note that the `UIColor` object here is declared optional—because a button can have its `backgroundColor` property set to `nil`. In this game that won't happen, but the declaration still needs to be made in this way because the type of `backgroundColor` is a `UIColor?` and not a `UIColor`.

The third variable, `highlightColor`, is the color that will be used to highlight the button. It is set to white by calling the `whiteColor` method of the `UIColor` class.

```
            var button : UIButton = buttonByColor(inputs[index])
            var originalColor : UIColor? = button.backgroundColor
            var highlightColor : UIColor = UIColor.whiteColor()
```

The following line of code is what actually causes the selected button to highlight. Here, the `animateWithDuration` method is used to perform the animation that indicates to the player that the button is to be touched. This special method, known as a *type method*, is called directly from the type itself, and not a variable of that type. They are typically done so out of convenience, where having an instance of a type is not necessary to perform a specific function.

A number of parameters are used to perform the animation, but the most relevant for the game are the highlightTime, which indicates how long the animation will run, and two closures: one that indicates what will be animated, and what happens after the animation is finished.

```
UIView.animateWithDuration(highlightTime,
          delay: 0.0,
          options: .CurveLinear & .AllowUserInteraction &
.BeginFromCurrentState,
```

The first closure simply sets the button's background color to the highlight color (white). This means that the button's color will change from its current color (either red, blue, green, or yellow) to white in 0.5 seconds, which you set when you created the highlightSquareTime variable.

```
          animations: {
              button.backgroundColor = highlightColor
```

After the animation has occurred and the duration has passed, the code in the second closure is executed.

In this closure, the button's backgroundColor property is restored to the original color that was obtained. In addition, a new variable, newIndex, is created and set to the value of the index passed to the method earlier, plus 1.

The final line of the closure actually calls back into the same method, playSequence, passing in the newIndex and the highlightTime. This action causes the next button in the inputs array to highlight.

If you find a method calling itself to be a little like a snake eating its tail, you're not alone. This concept in computer science is known as *recursion* and is useful when sequential operations such as this one are executed. The terminal point of the recursion is the return statement reviewed earlier—when all buttons have been highlighted.

```
          }, completion: { finished in
              button.backgroundColor = originalColor
              var newIndex : Int = index + 1
              self.playSequence(newIndex, highlightTime: highlightTime)
          })
     }
```

On to the next method. Here is the action method that is called when the player touches one of the four buttons (you'll hook up this action method shortly to the buttons in the storyboard). This is another fairly involved function that we'll dive into:

```
     @IBAction func buttonTouched(sender : UIButton) {
```

Every UIButton has a tag property. A tag is an integer property that can be set to a number. For convenience, all four buttons will link to this same action method. Soon, you'll set the tag of each button to correspond to the color code in the ButtonColor enumeration. This will assist the method in determining which button was touched.

```
// determine which button was touched by looking at its tag
var buttonTag : Int = sender.tag
```

This next line may look a little strange, but is actually a common way of conditionally executing a block of code based on the value of an assignment. Known in Swift as *optional chaining*, it assigns the result of the ButtonColor creation call and checks if the value is nil.

A new constant, colorTouched, is set to the appropriate ButtonColor enumeration member based on the value of buttonTag. Since buttonTag was declared as an Int type earlier, it must be converted to a ButtonColor using the rawValue parameter of the ButtonColor initialization method.

If in the unlikely circumstance ButtonColor(rawValue: buttonTag) were to return nil, the code inside the if statement would not get executed.

```
if let colorTouched = ButtonColor(rawValue: buttonTag) {
```

At this point, the player can touch the buttons while the computer is highlighting them. If this happens, this method will be called "out of order" and can interfere with proper gameplay. Therefore, you check to see who is the current player. If it is the computer, you simply ignore this touch and return immediately.

```
if currentPlayer == .Computer {
    // ignore touches as long as this flag is set to true
    return
}
```

The colorTouched constant, which was created and assigned earlier, is checked against the current button color in the inputs array. Here the determination is made whether the user has pressed the correct button in the sequence.

```
if colorTouched == inputs[indexOfNextButtonToTouch] {
```

If so, the indexOfNextButtonToTouch is incremented and checked against the size of the array (inputs.count).

```
// the player touched the correct button...
indexOfNextButtonToTouch++

// determine if there are any more buttons left in this round
if indexOfNextButtonToTouch == inputs.count {
```

If the above statement is true, the user has touched the last button in the round correctly. A call is then made to the advanceGame method (which you'll see shortly). The result of that call will determine whether there are more buttons to be touched. If not, false is returned and the user has won the game.

```
// the player has won this round
if advanceGame() == false {
    playerWins()
}
```

In either case, the round is over since the player has touched the buttons in sequence correctly, and the indexOfNextButtonToTouch variable is reset to zero.

```
    indexOfNextButtonToTouch = 0
}
```

For clarity, the else clause is placed here, but there is no specific action to take. The game keeps playing since the player has neither won nor lost, and there are more buttons to be pressed.

```
    else {
        // there are more buttons left in this round... keep going
    }
}
```

This else clause is the counterpart to the if statement earlier that checked if color-Touched was equal to inputs[indexOfNextButtonToTouch]. If control comes to this point in the code, the player touched the wrong button in the sequence and has lost the game. The appropriate method is called, and the indexOfNextButtonToTouch is reset to zero so the game can start over.

```
    else {
        // the player touched the wrong button
        playerLoses()
        indexOfNextButtonToTouch = 0
    }
}
```

WINNING AND LOSING

An important part of gameplay is the visual cues necessary to communicate to the player whether the game is won or lost. Cocoa Touch provides a class known as UIAlertView to do this. Both playerWins and playerLoses methods create the view with appropriate win and lose messages.

The following method is part of the UIAlertViewDelegate protocol, which is adopted by this class, and called when the user taps the button to acknowledge the message. Doing so in either case starts a new game.

```
func alertView(alertView: UIAlertView, clickedButtonAtIndex: Int) {
    startNewGame()
}
```

The next two methods are called depending on whether the player wins or loses the game. In both cases, the same UIAlertView object is created, taking a number of parameters, including a title, message, delegate (for calling the above method), and optional button titles.

Finally, the show method is called on the UIAlertView object, which causes the dialog to display.

```
func playerWins(Void) {
    var winner : UIAlertView = UIAlertView(title: "You won!", message:
    → "Congratulations!", delegate: self, cancelButtonTitle: nil,
    → otherButtonTitles: "Awesome!")
    winner.show()
}
```

```
func playerLoses(Void) {
    var loser : UIAlertView = UIAlertView(title: "You lost!", message:
    → "Sorry!", delegate: self, cancelButtonTitle: nil, otherButtonTitles:
    → "Try again!")
    loser.show()
}
```

The element of randomness is achieved through the following method, which takes no parameters and returns a ButtonColor. Inside the method, a variable is declared. Its value is derived from the arc4random_uniform method, which is provided by iOS to generate random numbers between zero and the passed parameter minus 1 (in this case, a value of 4 cast to a UInt32 type as mandated by the method).

As called, the arc4random_uniform method returns a random whole number between 0 and 3. The number 1 is added to shift the value to between 1 and 4, corresponding to the ButtonColor enumeration's raw values.

That Int value is then passed to the ButtonColor's rawValue creation method to return a ButtonColor? type. Since it's an optional, it is returned unwrapped (hence the exclamation point at the end of the last line).

```
func randomButton(Void) -> ButtonColor {
    var v : Int = Int(arc4random_uniform(UInt32(4))) + 1
    var result = ButtonColor(rawValue: v)
    return result!
}
```

This method starts a new game by initializing the inputs array to a set of empty ButtonColor objects, and calling the method advanceGame to start the gameplay.

```
func startNewGame(Void) -> Void {
    // randomize the input array
    inputs = [ButtonColor]()
    advanceGame()
}
```

This final method in the code is called as the gameplay advances from round to round.

```
func advanceGame(Void) -> Bool {
```

The assumption, based on the assignment of the result variable, is that there are more buttons for the player to touch. However, if the number of inputs in the inputs array is equal to the winningNumber constant, the game is effectively over.

```
var result : Bool = true

if inputs.count == winningNumber {
    result = false
}
else {
```

If the game is not over, a new random button is added to the inputs array using the concatenation notation. The randomButton method, which returns a random ButtonColor, is called. The returned value is wrapped and added to the end of the array, effectively increasing the button count by 1.

```
// add a new random number to the input list
inputs += [randomButton()]
```

After the addition of the random button, the playSequence method is called. This is how the computer shows the player the sequence of buttons that must be touched to continue gameplay:

```
// play the button sequence
playSequence(0, highlightTime: highlightSquareTime)
}
```

And finally, the result of the comparison at the top of the method is returned back to the caller.

```
return result
    }
}
```

BACK TO THE STORYBOARD

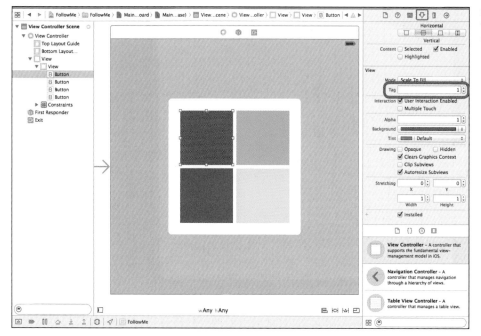

FIGURE 9.16 Setting the Tag property for the red button

With all the code added to the `ViewController.swift` class, we'll make a few hookups to the user interface in the storyboard.

Bring up the `Main.storyboard` file in the editor area, and then hook up the IBOutlets from the View Controller icon on the left of the editor area to the corresponding buttons in the view. To do this, right-click the View Controller icon, and then drag from the appropriate outlet to the button. Do this for all four outlets: blueButton, redButton, greenButton, and yellowButton.

Next, we'll set the tags for each button. In the view showing the four buttons, click the red button. From there, navigate to the utility area, click the Attributes inspector, and then scroll down and locate the Tag property. Set it to 1 (**Figure 9.16**). This value corresponds to the value Red in the `ButtonColor` enumeration.

Do the same thing for the green, blue, and yellow buttons, setting their tags to 2, 3, and 4, respectively. Setting up the tags this way allows the buttons to be found in the `button-Touched` method in the code.

Next, each button must link to the same `buttonTouched` action method. Start by single-clicking the red button, and then Command-click the green, blue, and yellow buttons. All four should be highlighted. Release the Command key and then right-click any of the four buttons.

FIGURE 9.17 Making the connections between the code and user interface elements

Locate the "Touch Up Inside" event in the heads-up display that appears, and then click the circle on the far right of the line. Drag the line up to View Controller to the left of the editor area, and attach it to the buttonsTouched method that appears in the second heads-up display (**Figure 9.17**). This links all four buttons to the same action method.

TIME TO PLAY

With the code typed in and the links made to the UI elements, it's time to play FollowMe! Run the app. If all goes well and you didn't make any typos, the iOS simulator should appear with the app running. Go through the game and play a few rounds.

If this isn't working, verify that all four buttons are attached to the action method, and that the outlet variables are connected back to the buttons. All the connections need to be made for the game to work.

Feel free to experiment with both the `highlightTime` and the `winningNumber` values to adjust the difficulty of gameplay.

There are number of other adjustments and enhancements you can consider making to improve the game as it currently stands. Consider doing the following to make playability more fun and interesting:

- Play sounds when the computer highlights each button.
- Keep a top score or a ranking based on the name of the player.
- When the user taps the wrong button, highlight the button that should have been tapped.

Congratulations on your very first iOS game written in Swift! Although somewhat simplistic in its presentation, the additional language concepts you've been exposed to in this chapter will become part of your foundation as you move forward into Swift development.

You've almost reached the end of your Swift journey... just one more chapter is left. We'll touch on some additional language features and delve into a few advanced topics.

CHAPTER 10

Advancing Ahead

It's been an exciting journey through the Swift language, and you've made it to the final chapter! Getting here, you've learned how to use the REPL, tested code in playgrounds, and created both a Mac OS and iOS app. Between all of that, you learned about the Swift language itself.

Your learning Swift doesn't stop with this chapter, or this book for that matter. You will continue to discover plenty about the language as you use it to craft apps. Then there's the ever-expansive collection of frameworks Apple continues to improve in Cocoa and Cocoa Touch. The sky is the limit, and the fun never ends.

This last chapter covers a range of Swift topics that should be the perfect ending to the heaping servings of text and code you've read through to get here.

MEMORY MANAGEMENT IN SWIFT

Every object, be it something as small as an `Int` type or as large as a blob of data, takes up memory resources. Even though your Mac, iPhone, or iPad comes with a large amount of memory, it is still a shared, finite resource that must be managed appropriately. Your app won't be the only app running on the system, so "playing nice" by using memory appropriately and wisely is part of being a good "app citizen."

If you have programming experience with other languages, you may have been waiting to see when and if this book would cover memory management. Indeed, that aspect of Swift hasn't been mentioned throughout the previous chapters. How memory is handled is usually a detail that other programming languages force the developer to deal with, but Swift was designed to make this detail as transparent as possible.

The secret weapon in Swift's seemingly invisible memory management is Apple's advanced LLVM compiler. More than just interpreting Swift statements into machine code, LLVM also traces code paths and determine where objects go out of scope and when their memory can be relinquished.

Even though memory management may seem transparent, you should be aware of some interesting twists as you embark on your Swift journey.

VALUE VS. REFERENCE

Early on, you were introduced to the concept of value types versus reference types. This is the notion of how types are used and passed around in the course of their lifetime.

Types such as `Int` and `String` as well as structures and enumerations are considered value types; when a value type is passed to a method, for instance, a copy of that value is made in memory, and the copy is passed. This makes for a relatively straightforward memory management style. By working with a copy of a `String` value, your method can modify it with impunity and not worry about it changing the original value that was passed.

Reference types, on the other hand, are not copied when they are passed around—instead, their *memory address* is provided to functions or methods that may use them. Closures and objects of instantiated classes are examples of reference types. If you pass a closure or object to a method, a copy is *not* made. Instead, a reference (in the form of the memory address) is passed.

Because reference types are not copied when passed around, special care must be taken to ensure that they are properly disposed of at the right time. If the memory occupied by a reference type is given back to the system's memory pool too early, a crash will result.

Conversely, if the memory occupied by a reference type is not given back to the system's memory pool after the type is no longer needed, that memory is essentially locked up and unavailable to be assigned to another type. This is known as a *memory leak*.

What's behind the reason for value versus reference types anyway? Why not make everything a value type? In constructs such as classes and closures where executable code exists, special memory protection constraints prohibit the copying of code. From a resource allocation and execution time point of view, passing an object as a reference instead of a value is also more efficient. Remember, values are copied, and copying data requires processor time, as well as extra memory to hold the copy.

THE REFERENCE COUNT

Swift uses a unique style of memory management for reference types. Devised by Apple and supported by the LLVM compiler, this memory management technique is known as ARC (automatic reference counting).

The basic premise of ARC is that every reference type has a number called a *reference count*. This number is set to 1 when a referenced object is created. As that object is passed around in your app, it may attain one or more "owners" who will use that object in some way or another. The owner of the object must increase the reference count by 1 when it attains ownership and decrease the reference count by 1 when it relinquishes ownership. When the reference count goes to 0 (presumably relinquished by the original owner), the object is destroyed, and the memory it occupied is returned to the free memory pool for reuse by other objects.

In Objective-C, this *retain/release* model of memory management used to be manually driven by the app developer. That is, the developer writing the code that used a referenced object would need to take care to both retain the object (increase its reference count by 1) and release the object (decrease its reference count by 1) when he was finished with it.

ARC was introduced sometime later, and the burden of retaining and releasing was lifted from the developer's shoulders and given to the compiler. Swift is a beneficiary of this memory management model, giving you total freedom from the tedium of keeping track of when your objects should be retained or released.

Not that you can safely ignore memory management when developing in Swift, however. Sometimes the use of reference types can get you into undue trouble, so having some appreciation for what ARC does is important. In fact, you've already seen hints of ARC in code you worked with in previous chapters. It just wasn't emphasized at that point.

FIGURE 10.1
Reference cycle

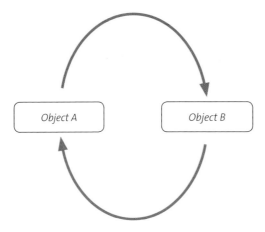

ONLY THE STRONG SURVIVE

For the most part, using classes and closures in your code involves nothing more than a simple declaration and creation. You can then pass the variable around as needed for work to be done. Although it's not obvious, when you declare a variable of a reference type and then assign an object to it, you are creating a *strong* reference to that variable, which means the variable's reference count will be incremented.

However, a unique problem— known as a *reference cycle*—can crop up when two objects reference each other, which is often the case when designing in Swift. Think of it as a deadly embrace, where object A has a reference to object B, and object B has a reference to object A (**Figure 10.1**). They both hold on to each other so strongly that when it's time to let go, they cannot.

The result of a reference cycle is that the referencing objects stay alive and the memory they occupy is never returned to the system as long as your app runs.

Let's look at a code example that exemplifies this problem. Start up Xcode if it's not already running and create a new OS X project by choosing File > New > Project. Select "Cocoa Application" from the OS X section. Be sure to select the Swift language and leave the "Use Storyboards" selection unchecked. Name this project **ReferenceCycleExample**.

PUT IT IN A LETTER

To demonstrate a reference cycle, you will create two Swift classes: a `Letter` class that models a letter addressed to someone, and a `MailBox` class that models the mailbox the letter will be put into.

```
class Letter {
    let addressedTo: String
    var mailbox : MailBox?

    init(addressedTo: String) {
        self.addressedTo = addressedTo
    }

    deinit {
        println("The letter addressed to \(addressedTo) is being discarded")
    }
}
```

This class contains a constant named `addressedTo`, which is the name of the person the letter will be addressed to. There is also a variable that is a reference to an optional `MailBox` object.

The `init` method takes a `String` that is assigned to the `addressedTo` member variable that is part of the `Letter` class. A new method named `deinit` is also present. This method is called when an object is about to be deinitialized and just before the memory it occupies is returned to the system. In this method, a message is printed to indicate that the letter is being discarded.

Now onto the `MailBox` class:

```
class MailBox {
    let poNumber: Int
    var letter: Letter?

    init(poNumber: Int) {
        self.poNumber = poNumber
    }

    deinit {
        println("P.O. Box \(poNumber) is going away")
    }
}
```

The MailBox class looks similar to the Letter class in structure. There is a member constant named poNumber, which is an Int representing the post office box number of the mailbox. A member variable named letter is a reference to an optional Letter object.

THE TEST CODE

The code to exercise the two classes and demonstrate the reference cycle is next.

In the following code segment, two variables are declared: an optional Letter variable named firstClassLetter and an optional MailBox variable named homeMailBox.

```
var firstClassLetter: Letter?
var homeMailBox: MailBox?
```

The objects are then created with appropriate parameters and assigned to the variables:

```
// initialize the objects
firstClassLetter = Letter(addressedTo: "John Prestigiacomo")
homeMailBox = MailBox(poNumber: 355)
```

Here is where the homeMailBox object reference is assigned to the mailbox member variable of the firstClassLetter object, as well as assigning the firstClassLetter object to the letter member variable of the corresponding homeMailBox object.

```
firstClassLetter!.mailbox = homeMailBox
homeMailBox!.letter = firstClassLetter
```

Lastly, both the firstClassLetter object and homeMailBox objects are assigned to nil. This is allowable since both member variables were declared optionals. When nil is assigned to a variable holding an optional reference, that object is destroyed, its deinit method is called, and the memory the object occupied is released back to the system.

```
// deinitialize the objects
firstClassLetter = nil
homeMailBox = nil
```

Figure 10.2 shows the placement of this code in the AppDelegate.swift file of your newly created project. The Letter and MailBox classes go at the bottom of the file on lines 41 through 65, while the test code is located on lines 19 through 31 in the applicationDidFinishLaunching method.

Because the app uses the println method to show when the objects are discarded in their respective deinit methods, the debug area must be visible. This is where the output of the println methods will be directed. Before running the code, ensure that the debug area is visible at the bottom of the Xcode window. If it isn't visible, just click the Debug area icon (**Figure 10.3**).

```
13
14      @IBOutlet weak var window: NSWindow!
15
16
17      func applicationDidFinishLaunching(aNotification: NSNotification) {
18          // Insert code here to initialize your application
19          var firstClassLetter: Letter?
20          var homeMailBox: MailBox?
21
22          // initialize the objects
23          firstClassLetter = Letter(addressedTo: "John Prestigiacomo")
24          homeMailBox = MailBox(poNumber: 355)
25
26          firstClassLetter!.mailbox = homeMailBox
27          homeMailBox!.letter = firstClassLetter
28
29          // deinitialize the objects
30          firstClassLetter = nil
31          homeMailBox = nil
32      }
33
34      func applicationWillTerminate(aNotification: NSNotification) {
35          // Insert code here to tear down your application
36      }
37
38
39  }
40
41  class Letter {
42      let addressedTo: String
43      var mailbox : MailBox?
44
45      init(addressedTo: String) {
46          self.addressedTo = addressedTo
47      }
48
49      deinit {
50          println("The letter address to \(addressedTo) is being discarded")
51      }
52  }
53
54  class MailBox {
55      let poNumber: Int
56      var letter: Letter?
57
58      init(poNumber: Int) {
59          self.poNumber = poNumber
60      }
61
62      deinit {
63          println("P.O. Box \(poNumber) is going away")
64      }
65  }
66
67
```

FIGURE 10.2 Placement of the reference cycle example code in AppDelegate.swift

FIGURE 10.3 The Debug area icon
shows or hides the debug area.

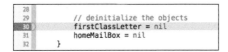

FIGURE 10.4 The breakpoint encountered on line 30

FIGURE 10.5 The Continue program execution button

With the code in place, set breakpoints on the following lines by clicking on the line number to the left of the editor display (remember, the blue arrow indicates the breakpoint is set):

Line 30:

```
firstClassLetter = nil
```

Line 50:

```
println("The letter address to \(addressedTo) is being discarded")
```

Line 63:

```
println("P.O. Box \(poNumber) is going away")
```

With the breakpoints set, run the app in Xcode by choosing Product > Run. The breakpoint at line 30 will pause execution (**Figure 10.4**).

The firstClassLetter object is about to be set to nil. This action, once it takes place, causes the Letter class's deinit method to be called, thus triggering the second breakpoint. Will it? To find out, click the Continue program execution button just above the debug area (**Figure 10.5**). Instead of encountering the second breakpoint, control will continue.

A blank window appears, but since the focus of this simple app is to view the log information only, you can safely ignore it. Use Command Q to quit the app.

At this point, both the firstClassLetter and homeMailBox variables have been set to nil, but the deinit methods corresponding to the objects were not called. This is a clear indication that a reference cycle is in place and that the objects, though no longer referenced, are still alive and holding memory.

BREAKING THE CYCLE

Now that the reference cycle exists, how do you break it?

The problem stems from the fact that by default, variables that point to reference objects are strong references. The solution is to convince one of the variables—either letter in the Letter class or mailbox in the MailBox class—to **not** increment the reference count. This is known as a *weak reference,* and you have actually seen this keyword in code from an earlier chapter.

Declaring a reference variable as weak means that the variable does not "own" the referenced object, but merely "refers" to it. The assignment does not cause the retain count to increment, which breaks the deadly embrace that two objects can have on each other.

In the previous code example, it does not matter which variable is declared as weak, as long as one of them is. Modify the `mailbox` member variable on line 43 as follows:

```
weak var mailbox : MailBox?
```

Just adding the weak keyword in front of the var keyword is enough to let Swift know that `mailbox` is a weak variable. With the change in place, rerun the application.

The breakpoint on line 30 will stop execution as it did before. Now when you continue execution, you'll notice that the breakpoint on line 63 is encountered. This is the `deinit` method of the `MailBox` object being called as part of its deinitialization. Clicking the Continue program execution button then stops at the third breakpoint on line 50, corresponding to the `Letter` object's `deinit` method. Now the cycle is broken, and both objects have been properly terminated. The output from the `println` methods also appears in the debug area, indicating that both objects have been deinitialized.

CYCLES IN CLOSURES

Closures are also reference types, and as such, can fall victim to the reference cycle, albeit in a slightly different way. Take for example the following class, which creates a `MailBox` object and a `Letter` object:

```
class MailChecker {
    let mailbox: MailBox
    let letter: Letter

    lazy var whoseMail: () -> String = {
        return "Letter is addressed to \(self.letter.addressedTo)"
    }

    init(name: String) {
        self.mailbox = MailBox(poNumber: 311)
        self.letter = Letter(addressedTo: name)
    }

    deinit {
        println("class is being deinitialized")
    }
}
```

In addition to the `mailbox` and `letter` properties, this class has something new: a *lazy property* named `whoseMail` to check the letter's addressee. The `lazy` keyword is used to defer the evaluation of the property until it is actually used somewhere in the code. For this example, the reference to `self.letter.addressedTo` inside the closure that makes up the `whoseMail` property mandates the `lazy` keyword; otherwise a compiler error would result.

FIGURE 10.7 Setting
the breakpoint in
MailChecker's deinit
method

```
29        // deinitialize the objects
30        firstClassLetter = nil
31        homeMailBox = nil
32
33        // create and destroy a MailCheck object
34        var checker : MailChecker? = MailChecker(name: "Mark Marlette")
35        var result : String = checker!.whoseMail()
36        println(result)
37        checker = nil
38    }
```

Because the closure is referencing its enclosing MailChecker object as self, Swift insists on capturing the object as a strong reference. Likewise, the closure itself is strongly referenced by the MailChecker object that owns it, showing another example of the deadly embrace that can occur between two objects that strongly reference each other (in this case, those two objects are a class and a closure).

To illustrate this, type in the MailChecker class at the bottom of the AppDelegate.swift file, insert a blank line at line 32, then add the following lines of code starting at line 33 inside the applicationDidFinishLaunching method (**Figure 10.6**):

```
// create and destroy a MailCheck object
var checker : MailChecker? = MailChecker(name: "Mark Marlette")
var result : String = checker!.whoseMail()
println(result)
checker = nil
```

This code instantiates an optional MailChecker object and assigns it to the checker variable and then prints the contents of the object's whoseMail variable (which is composed of the closure we just discussed). Lastly, the checker variable is set to nil, which should cause the deinit method of the MailChecker object to be called and its memory returned to the system.

With all the code in place, set a breakpoint on the line of the MailChecker class's deinit method (line 87 as shown in **Figure 10.7**) and then run the application from Xcode.

When the application runs, the previously set breakpoints will be encountered. Just click the Continue program execution button to continue over them. However, the breakpoint on line 87 is not encountered. That's because of the reference cycle.

To break this cycle, a special notation has to be added to the closure declaration in the MailChecker class. Change line 77 to read:

```
lazy var whoseMail: () -> String = { [unowned self] in
```

The addition of [unowned self] in to the closure definition alerts Swift that the self object should not be retained, thus breaking the reference cycle.

With the addition in place, run the application one more time in Xcode. Execution will stop on the breakpoint at line 87, confirming that the reference cycle no longer exists, and the MailChecker object is properly deinitialized and terminated.

FIGURE 10.6 Adding the code to the applicationDid FinishLaunching method

THANKS FOR THE MEMORIES

Aside from needing to be cognizant of problems like reference cycles, memory management in Swift is mostly a hidden detail that is handled behind the scenes thanks to the LLVM compiler. It's one of the many things that make developing in Swift simple and straightforward. You focus on your app, and the language and compiler worry about the rest.

THINKING LOGICALLY

Although Swift has new and innovative features, in some ways it remains a beneficiary of computer languages that came before it. That's particularly true regarding basic things like mathematical expressions, which have a common, recognizable syntax across many different languages.

Another area where Swift inherits from other languages is in the use of *logical operators*. Logical operations involve determining the truth or falseness of a statement based on words like *and*, *or*, and *not*. We use these in our every day spoken language all the time. For example:

If it is past 10 P.M. and the living room lights are on, turn them off.

or:

While it is not raining, leave the windows open.

These statements involve evaluating the truth of a clause in the statement and performing some action based on the outcome of the evaluation.

When programming, these types of constructs come up often, and Swift provides logical operators you can use to build expressions that evaluate to either true or false.

Let's move back to playgrounds to test out some of these ideas. In Xcode, create a playground using File > New > Playground and select the OS X platform. Save the playground as `Chapter 10.playground`.

TO BE OR NOT TO BE...

A common operator is the *logical NOT*, which is used to negate the outcome of an evaluation. It uses the exclamation point (!) operator and precedes an expression.

Type the following code into your newly created playground:

```
// logical NOT
var a : String = "pumpkin"
var b : String = "watermelon"

if a == b {
    println("The strings match!")
}
```

This code snippet compares the value of a and b using the equality comparison operator (==) you learned about in Chapter 1. Obviously, "pumpkin" and "watermelon" are not equal strings, so the result is false, and the code inside the curly braces does not execute.

But by simply using the NOT operator, the logical outcome can be inverted, causing the block to execute. Type the following code into the playground and observe the Results sidebar:

```
if !(a == b) {
    println("The strings don't match!")
}
```

As you would expect, the NOT character inverts the false result, making it true, and the `println` method is executed. Also, the parentheses surround the comparison by necessity so that the NOT operator can invert the result of the comparison.

COMBINING WITH AND

The second logical operator that you should know about is the *logical AND*, which is used to combine two or more Boolean expressions. If any of the Boolean expressions are false, the entire expression is considered false as well.

Two consecutive ampersand characters (&&) are used to denote the logical operation. The following code snippet illustrates how to use the operator. Type the code into your playground:

```
// logical AND
let c = true
let d = true

if c == true && d == true {
    println("both are true!")
}
```

Here, the logical AND is used when the predicate is evaluated. Both c and d are set to true, therefore the result of the logical AND is also true, and the println method is called.

If either variable were set to false instead of true, the predicate result would be false, and the code inside of the curly braces would not execute.

ONE WAY OR THE OTHER

The third and final logical operator is the *logical OR*. Like the logical AND, the logical OR also combines two or more Boolean expressions, but only one of the expressions needs to be true for the entire expression to be true.

The logical OR is denoted with two vertical bar characters (||). Type in the following code in your playground to see the logical OR in action:

```
// logical OR
let e = true
let f = false

if e == true || f == true {
    println("one or the other is true!")
}
```

FIGURE 10.8 Code demonstrating the logical operators

```
1   // Playground - noun: a place where people can play
2
3   import Cocoa
4
5   var str = "Hello, playground"                          "Hello, playground"
6
7   // logical NOT
8   var a : String = "pumpkin"                             "pumpkin"
9   var b : String = "watermelon"                          "watermelon"
10
11  if a == b {
12      println("The strings match!")
13  }
14
15  if !(a == b) {
16      println("The strings don't match!")                "The strings don't matc...
17  }
18
19  // logical AND
20  let c = true                                           true
21  let d = true                                           true
22
23  if c == true && d == true {
24      println("both are true!")                          "both are true!"
25  }
26
27  // logical OR
28  let e = true                                           true
29  let f = false                                          false
30
31  if e == true || f == true {
32      println("one or the other is true!")               "one or the other is tru...
33  }
34
```

This code illustrates that even though f is set to false, e is true; therefore, the predicate evaluates to true and the println is executed.

Figure 10.8 shows the sample code in the playground along with the results. Feel free to change the values of the variables to see how they affect the outcome of the if statements.

GENERICS

Many times in software development, you will encounter situations where you need a function or method to perform similar behavior on more than one type. In other languages, this usually means writing one method or function for every type supported.

For example, consider a simple function that takes two parameters of the same type and returns a Boolean indicating if the first value is equal to the second value. Writing such a function for Int, Double, and String types would require three functions:

```
// check for equality between Int values
func areValuesEqual(value1: Int, value2: Int) -> Bool {
    return value1 == value2
}


// check for equality between two Double values
func areValuesEqual(value1: Double, value2: Double) -> Bool {
    return value1 == value2
}


// check for equality between two String values
func areValuesEqual(value1: String, value2: String) -> Bool {
    return value1 == value2
}
```

Swift provides a feature known as *generics* that makes this repetitiveness a thing of the past. A generic function or method doesn't specify the type but instead specifies a placeholder.

All three functions just listed could be replaced by the following function, which makes the type a generic:

```
func areValuesEqual<T: Equatable>(value1: T, value2: T) -> Bool {
    return value1 == value2
}
```

The generic method has a special syntax, with the generic placeholder T encompassed in < and >. Normally just the placeholder is required, but since the values are being used in a comparison context with ==, the placeholder is followed by a colon and the word Equatable, which is a Swift-provided protocol that requires arguments to be of types which support equality comparisons.

FIGURE 10.9

The generic method and the code that exercises it

```
 9   var b : String = "watermelon"                                        "watermelon"
10
11   if a == b {
12       println("The strings match!")
13   }
14
15   if !(a == b) {
16       println("The strings don't match!")                             "The strings don't matc..."
17   }
18
19   // logical AND
20   let c = true                                                        true
21   let d = true                                                        true
22
23   if c == true && d == true {
24       println("both are true!")                                       "both are true!"
25   }
26
27   // logical OR
28   let e = true                                                        true
29   let f = false                                                       false
30
31   if e == true || f == true {
32       println("one or the other is true!")                            "one or the other is tru..."
33   }
34
35   func areValuesEqual<T: Equatable>(value1: T, value2: T) -> Bool {
36       return value1 == value2                                         (3 times)
37   }
38
39   areValuesEqual(3, 3)                                                true
40   areValuesEqual(3.3, 1.4)                                            false
41   areValuesEqual("first", "second")                                  false
42
```

Now, you simply need to exercise the generic function with Int, Double, and String values:

```
areValuesEqual(3, 3)
areValuesEqual(3.3, 1.4)
areValuesEqual("first", "second")
```

Figure 10.9 shows the code and the results.

OVERLOADING OPERATORS

Early on, you learned how to enhance classes with new methods using extensions. This ability to bring new functionality into a language construct also extends to the most basic elements in Swift: operators.

With *operator overloading*, you can define how basic math operations such as addition, subtraction, multiplication, and division operate among custom classes or structures by redefining how their operators behave.

You may be wondering why you would even consider redefining the operation of the + (addition) sign or the * (multiplication) sign? Wouldn't it be confusing to change the meaning of these very basic operators and how they are used in Swift source code?

Although this is a valid observation, in some cases these basic operators can be useful outside of regular integer or floating-point mathematics. Consider linear algebra, for example, which concentrates on mathematical operations between matrices.

Addition and multiplication operations are more involved and complex in matrices than regular numbers. Although some computer languages can inherently perform math on matrices, they are typically domain-specific languages that focus specifically on scientific computing.

With operator overloading in Swift, providing support for matrices natively is possible. Although a more general class could be constructed to perform operations on matrices of different sizes, let's keep it simple and focus on a specific case: the 2 x 2 matrix. In linear algebra, the procedure for adding two 2 x 2 matrices is as follows:

$$\begin{bmatrix} a11 & a12 \\ a21 & a22 \end{bmatrix} + \begin{bmatrix} b11 & b12 \\ b21 & b22 \end{bmatrix} = \begin{bmatrix} a11 + b11 & a12 + b12 \\ a21 + b21 & a22 + b22 \end{bmatrix}$$

Each member of the first matrix is added to the corresponding member of the second matrix, and the result placed in the corresponding location of the result matrix.

Matrix multiplication is a little more involved. The procedure is as follows:

$$\begin{bmatrix} a11 & a12 \\ a21 & a22 \end{bmatrix} + \begin{bmatrix} b11 & b12 \\ b21 & b22 \end{bmatrix} = \begin{bmatrix} a11 * b11 + a12 * b21 & a11 * b12 + a12 * b22 \\ a21 * b11 + a22 * b21 & a21 * b12 + a22 * b22 \end{bmatrix}$$

Swift's ability to enhance basic operator behavior is useful in such a case. Consider the following structure, which is a 2 x 2 matrix:

```
struct Matrix2x2 {
    var a11 = 0.0, a12 = 0.0
    var a21 = 0.0, a22 = 0.0
}
```

The structure contains four variables of type Double. The variable name's first number is the row number, and the second number is the column number.

In Swift, defining a function with the operator's name as the function name is all you need to create new functionality for that operator. Below is the function that overrides the plus operator. Two Matrix2x2 structures are passed as parameters, and the same type is returned, representing the summation of the two matrices.

```swift
func + (left: Matrix2x2, right: Matrix2x2) -> Matrix2x2 {
    return Matrix2x2(a11: left.a11 + right.a11,
        a12: left.a12 + right.a12,
        a21: left.a21 + right.a21,
        a22: left.a22 + right.a22)
}
```

This function returns a new Matrix2x2 object with its a11, a12, a21, and a22 members set to the sums of the left and right matrices.

The next function defines matrix multiplication on the multiplication operator. The parameters are identical to the addition function. The code performs matrix multiplication and returns a new Matrix2x2 representing the product of the left and right matrices.

```swift
func * (left: Matrix2x2, right: Matrix2x2) -> Matrix2x2 {
    return Matrix2x2(a11: left.a11 * right.a11 + left.a12 * right.a21,
        a12: left.a11 * right.a12 + left.a12 * right.a22,
        a21: left.a21 * right.a11 + left.a22 * right.a21,
        a22: left.a21 * right.a12 + left.a22 * right.a22)
}
```

Using these operators on the Matrix2x2 structure is as natural as expressing regular math in Swift. Here, two matrices, A and B, are defined, and their sum is placed in C:

```swift
var A : Matrix2x2 = Matrix2x2(a11: 1, a12: 3, a21: 5, a22: 6)
var B : Matrix2x2 = Matrix2x2(a11: 2, a12: 6, a21: 4, a22: 8)

var C = A + B
```

This same pattern is used to demonstrate matrix multiplication:

```swift
var E : Matrix2x2 = Matrix2x2(a11: 2, a12: 3, a21: 1, a22: 4)
var F : Matrix2x2 = Matrix2x2(a11: 3, a12: 2, a21: 1, a22: -6)

var G = E * F
```

To see the code in action, type it into your playground and notice the results, which should match those shown in **Figure 10.10**.

FIGURE 10.10
The matrix addition
and multiplication
code in action

```
 37    }
 38
 39    areValuesEqual(3, 3)                                          true
 40    areValuesEqual(3.3, 1.4)                                      false
 41    areValuesEqual("first", "second")                            false
 42
 43    struct Matrix2x2 {
 44        var a11 = 0.0, a12 = 0.0
 45        var a21 = 0.0, a22 = 0.0
 46    }
 47
 48    func + (left: Matrix2x2, right: Matrix2x2) -> Matrix2x2 {
 49        return Matrix2x2(a11: left.a11 + right.a11,               {a11 3.0, a12 9.0, a21 9.0, a22 14.0}
 50            a12: left.a12 + right.a12,
 51            a21: left.a21 + right.a21,
 52            a22: left.a22 + right.a22)
 53    }
 54
 55    func * (left: Matrix2x2, right: Matrix2x2) -> Matrix2x2 {
 56        return Matrix2x2(a11: left.a11 * right.a11 + left.a12 * right.a21,   {a11 9.0, a12 -14.0, a21 7.0, a22 -22.0}
 57            a12: left.a11 * right.a12 + left.a12 * right.a22,
 58            a21: left.a21 * right.a11 + left.a22 * right.a21,
 59            a22: left.a21 * right.a12 + left.a22 * right.a22)
 60    }
 61
 62    var A : Matrix2x2 = Matrix2x2(a11: 1, a12: 3, a21: 5, a22: 6)    {a11 1.0, a12 3.0, a21 5.0, a22 6.0}
 63    var B : Matrix2x2 = Matrix2x2(a11: 2, a12: 6, a21: 4, a22: 8)    {a11 2.0, a12 6.0, a21 4.0, a22 8.0}
 64
 65    var C = A + B                                                   {a11 3.0, a12 9.0, a21 9.0, a22 14.0}
 66
 67    var E : Matrix2x2 = Matrix2x2(a11: 2, a12: 3, a21: 1, a22: 4)    {a11 2.0, a12 3.0, a21 1.0, a22 4.0}
 68    var F : Matrix2x2 = Matrix2x2(a11: 3, a12: 2, a21: 1, a22: -6)   {a11 3.0, a12 2.0, a21 1.0, a22 -6.0}
 69
 70    var G = E * F                                                   {a11 9.0, a12 -14.0, a21 7.0, a22 -22.0}
 71
```

EQUAL VS. IDENTICAL

Early on you learned about testing for equality among types such as Int, Double, and String.
Testing if two integers are equal is as simple as typing the following into your playground:

```
1 == 3
```

The result of such a comparison of course, would be false. What about other types?
Can those objects be compared for equality? They certainly can, and such a test indicates
whether two objects are *identical* as opposed to equal.

Sometimes comparing two variables to see if they are referring to the same object, rather
than to two separate objects which have equal values, can be useful. Swift lets you perform
this comparison by using === and !==, which are slight variants of the of the == and !=
operators used for comparisons between numeric and string types.

To illustrate how to determine if objects are identical or not, type the following code into your playground:

```
// testing the identity of objects
class Test1 {
}

class Test2 {
}

var t1 : Test1 = Test1()
var t2 : Test2 = Test2()
var t3 : Test2 = Test2()
var t4 = t2

t1 === t2
t2 === t3
t4 === t2
t4 !== t2
```

The Test1 and Test2 classes are empty classes that exist merely for illustration. They could just as easily be large classes with plenty of member variables and methods.

Four variables (t1, t2, t3, and t4) are defined. Both t2 and t3 are set to new instances of the Test2 class, while t1 is set to a fresh instance of the Test1 class. The variable t4 is set equal to t2.

Three comparison tests for object identity are followed by an opposite test. **Figure 10.11** shows the results of the comparisons.

The statements on lines 85 and 86 evaluate to false, because t1 and t2 hold references to separate objects (which also happen to be different classes). On line 87 is the sole test that returns true. The variables t4 and t2 indeed point to the same object, since t4 was assigned to t2 on line 83. Lastly, the test on line 88 is false. The variable t2 is equal to t4 as was just established on the previous line.

Remember that the object identity test is based on the instantiated object and not the class. Two variables can be of the same class but pointing to different instances of that class, and they would not be considered identical.

FIGURE 10.11 Testing for identity among objects

SCRIPTING AND SWIFT

If you have ever used command-line tools in the Terminal app, you have interacted with the shell. In fact, when you ran the command to launch the REPL in Chapter 1, you were using the *Bash shell*. You can run several different shells on your Mac, but Bash is the most popular.

Shell scripts are files that contain a list of executable lines of code in the language of the shell. Instead of typing a number of lines at the shell prompt, you can type those lines in a file as a shell script and then invoke that filename as though it were a command. For many developers who are command-line savvy, shell scripts are useful for repetitive tasks that are composed of many lines that need to run from time to time.

As useful as shell scripts can be, the one impediment to their adoption is that you must learn and master yet another language in order to take full advantage of them. Add to that the possibility of shell scripts also being written in other shell languages such as C shell or KornShell, and writing, let alone reading, an existing shell script can be a challenge.

FIGURE 10.12 Creating a shell script under Xcode

This discussion about shell scripts, of course, is leading up to the fact that Swift code can run inside of a shell script! This is quite an interesting achievement given that Swift is also a compiled language, and it speaks to the power and flexibility that Apple has designed into the language. If you've used C, C++, or Objective-C, you can imagine how convenient it would be if you could use those languages in a shell script (hint: you can't).

Writing a shell script involves several steps:

1. Using an editor to create the script.

2. Setting the script's permissions so it can be executed.

3. Executing the script.

EDITING THE SCRIPT

Xcode makes a great editor, so why not use it to create a shell script?

Choose File > New > File and then select Shell Script under the OS X Other section (**Figure 10.12**).

Click Next. In the file save dialog, name the file **SwiftScript**, and save it to your desktop (Xcode will automatically append .sh to the shell script filename). A window then appears where you can edit your script.

Xcode helps you by placing several default lines at the top of the file. The first line is the most important:

```
#!/bin/sh
```

This is known as "hash bang" syntax and specifies the full pathlist in your file system to the shell that will run the subsequent lines of code. In this case, /bin/sh (which is the Bash shell) is specified. For Swift scripting, you'll remove this line. In fact, delete all the lines and replace them with the following lines:

```
#!/usr/bin/env xcrun swift
import Foundation

class Execution {
    class func execute(#path: String, arguments: [String]? = nil) -> Int {
        let task = NSTask()
        task.launchPath = path
        if arguments != nil {
            task.arguments = arguments!
        }
        task.launch()
        task.waitUntilExit()
        return Int(task.terminationStatus)
    }
}

var status : Int = 0

status = Execution.execute(path: "/bin/ls")
println("Status = \(status)")

status = Execution.execute(path: "/bin/ls", arguments: ["/"])
println("Status = \(status)")
```

I'll go over the details of the script shortly. For now, type the lines into the Xcode editor and then save the file by choosing File > Save.

SETTING PERMISSIONS

Scripts are run from the command line, so launch the Terminal app (remember you used Spotlight in Chapter 1 to do this). When the terminal and shell prompt appears, type the following lines:

```
cd ~/Desktop
chmod +x SwiftScript.sh
```

The first line changes the current directory to your Desktop folder (where you saved the script). The second line is needed only once to set the permissions of the script file so that it can be executed by the shell.

Now you're ready to run the script.

RUNNING THE SCRIPT

Running the script is as simple as invoking the script's name at the prompt with a little extra typing at the beginning:

```
./SwiftScript.sh
```

The `./` tells the shell that the script is in the current directory; you have to be explicit about this because if you leave it off, the shell won't be able to locate the script.

When the script runs, you'll see a listing of files in both your Desktop folder and in the root folder of your disk. You'll also see a `Status = 0` message that indicates the commands that were used to show the files worked without issue.

Now that the script has executed, let's look a little closer at what this script does.

HOW IT WORKS

The first line is the "hash bang" mentioned earlier. In this case, the application path is `/usr/bin/env`, which is a special command to set up the environment for the shell script. Following that is a command that should be familiar to you: the same command you used to run the REPL:

```
#!/usr/bin/env xcrun swift
```

The next line should also look familiar to you. It's the `import` statement that you've seen in source code examples up to now. Just as in an application context, Swift scripts require a base of code to run from. Foundation is the framework that brings base functionality to Swift apps, so it is included here:

```
import Foundation
```

Next is a Swift class named `Execution`. Its purpose in life is to execute a command, which is something that scripts do a lot of. As you can see, setting up to execute a command in Swift takes a bit of work. Encapsulating this functionality into a class makes subsequent command execution much easier.

```
class Execution {
```

The one and only method in this class is named `execute`, and it takes two parameters: a `String` named `path` to an executable to run, and an array of `String` arguments that can be optionally passed. An `Int` is returned that will reveal the executed command's status.

You may recall that optional arguments allow you to either pass or not pass a parameter to a method or function. In this case, the array is also an optional, which means it can be assigned to `nil`.

What may look a little different to you is the keyword class in front of the method definition. This is a special method known as a *type method*. Type methods are called differently than instance methods, which is what you've been familiar with up to now.

A type method can be called directly from the class without creating an instance. Type methods are mostly for convenience, as you will see shortly.

```
class func execute(#path: String, arguments: [String]? = nil) -> Int {
```

Within the method are the steps to launch a command. A Foundation class named NSTask is used set up the launch path and arguments:

```
let task = NSTask()
task.launchPath = path
```

In the case of the arguments parameter, there is a necessary check for the value being nil. Only if it is not nil is the parameter assigned to the arguments property of the task object, where it is unwrapped using the exclamation point (!).

```
if arguments != nil {
    task.arguments = arguments!
}
```

Once the task object has been set up, the launch method is called to invoke the command:

```
task.launch()
```

And as per the documentation for NSTask, the waitUntilExit method must be called to allow the task to complete:

```
task.waitUntilExit()
```

Finally, the terminationStatus property of the task object is returned as an Int (originally it is an Int32, so we just cast it here for the caller's convenience):

```
    return Int(task.terminationStatus)
    }
}
```

What follows the class definition is the code that actually uses the class. The variable that will hold the return status of the execute method is defined:

```
var status : Int = 0
```

Then, the execute method is used to execute the command /bin/ls (which shows files in a directory). Note the named parameter path:, which is mandated in the method's definition by use of the # character. Insisting that the user specify the parameter name reinforces its purpose and makes the use of the method clear.

Also note that in this case, no arguments are being passed.

The status is returned and printed on the following line as well.

```
status = Execution.execute(path: "/bin/ls")
println("Status = \(status)")
```

The method is used again to execute the same command, but this time with an argument indicating the root path /.

```
status = Execution.execute(path: "/bin/ls", arguments: ["/"])
println("Status = \(status)")
```

What you've just witnessed is the ultimate in language flexibility. You can write a class in Swift and then utilize it in the context of a shell script, which is superbly convenient. Time you invest in developing code in Swift for your apps isn't lost on scripting—the sky is the limit!

CALLING S.O.S.

Having world-class documentation is one thing, but knowing how to get to it and use it is another. Apple has invested significant resources to bring you top-notch documentation on their tools and classes, so use it. In Xcode simply choose Help > Documentation and API Reference (**Figure 10.13**). The documentation browser appears, where you can read everything you need to know about all of Apple's technologies, including Swift, Cocoa, Cocoa Touch, and more (**Figure 10.14**).

Besides the Help menu, you have other venues for accessing documentation. You were introduced earlier to Xcode's Command-click and Option-click shortcuts for viewing details of Apple-provided Swift classes. Recall from Chapter 8 that you can hover over a Cocoa or Cocoa Touch class name in your source code and then hold down the Command key and click the underlined class name to view all the details of that class.

Get into the habit of using these shortcuts—they will save you time and get you to the right place in the documentation to help you complete your work. Remember, if you hold down the Option key while hovering the mouse pointer over a type name, variable, or constant in your source, the pointer changes to a question mark. You can then click and receive a popover that shows relevant information about the item. See **Figure 10.15** for a refresher on this handy feature.

FIGURE 10.13 Xcode's Help menu gives you access to all of Apple's documentation resources.

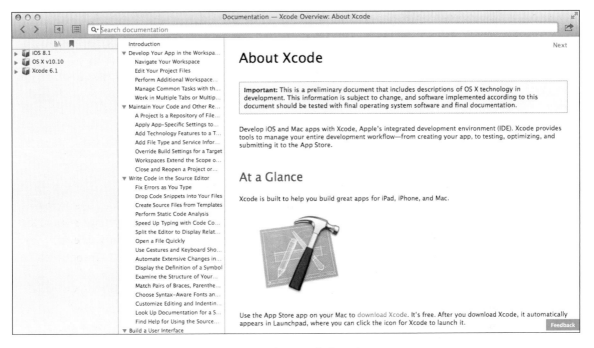

FIGURE 10.14 The Xcode documentation browser is your central source of information.

FIGURE 10.15 Using Xcode's Option-click shortcut to view documentation on NSNotifcation

AND NOW, YOUR JOURNEY BEGINS

Congratulations! You've reached the end of *Swift for Beginners*. In all honesty though, your journey into Swift has really just begun. The investment you have made in reading the pages of this book, following the examples, and typing and running code will begin to pay off as you start to practice what you've learned.

Before I send you off on your Swift adventure, I've compiled some "words of wisdom" I hope will guide you going forward.

STUDY APPLE'S FRAMEWORKS

Cocoa and Cocoa Touch are composed of many, many frameworks and libraries. Along with all of those frameworks are pages and pages of documentation available from Xcode's Help menu. It may seem overwhelming at first, but over time your knowledge of them will increase. Like a skilled carpenter who knows which tool is best to use for the job at hand, you too will learn to select the right framework and class to perform the task you need.

JOIN APPLE'S DEVELOPER PROGRAM

If writing an app for the App Store is in your plans, being a part of one of Apple's Developer Programs is essential. Currently the Mac Developer Program and iOS Developer Program are $99/year each. Depending upon your development goals, you may need to be a part of only one, but in doing so you are prepared for eventual launch of your app. You also gain access to the latest beta builds of the software, development tools, and a host of other goodies, including sample app code from Apple. Finally, the iOS Developer Program provides you with the ability to run apps on actual devices, and not just the simulator.

Besides the obvious benefits of being a member of the Developer Program, you also receive a number of technical support incidents that are handled by Apple Support engineers so you can have direct access to personalized support to resolve difficult problems. You also gain access to the developer forums, where developers and Apple engineers alike participate in helping each other with problems.

BECOME A PART OF THE COMMUNITY

Whether you're in a big city where there are other like-minded Swift developers, or in the solitude of the country, miles away from civilization, consider joining the growing number of online communities that focus on Swift and Apple development. Join publicly available forums, mailing lists, and any other online resources you can find.

If your budget allows, considering traveling to one of the many conferences that focus on iOS and Mac development. Traditionally, stateside conferences such as CocoaConf and MacTech Conference have focused on Objective-C development, but that will undoubtedly change as Swift becomes the dominant language for Apple's family of devices. Attending conferences like these gives you the opportunity to focus on specific areas by speakers who are well known in the community. I can personally vouch that they are terrific folks who are very approachable and willing to help.

NEVER STOP LEARNING

The key to any investment's success is continued and sustained growth. I encourage you to continue expanding your knowledge of Swift by reading and studying the proliferation of example code on Apple's developer site and throughout the Internet. Ask questions, share knowledge and ideas, and continue to focus on the basics. Leave yourself some room to poke and prod some of the esoteric nooks and crannies of the Swift language.

A number of websites are dedicated to helping you get past a compiler error or an issue with a particular class. Use the crowd-sourced wisdom of other Swift developers on the Internet to help expand your understanding of the language—and don't forget to give back when someone else needs help.

BON VOYAGE!

It's been fun having you along for the ride; now it's time for you to go out there and use Swift to bring great products to people. You've been given a solid foundation—continue to study and explore the language. The rest is up to you.

Now go out there and change the world!

INDEX

SYMBOLS

+ (addition), performing, 21

&& (ampersands), using with logical AND, 261

[ ] (brackets), using with arrays, 37

: (colon), using with arrays, 37

, (comma), using with arrays, 34

/ (division), performing, 21

== (double equal), using in comparisons, 68

! (exclamation) point
  explained, 188, 197
  using with logical NOT, 260

> (greater-than) symbol, effect of, 69

< (less-than) symbol, effect of, 69

* (multiplication), performing, 21

(pound) sign, prepending to parameter
    names, 103

? (question mark), using with Int
    declarations, 43

(subtraction), performing, 21

... (three periods), using with for-in loop,
    58–60

_ (underscore), using, 168

| | (vertical bar), using with logical OR, 261

A

account balances, adding, 89–90

account tuple, example of, 93

actions and outlets, connecting, 190–191

addition (+)
  and multiplication code, 266–267
  performing, 21

administrator password, entering, 9

aliases, using, 27

ampersands (&&), using with logical AND, 261

AND operator, using, 261

API Reference, accessing, 274

App Delegate object, using, 190

AppDelegate.swift source file, 178–179, 187

append method, adding, 165

append( ) method, using with arrays, 36, 38–39

ARC (automatic reference counting), 251

array index, explained, 35

array iteration, 52–54

array values
  inserting, 40–41
  removing, 39–40
  replacing, 39–40

arrays. *See also* empty arrays
  accessing elements in, 36
  adding values to, 36
  of arrays, 48–50
  combining, 41–42
  confirming values in, 35
  declaring to hold type values, 37
  defined, 34
  versus dictionaries, 42, 48, 50
  extending, 38–39
  using colon (:) with, 37
  using commas with, 34

attributes, explained, 116

Attributes inspector, using in Xcode, 226

B

balances, finding, 91–92

bank account, depositing check into, 92–93

bank balances, finding, 91–92

base class, modeling, 129–132

Bash shell, 269

behaviors, explained, 116

binary notation, 23

"Bonjour, monde," 10

Bool variable type, 15, 24–25

brackets ([ ]), using with arrays, 37

break keyword, using, 81

subtraction (-) performing, 21
superclass, explained, 128
Swift programming language. *See also* OOP
    (object-oriented programming)
   interacting with, 7
   running code samples, 7
Swift REPL, starting, 9. *See also* REPL
    (Read-Eval-Print-Loop) environment
switch statement, using, 72–75
switch-case statement, using, 72–75

T

temperature conversion, performing, 85–87
temperature units, computing, 164
temporary variables. *See also* variable types
   assigning values to, 25
   creating, 106
Terminal application
   finding, 8
   launching, 8
test methods, variables used with, 214
tests. *See also* unit tests
   failure of, 215–216
   passing, 214
   running, 214, 216–217
   writing, 212–214
text fields, using in Xcode, 184
three periods (...) using with for-in loop,
   58–60
Timeline pane, accessing, 80
Tractor class
   convenience initializers in, 139
   using, 141
traffic light analogy, setting up, 67
tuples
   grouping data with, 28–29
   returning for dictionaries, 55
type alias, explained, 27
type conversion, explained, 17. *See also*
   variable types
type method
   in games, 239
   in shell scripts, 273

type promotion, explained, 22
types. *See* variable types

U

UI (user interface)
   building in Xcode, 181–184
   connecting actions to, 189–190
   connecting outlets to, 189–190
UIButton object
   tag property for, 241
   using in Cocoa Touch, 225
UIKit frameworks, importing, 231, 236
UInt* variable type, 15
unary operators, using, 21
underscore (_), using, 168
unit tests. *See also* tests
   framework, 213
   performing, 211–212
unlock function, declaring, 152
unlock method, using, 138
unsigned integers, 15

V

value types versus reference types, 145–147,
   250–251
values
   comparing, 68
   displaying, 13
var declaration, using on parameter, 106
var keyword
   changing let keyword to, 125, 127
   using, 11
variable declaration, displaying in
   playground, 65
variable modification, reflecting to caller,
   108–109
variable parameters, using, 106–107
variable types. *See also* temporary variables;
   type conversion
   adding .max to, 16
   adding .min to, 16
   Bool, 15, 24–25
   Character, 15